Microfinance in India

A State of the Sector Report, 2007

Microfinance in India

A State of the Sector Report, 2007

By

Prabhu Ghate

Sai Gunaranjan
Vijay Mahajan
Prasanth Regy
Frances Sinha
Sanjay Sinha

SAGE   Los Angeles • London • New Delhi • Singapore
www.sagepublications.com

First published in 2008 by

 SAGE Publications India Pvt Ltd
B1/I-1 Mohan Cooperative Industrial Area
Mathura Road, New Delhi 110 044, India
www.sagepub.in

SAGE Publications Inc
2455 Teller Road
Thousand Oaks, California 91320, USA

SAGE Publications Ltd
1 Oliver's Yard
55 City Road
London EC1Y 1SP, United Kingdom

SAGE Publications Asia-Pacific Pte Ltd
33 Pekin Street
#02-01 Far East Square
Singapore 048763

Published by Vivek Mehra for SAGE Publications India Pvt Ltd, typeset by Televijay and printed at Chaman Enterprises, New Delhi.

Library of Congress Cataloging-in-Publication Data

Microfinance in India: a state of the sector report, 2007/by Prabhu Ghate... (et al.).
     p. cm.
1. Microfinance—India. 2. Rural development—India. I. Ghate, Prabhu, 1941–

HG178.33.I4M534	332—dc22	2008	2008039413

ISBN: 978-81-7829-893-1 (Pb)

The SAGE Team: Rekha Natarajan

This report represents the personal views of the chapter authors. It does not represent the views of Microfinance India, or of its sponsors, or of the Microfinance India Advisory Group.

Contents

Foreword

This report is the published version of the second in a series of annual reports on the micro-finance sector in India, presented at the Microfinance India Conference organized by ACCESS Development Services every year. The conference has become established as an important sector event, and attracts large-scale interest from a diverse set of stakeholders and interested observers from within and outside the country. The report was presented to the fourth in the series of conferences, held in New Delhi on 9–10 October 2007. New material presented at the conference as well as feedback received on the conference version have been incorporated in this final published version.

Like last year, the State of the Sector report contains two chapters on progress under each of the two main models of microfinance in India, viz. linkage banking and MFIs. These two chapters are proposed to be carried every year and contain updates on how the two models have progressed during the year. In addition, the report includes five chapters on new topics and themes that could not be covered last year but are of current and future significance. These topics relate to SHG federations, evaluation of social performance, urban microfinance, developments in technology, and perspectives on regulatory issues, including the pending microfinance bill. A few topics such as developments in commercial bank lending to MFIs, equity investments, and issues relating to the need for quality human resource for the sector could not be covered again in this year's report for reasons of space, but are proposed to be taken up in subsequent years. In future years, we also hope to include themes, which have yet to be covered, such as livelihood finance, the challenge of financial inclusion, and financial literacy.

In order to broad-base participation in the preparation of the report and take full advantage of the rich expertise available in the sector, four of the chapters contained in this year's report have been contributed by well-known sector experts. I am grateful to them for taking valuable time off from their other responsibilities. I acknowledge support extended for one of these chapters, that on the MFI model, by the MIX.

I am also grateful to our sponsors Swiss Development Cooperation and Ford Foundation, and the close association of Adrian Marti and Ajit Kanitkar at all stages of the report's progress. And finally, I am grateful to Prabhu Ghate, who, exhausted from the first effort, agreed, with some persuasion, to author the 2007–08 report. I also would like to thank my team at ACCESS for the support provided to this effort. Most importantly, I am grateful to the sector at large for their very positive response to last year's report, which encouraged us to persist with the idea of publishing the report annually.

To ensure widespread distribution of the State of the Sector report for 2006–07, it has been published as a book under the title of *Indian Microfinance: The Challenges of Rapid Growth*. The book has been published by Sage Publications as a paperback so as to enhance affordability. I hope the sector will find the State of the Sector Report 2007–08 as valuable. The two reports between them cover the Indian microfinance sector fairly comprehensively, and constitute the base line, so to speak, against which future progress can be measured. I urge the sector to continue supporting this effort by sharing information, contributing experiences from the field, and bringing in diverse perspectives on the sector.

Vipin Sharma
CEO, ACCESS Development Services, New Delhi

Preface

Like last year's report on the state of the Indian microfinance sector, this year's seeks to document developments, clarify issues, publicize studies, stimulate research, identify policy choices, generate understanding, and enhance support for the sector. Given the increasing complexity and diversity of the sector, each annual edition of the report can try, but is unlikely to succeed, in being a comprehensive record of everything that happened during the year. In its choice of topics, this year's report tries to complement last year's. Thus, it covers five topics not covered last year, two of them contained in chapters by practitioners (those on technology and social performance) and three of them in chapters by the lead author (those on SHG federations, urban microfinance, and regulation). A third chapter on insurance is also by a practitioner. I am grateful to Vijay Mahajan, Sai Gunaranjan, and Prasanth Regy for giving the report a more practical flavour by drawing on the experience of BASIX, an industry leader in the adoption (and adaptation) of both technology and micro insurance. Frances Sinha leads M-CRIL's pioneering efforts in introducing social performance assessment to India (and indeed to many other countries), and Sanjay Sinha is one of India's leading analysts of the MFI model through M-CRIL's rating work and the periodic M-CRIL Reviews.

Many of the people whose help I gratefully acknowledged last year were generous again in sharing their time and understanding. I hope they will understand if I do not thank them individually again. Among those I had not managed to contact last year but were an invaluable source of information and guidance this year were Vikram Akula, Ramesh Arunachalam, Anjali Banthia, Mukti Bosco, Arabdha Das, T Dhanaraj, BR Diwakar, Malini Eden, Aloysius Fernandez, Suvarna Rani Gandham, Aseem Gandhi, Chandra Shekhar Ghosh, Samit Ghosh, Gita Goel, Marie-Luise Haberberger, Pradeep Jena, Mohd Ali Karim, KG Karmakar, Jugal Kataria, S. Kathiresan, Manish Khera, Sudha Kothari, Aparna Krishnan, Ajit Kumar Maity, Veena Mankar, Jan Meissner, Amulya Mohanty, Nayana Mohanty, R Murali, Ravi Narasimhan, Venky Natarajan, Anant Natu, Parashuram Nayak, LB Prakash, Vidya Ramachandran, RV Ramakrishna, S Ramamurthy, Abhijit Ray, Chinappa Reddy, Rama Reddy, Suma Reddy, Shubhankar Sengupta, HP Singh, Jaipal Singh, Usha Somasundaram, Girija Srinivasan, Mark Straub, Yusuke Taishi, Usha Thorat, and Srikrishna. My apologies to the many others who have been left out. My thanks to all of you.

I would like to thank the following institutions for their support: Sa-Dhan for coming out in such timely fashion with this year's *Quick Report 2007: A Snapshot of MFIs in India*," which forms the basis of an important table in the statistical appendix; the Center for Micro Finance, Chennai, for useful interactions over the year; and M2i through Deepak Alok and Avishek

Sarcar, who helped put together the statistical appendix, brief though it is because of the paucity of time and the scattered nature of the data available.

I would like to thank also the sponsors for giving me this opportunity to immerse myself for another year in a sector peopled by so many creative and inspiring individuals. I am grateful to Vipin Sharma of ACCESS India for his encouragement, and the freedom and flexibility he gave me while I tried to put together the various pieces of the complicated puzzle that is Indian microfinance; to his team consisting of Nishant Tirath and Yeshu Bansal and other colleagues for help provided; and to Malcolm Harper and Brij Mohan, two of our resource persons, for being on tap once again with a constant flow of good advice and stimulating comments.

In order to establish continuity and avoid duplication with last year's report, I refer back to it frequently as "last year's report." It is now conveniently available as a paperback under the title of "*Indian Microfinance: The Challenges of Rapid Growth*" published by Sage Publications New Delhi in 2007 (ISBN 978-0-7619-3643-5(PB)).

In my presentation at the Microfinance India Conference where this report was first presented, I requested readers to bring any comments or corrections to my notice, or any developments or materials that may have escaped my attention. In preparing the report for final publication, the feedback received, as well as new materials presented at the conference itself, have necessitated several revisions to the conference version. Most of the changes are contained in Chapter 1 and in Table A.1 (the Fact Sheet on the sector). Apart from changes to the text, several new footnotes and references have been added. Needless to say, the views expressed by the authors in their respective chapters are entirely their own.

Prabhu Ghate
pghate1@gmail.com

Abbreviations

AIDS	Acquired Immune Deficiency Syndrome
ALW	A Little World
AMMACTS	Acts Mahila Mutually Aided Cooperative Thrift Society
AMUL	Anand Milk-producers Union Limited
AP	Andhra Pradesh
APMACS	Andhra Pradesh Mutually Aided Cooperative Societies
APMAS	Andhra Pradesh Mahila Abhivruddhi Society
APR	Annualized Percentage Rate
ASP	Ankuram Sanghamam Poram
ATM	Automated Teller Machine
AWA	Assistant Anganwadi Worker
AWW	Anganwadi Worker
BC	Business Correspondent
BDS	Business Development service
CASHE	Credit and Savings for Household Enterprise
CASHPOR	Credit and Savings for the Hardcore Poor
CBHI	Central Bureau of Health Intelligence
CBMFI	Community Based MFI
CBO	Capacity Building Organization
CBS	Core Banking Solution
CDF	Cooperative Development Foundation
CGAP	Consultative Group to Assist the Poor
CIF	Community Investment Funds
CM	Computer Munshi
CMF	Center for Microfinance
CMRC	Community Managed Resource Centres
CRAR	Capital to Risk Weighted Assets Ratio
DCCB	District Central Cooperative Bank
DF	DHAN Foundation
DFID	Department for International Development
DRDA	District Rural Development Authority
DWCD	Department of Women and Child Development
EIR	Effective Interest Rate
EWI	Equated Weekly Installment
FAMIS	Financial Accounting and Management Information System
FGD	Focus Group Discussion
FINO	Financial Information Network & Operations Ltd
FLDG	First Loss Deficiency Guarantee
FWWB	Friends of Women's World Banking
GCC	General Purpose Credit Cards
GNI	Gross National Income

GRADES	G stands for governance, R for resources, A for asset quality, D for design of systems, E for efficiency and profitability, and S for services to member SHGs and their performance
GTZ	Deutsche Gesellschaft für Technische Zusammenarbeit
HDFC	Housing Development Finance Corporation
HIV	Human Immunodeficiency Virus
HO	Head Office
HR	Human Resources
HUDCO	Housing Urban Development Corporation
IB	Individual Banking
ICT	Information Communication Technology
IFAD	International Fund for Agricultural Development
IGS	Indian Grameen Services
IKP	Indira Kranti Patham
ILO	International Labour Organization
IPO	Initial Public Offering
IRDA	Insurance Regulatory and Development Authority
IT	Information Technology
JLG	Joint Liability Group
KBSLAB	Krishna Bhima Samruddhi Local Area Bank
KDFS	Kalanjiam Development and Financial Services
KSDF	Kalighat Society for Development Facilitation
KVK	Krishi Vigyan Kendras
KYC	Know Your Customer
LAB	Local Area Bank
LAN	Local Area Network
LSS	"Lights and Shades" Study
MACS	Mutually Aided Cooperative Society
MBT	Mutual Benefit Trust
MCRA	Micro Credit Regulatory Authority
M-CRIL	Micro-credit Ratings International Ltd
MFDC	Microfinance Development Council
MFDEF	Micro Finance Development and Equity Fund
MFI	Microfinance Institution
MFO	Microfinance Organizations
MIFOS	Microfinance Open Source
MIS	Management Information System
MIX	Microfinance Information Exchange
MSDF	Michael & Susan Dell Foundation
NABARD	National Bank for Agriculture and Rural Development
NABFINS	NABARD Financial Services
NBFC	Non-Banking Financial Company
NBJK	Nav Bharat Jagriti Kendra
NCAER	National Council for Applied Economic Research
NDA	National Democratic Alliance
NDDB	National Dairy Development Board
NE	North East
NFC	Near Field Communication
NGO	Non-Governmental Organization
NOF	Net Owned Fund
NPA	Non-Performing Assets
NREGA	National Rural Employment Guarantee Act
NSSO	National Sample Survey Organization
OER	Operating Expense Ratio
OSS	Operating Self-Sufficiency
PACS	Primary Agricultural Credit Societies

PAR	Portfolio at Risk
PC	Personal Computer
PDA	Personal Digital Assistant
PHC	Public Health Centre
PLR	Prime Lending Rate
POS	Point of Sale
PPP	Purchasing Power Parity
PRADAN	Professional Assistance for Development Action
PSS	Pragathi Sewa Samithi
PWMACTS	The Payakaraopta Women's Mutually Aided Cooperative Thrift and Credit Society Ltd.
RBI	Reserve Bank of India
RGVN	Rashtriya Grameen Vikas Nidhi
RMK	Rashtriya Mahila Kosh
RRB	Regional Rural Bank
RSRO	Recognized Self-Regulatory Authority
RV	Roshan Vikas
SBLP	SHG–Bank Linkage Program
SC	Scheduled Caste
SCB	State Cooperative Bank
SEEP	Small Enterprise Education and Promotion
SERP	The Society for Elimination of Rural Poverty
SEWA	Self-Employed Women's Association
SGSY	Swarna Jayanti Gram Swarozgar Yojna
SHG	Self-Help Group
SHPA	Self-Help Promotion Agency
SHPI	Self-Help Promoting Institution
SIDBI	Small Industries Development Bank of India
SIM	Subscriber Identity Module
SKDRDP	Shri Kshetra Dhamrmasthala Rural Development Project
SKS	Swayam Krishi Sangam
SNFL	Sarvodaya Nano Finance Limited
SPM	Social Performance Management
SPMS	Sri Padmavathy Mahila Abyudaya Sangh
SPOT	Specified Point of Transaction
SQL	Structured Query Language
SRO	Self-Regulatory Authority
ST	Scheduled Tribe
STEP	Strategies and Tools against social Exclusion and Poverty
SWAWS	Sharadas Women's Association for Weaker Section
TAFI	Technology Assisted Financial Inclusion
TNCDW	Tamil Nadu Corporation for the Development of Women
UCB	Urban Cooperative Bank
UNDP	United Nations Development Program
UPS	Uninterruptible Power Supply
USP	Unique Selling Proposition
VO	Village Organization
VWS	Village Welfare Society

NOTE: 1 CRORE = 10 MILLION, 1 LAKH = 100,000, US$1 = RS 40 APPROXIMATELY

CHAPTER 1

Overview

1.1 Growth of the sector continues to be rapid...

The SHG–Bank Linkage Programme (SBLP) covered a further 9.6 million persons in 2006–07, over 90 percent of them women, and about half of them are poor. The total number of SHG members who have ever received credit through the programme has grown therefore to 41 million persons (Chapter 2). Microfinance Institutions (MFIs), the other model of microfinance in India, grew even more strongly, and added an estimated 3 million new borrowers to reach a total coverage of about 11.5 million borrowers. Both programmes taken together have therefore reached about 50 million households (Appendix Table A.1, The Fact Sheet).

1.2 However, not all microfinance borrowers are poor

About half of SHG members, and only 30 percent of MFI members, are estimated to be below the poverty line.[1] Thus about a fifth of all poor households (about 75 million persons) are currently receiving microfinance services, or at least microcredit.[2] Given limitations in the database that continue to afflict the sector, these are only rough estimates, but they indicate the sector continues to make strong progress towards the goal of extending financial inclusion to roughly four-fifths of the population who do not receive credit from the banks, although there is still a long way to go. Slower progress is being made in reaching out to poor households.[3]

MFI borrowers receive larger first loans than SHG members, but since (i) the average duration of MFI loans is shorter (generally one year instead of two), (ii) MFIs have been expanding rapidly, bringing down average MFI loan size (Chapter 4), and (iii) the size of repeat loans to SHGs has been growing even faster than first loans (Chapter 2), the difference in average loans outstanding per borrower in the two models no longer appears to be significant.[4]

...estimates indicate... the sector continues to make strong progress towards the goal of extending financial inclusion to roughly four-fifths of the population who do not receive credit from the banks although there is still a long way to go. Slower progress is being made in reaching out to poor households

1.3 The sector needs to pay more attention to the depth of outreach and other quality issues

Both models continue to do relatively well on loan repayment performance[5] and on empowering women by improving their economic status in the household. The SHG model has the additional empowerment benefit of bringing almost a million SHG leaders into direct contact with the banks, and in a few states giving them an opportunity to represent their groups in SHG federations at the village and higher levels. While SHG federations are still being formed in most states, in a few states such as Andhra Pradesh they have started playing an increasingly active role in delivering economic and social services (Chapter 3). Last year's report made the point that now that the goal of making a significant dent on the challenge of financial inclusion seems attainable, the sector should pay more attention to quality issues. It expressed the concern that growth in the SBLP in particular was running ahead of the programme's capacity to ensure quality. The programme has decelerated only slightly this year in terms of growth of new groups linked, and not at all in respect of loans disbursed (which now amount to a cumulative amount of Rs. 18,000 crores (Chapter 2)). Indeed, the SBLP is now growing under its own momentum.

Although there are some well-known exceptions, including MFIs who rely on methods such as an easy-to-use housing index to target the poor, most MFIs, while contributing to the financial inclusion objective, are making no special efforts to target the poor

There is, of course a need to accelerate growth in the underserved states, which are mostly in the central and eastern regions, and slower growth in the programme as a whole will not in itself lead to higher quality in terms of the depth of outreach (the proportion of SHG members below the poverty line), or in book-keeping capacity, which is crucial for a whole range of performance variables such as the drop-out rate, the equity of loan distribution within groups, and indeed of the longevity of groups themselves. There have been no reported new approaches by NGOs promoting SHGs, or by NABARD, in tackling the phenomenon of self-exclusion, by introducing lower and more flexible monthly savings requirements in keeping with the variable and uncertain incomes of the poor. Assistance to promoting NGOs remains inadequate to enable them to provide training inputs for long enough to ensure group sustainability. Studies show that groups promoted by field level government functionaries who are given targets in addition to their regular duties, tend to be the weakest, and receive the lowest hand-holding inputs after the groups have been formed. While progress is being made in expanding the programme in 13 priority states as discussed in Chapter 2, it is being achieved on the basis of government-promoted groups, since these are the states where good NGOs tend to be thinnest on the ground. It would enhance quality consciousness at all levels of the programme if NABARD could include in its annual report on the programme, information on the quality of groups. A grading system has already been prescribed for purposes of loan appraisal by the banks, but it is not being used in monitoring the programme. Of course, grading would have to be done on a sample basis given the immensity of the task of grading all groups.

Increasing the depth of outreach is equally urgent for MFIs, although it could be argued that as the SHG programme expands to all parts of the country, SHGs should attempt to meet the demand for household consumption and emergency loans and for relatively small investment loans for income-generation activities, while allowing MFIs to cater to the market for larger loans, which is growing rapidly in the rural areas. The emergence of some such division of labour will help reduce MFI transactions costs and therefore, interest charged to MFI borrowers. SHGs are designed to internalize these costs. Although they do so, they end up charging their borrowers about the same rates as MFIs, in order to build up the group capital. The modal SHG charges 2 percent per month, or 24 percent per annum, as against average MFI rates for the country as a whole of 21 percent as self-reported by 129 MFIs in Sa-Dhan (2007), or about 25 percent according to a smaller M-CRIL sample (Chapter 4).[6]

However, until some such division of labour takes place, it would be unfortunate if MFIs in their urge to expand and reduce unit costs increasingly neglect the poorest borrowers, as seems to be already happening. Although there are some well-known exceptions, including MFIs who rely on methods such as an easy-to-use housing index to target the poor,[7] most MFIs, while contributing to the financial inclusion objective, are making no special efforts to target the poor.[8]

Depth of outreach is one of the social performance variables that the new social rating tools being developed in India and elsewhere seek to monitor (Chapter 6). Client satisfaction and client protection issues are other social performance quality variables that have come to the fore in India after last year's Krishna district episode (Chapter 4 of last year's report).

1.4 The on-lending funds constraint makes a reappearance

As last year's report points out, there was a time when MFI managers had to devote most of their time and energy in dealing with the uncertainty of where the next loan for on-lending funds was going to come from. However, the rapid expansion of commercial bank lending to the sector from 2004 led to the happy situation in which this was no longer the case. MFI lending grew rapidly, both through the expansion of existing MFIs and the incubation of new ones, and the Indian microfinance sector became one of the most highly leveraged sectors in the world (Chapter 3, last year's report).

The partnership model in effect removed both the equity and the on-lending funds constraints at one stroke... This major innovation unfortunately came unstuck during the year

However, developments during the year have made it more difficult to be as sanguine as before that the on-lending funds constraint on continued growth of MFI's has for once and all been removed. The rapid expansion of lending to MFIs was due largely to the introduction by ICICI Bank of its "partnership model", under which loans to borrowers remained on the books of the bank, off the balance sheet of the MFI partner, which only undertook loan origination, monitoring, and collection services for a fee. Thus, the MFI performed the role of a social intermediary, while credit risk was borne largely by the bank, although the MFI had to share the risk of default up to a specified level, by providing a "first loss guarantee". This greatly reduced the amount of equity with which an MFI required to support its borrowings, and the partnership model in effect removed both the equity and the on-lending funds constraints at one stroke.

This major innovation unfortunately came unstuck during the year, initially due to the AP crisis in March 2006 and regulatory concerns about Know Your Customer (KYC) requirements, but thereafter because ICICI changed its own requirements under the partnership model, and indeed its whole vision of the nature of the relationship it wants to have with its partners. By March 2006, ICICI Bank's lending had grown to constitute about two-thirds of total lending to the sector, with about 60 percent of its lending coming under the partnership model.[9]

However, instead of increasing sharply again as in previous years, ICICI's lending declined in 2006–07, and is likely to stay relatively low in the current year. One of the concerns raised by the AP crisis was the possibility of multiple borrowing by MFI customers from both the major MFIs in the district concerned, both of who were major partners of the bank under the partnership model. While there is no evidence that this led to over-lending as reflected in an inability to repay loans,[10] ICICI was urged by the RBI to strengthen its KYC procedures now that the loans were on the bank's own books and not on those of the partner.[11]

It took some time for ICICI's partners to furnish the relevant information, during which time fresh lending under the partnership model was suspended. It was partly substituted by term loans, but not in sufficient amounts to alleviate the stress being experienced by partners who were now strapped for funds. While other banks increased their lending, it was mostly to existing partners, although some switching may have taken place. Box 1.1 describes the loan fund stringency caused to a major partner of the bank, an experience not untypical of that undergone by a number of former partners, especially the smaller ones.[12]

Box 1.1   CASHPOR: Stoppage of Partnership Funding

This was an unexpected and major challenge for the Company during the last Fiscal. Funds stopped flowing, suddenly and without notice, from our major off-balance sheet funder in early September. As about half (47%) of our total portfolio was under Partnership, and it amounted to Rs. 29.2 crore, danger signals started flashing. To make things worse, we could not get a clear explanation from the Bank, nor any indication as to when the funds would flow again. Normally under Partnership, our portfolio grows over-time according to demand from clients, as the funds are on tap. For efficient fund management the practice is to contra due repayments against new loan disbursement. If there are no longer any funds for new disbursement, however, due repayments still have to be made – taking funds out of circulation in the field. With the stoppage of funds, not only did we have to find new funds for new clients but also for subsequent loans of existing clients. Suddenly we needed about Rs. 6 crore of new funds, every month! Fortunately, we had been negotiating with two other banks to provide funding under Partnership, so as to diversify our sources of that important category of funding. They agreed to start funding under Partnership, and we transferred 4 of the 6 districts funded under partnership to them. One of them got cold feet, however, at the last moment, as there were rumours circulating that the RBI was not happy with Partnership funding, and had directed the major bank involved to stop it. Similar rumours have continued to circulate and have even appeared in the press; but RBI has not issued any public clarification.

Meanwhile, after a month and a half, our original Partner Bank, offered a term loan to replace its Partnership funding, which the Company accepted. Then in December, funds started flowing again under Partnership. Then, just as suddenly and without notice, the flow stopped again in early January. It had not resumed by end of the Fiscal; but the Bank has made an additional term loan available. Nevertheless, the irregularity and uncertainty over the flow of Partnership funds have caused considerable delay and confusion on the ground among clients and staff of the Company. The continuing failure of the Bank and RBI to inform the MFIs and the public as to the reasons for the stoppage and if and how the flow of funds could be resumed is creating uncertainty which is unhealthy for the financial system...Partnership funding was a break-through to reach increasing numbers of BPL households with financial services. Its stoppage removes economic opportunity from them.

Informally we have discovered that the proximate reason for the stoppages in Partnership funding last Fiscal was strict new guidelines that RBI insisted for it. It seems that the main Bank involved was slow to meet these requirements, did not inform its partner MFIs clearly about them and their deadlines, and finally was instructed by their own legal department that they were in violation and had to stop.

We are now clear that Partnership funding can resume when RBI's KYC requirements are fully-met and compliance is maintained, and when the banks involved receive day-end transaction information for clients under Partnership. KYC requirements are being fully complied with by CMC; and we will soon test the FINO technological solution for providing day-end transaction

---

information to the banks. Partnership funding is expected to resume as the new technology spreads.

It might be asked as to why the Company wishes to resume Partnership funding, when it and the main Bank involved have been unreliable? The answer is simple. Our overriding objective is to increase our outreach to BPL households. Partnership funding, as imperfect as it has been, enables us to expand that outreach twice as much as we could without it.

Extract from "Highlights from the Chairman," in "CASHPOR Annual Report, 2006–07: Crossing Two Lac BPL Clients," CASHPOR, Varanasi, 2007

1.5 And technology makes an entry

During this period, it seems ICICI's own thinking underwent a change as it gained a better understanding of the limitations of the MIS systems of most of its partners. Many MFIs are still putting in place computerized information systems that can track ever-increasing number of transactions and branch accounts. MIS systems are the foundation of other technology applications, and are discussed in Chapter 8. It came around to the view that without major reliance on technology (and renewed inputs of capacity-building) most partners would not be available to furnish KYC information in a timely fashion, and certainly not by the "end of day", as required under the guidelines of the business correspondent model (see below). However, there was an even more important reason for why ICICI Bank came to feel the need to reflect all transactions in its books on a real-time basis, which had to do with the bank's own rethinking of its stance towards microfinance.

The bank has always been interested in developing what it has called the "missing markets" of complementary infrastructure, including shared borrower information systems. It is making a major effort to introduce smart cards bearing unique ID numbers and biometric information (finger prints) that will help identify customers, track service usage, and build up customer histories. In the longer term, this will be an essential element in the creation of credit infor-mation systems such as credit bureaus. The "front-end" technology will have to be supported, however, by "back-end" "core banking" infrastructure consisting of "hosted" or centralized software, which can be shared by several customers, and which can communicate with hand-held devices (or POS or "point-of-sale" terminals) in the field, which read and record transaction information on the customer's smart cards. If internet connectivity is available, the smart cards can be used on a real-time basis, enabling real-time sharing of credit infor-mation across the branch network. ICICI is supporting such a system through FINO, a company which seeks to provide a core banking solution, not just to MFIs but to other banks and finan-cial institutions and even state governments (Chapter 8).[13]

Many MFIs are still putting in place computerized information systems that can track ever-larger number of transactions and branch accounts. MIS systems are the foundation of other technology applications

Partnership loans are being extended only to existing or new partners who are willing to sign up for FINO, or any alternative core banking system.[14] Only a small proportion of the bank's former 100 odd partners are reported to have joined so far.[15] As we have seen, for those for-mer partners who have decided not to join, lending flows have declined because term loans are not intended to fully substitute for the former level of partnership flows.

While ICICI Bank continued to make term loans as an interim measure to alleviate distress, it has veered around to a strong preference for partnership lending supported by technology for the long-term advantage of the combination of partnership lending and ICT holds out of being able to generate customer information, not just on credit, but also on savings, insurance, remittance, and other transactions, built up through the use of smart cards. Smart cards are being issued through partners to all borrowers. ICICI has also launched pilots to collect savings through smart cards and POS devices through several partners around the country under the business correspondent scheme, and expects eventually to be able to make individual loans to the same customers on the basis of the customer information built up.[16]

Conversely it has lost interest in making term loans to MFIs conducting group lending along traditional minimalist lines.

Given the radically changed perspective on the part of the major lender, it is possible that we are in the midst of at least a temporary hiccup in the growth rate of lending under the MFI model, especially to medium-sized and small MFIs, until other banks and bulk lenders such as SIDBI, FWWB, and others can step in to fill the breach.[17] While banks other than ICICI have been increasing their lending quite sharply, they are doing so from a relatively small base.[18]

Independently of these developments, the World Bank is reported to be considering making a loan to SIDBI which would enable SIDBI to further step up its lending, and make longer term loans with the grace periods necessary to finance MFI deficits in the initial years. Demand for such loans is certainly likely to strengthen, especially on the part of smaller MFIs who may not be able to attract the equity investments which could temporarily alleviate credit stringency for larger MFIs. A greater diversity of lenders will reduce unhealthy dependence on a single large lender. Another possible source of funds are member savings which in Bangladesh contribute about a third of the funding base, while lowering at the same time the average cost of funds (Chapter 9). However, this option is not proposed to be made available to the bulk of the sector consisting of NBFCs and S25 companies by the emerging regulatory regime for the sector, as discussed below.

1.6 Private equity also makes an entry

Two landmark private equity investments in Indian MFIs took place in the first part of the year; a $11.5 million investment in SKS, led by Sequoia Capital, at the end of March, followed soon after by a $25 million investment in SHARE, by Legatum Capital. Hyderabad-based SKS is the third largest MFI in India (Table A.2) and is growing perhaps the most rapidly, hoping to end the current financial year with an outreach of about 1.5 million borrowers in 11 states. Sequoia was joined by Unitus equity fund, which already has two equity investment partners in India and eight other "capacity building" partners through an associated foundation with offices in Bangalore, as well as by Vinod Khosla and other investors. This infusion of fresh equity enabled SKS to leverage a Rs. 180 crore financial arrangement with Citibank India to finance its expansion plans. Under the deal, Citibank will purchase loans originated by SKS under a limited guarantee provided by US-based Grameen Foundation, which also has an office in India.[19]

In an even more unusual and rapid development, the SHARE investment has occasioned the first change of control of a major MFI in India. SHARE is India's largest MFI with over 1 million clients and has plans to grow to 6 million over the next 5 years. When lending under ICICI Bank's partnership model was suspended at the beginning of the year, until partners could fulfill KYC requirements, SHARE found itself strapped not just for lending funds, but short of the equity capital with which to borrow them as term loans from the banks. Legatum's investment was accompanied by a $2 million investment by Aavishkaar Goodwell Microfinance Development Company, an Indo-Dutch joint venture,[20] which becomes the fifth social venture capital company to have a presence in India (Table A.4, and Chapter 7B, last year's report). The joint investment has given Legatum and Aavishkaar majority control of SHARE.

The size of the SKS and SHARE investments is unusual even by Latin American standards. One came just before, and the other just after Banco Compartamos, a Mexican bank specializing in microfinance, that had started life as an NGO, made an initial public offering of 30 percent of its stocks on Wall Street, in April. The success of the Compartamos floatation, and the size of the SKS and SHARE private placements occasioned considerable excitement worldwide. These were investments by mainstream commercial (as opposed to socially motivated) investors, whose support would accelerate the mobilization of private capital for massive expansion of outreach. They were seen as heralding the beginning of large private placements in microfinance as "investors now have a clear line of sight towards an exit" (Satterthwaite 2007).

However, the huge profits made by the shareholders of Compartamos also stirred worldwide debate about "whether this was what microfinance was all about." The IPO was oversubscribed 13 times and the share price surged by 22 percent on the first day of trading alone. Two-thirds of the shares were held by public-purpose institutions and a third were held by private individuals, including the co-founders of the NGO.[21] The issues raised by Compartamos have been discussed comprehensively in a CGAP study. It points out the extremely high profitability of Banco (resulting in a return to equity of over 50 percent a year) was based on interest rates that were high even by Mexican standards (CGAP 2007). The study felt that that as long as Compartamos was an NGO, its strategy of funding growth on the basis of unusually high profits and retained earnings so as to expand coverage rapidly to new borrowers, was justified. But once it commercialized in 2000,[22] and private investors stood to benefit, it should have funded further growth by tapping into the rapidly expanding flow of funds from socially minded investors and development-oriented lenders. This would have enabled it to decrease interest rates considerably. As the report says "it seems to us at CGAP that after 2000 there was a direct conflict between the profits of private investors and the financial interest of Compartamos borrowers. We don't think that Compartamos and its pro-bono majority shareholders gave enough weight to borrowers when setting its prices."

It pointed out further that the high IPO prices sets in place expectations and alters the ownership structure of Compartamos in such a way that will make it even harder for the company to balance social and commercial objectives in the future. The not-for-profit institutional shareholders are now in a minority by a tiny margin, although they can still exercise effective control if they vote together. However, the "... practical implication is that new purchasers cannot realize a respectable return on their investment unless future profitability is considerably higher than it already was in 2006...new investors...will have little sympathy for interest rate policies that do not stretch profits to the maximum..."

The report is candid enough to admit that "those of us who are involved in MFI transformations may need to be clearer about the inevitable governance consequences of those transformations...since our founding in 1995, CGAP has been vocal about the need for interest rates that are high enough to cover costs, but we have been less emphatic about the loss to clients when interest rates are driven by inefficiency or exorbitant profits. We never made concrete predictions about how quickly competition would fix these problems, but

The study felt that that as long as Compartamos was an NGO, its strategy of funding growth on the basis of unusually high profits and retained earnings so as to expand overage rapidly to new borrowers, was justified. But once it commercialized in 2000, and private investors stood to benefit, it should have funded further growth by tapping into the rapidly expanding flow of funds from socially minded investors and development-oriented lenders

. we were probably too optimistic on this score. The Compartamos IPO gives all of us an opportunity to take another look at these questions."

Some of the issues raised in the Compartamos debate were reflected in India too, for example in the debate carried by *Microfinance Insights*, a quarterly publication by Intellecap, the microfinance consultancy company, between the founders of SKS, SHARE, and the BASIX group of companies. The flavour of the debate is conveyed by extracts in Box 1.2. The key question is what is the impact of large commercial investments likely to be on the Indian microfinance sector and the borrower? India already has a group of microfinance venture capital funds driven by a mix of social and commercial objectives[23] and they have been active during the year, investing both in "transformees" (see below) and start-ups. They constitute a class of specialist investors in microfinance who can aid the growth of the industry by adding value in a whole variety of areas such as capital adequacy, financial and accounting correctness, corporate governance, access to and understanding of new sources of debt and debt instruments, and best practices in management accounting, IT and HR systems. SVCs can work in partnership with larger PE investors as in the cases above, and in an investment in July 2007 of $2.5 million by Lok Capital in conjunction with a Rs. 40 crore (approximately $10 million) investment in Spandana by JM Financial India Fund. As a group, they have longer time horizons and probably lower-return expectations than the new private equity investors.[24] However, they cannot hope to match the scale of investments required by the larger MFIs or the sector as a whole, especially after the sharp decline in the number of MFIs under the partnership model.

Box 1.2 The Challenges of Raising Capital: Inside the Entrepreneur's Mind

MICROFINANCE INSIGHTS: As the SHARE deal showed, microfinance is becoming more and more accepted by mainstream investors. Do you have any personal concerns about the pressure for financial performance and its possible impact on the social mission of MFIs?

UDAIA KUMAR: Actually there is no conflict between both of them ... what we are trying to do at SHARE is focus on the poorest of the poor, trying to help them come out of poverty. In the process, we run a viable program where we cover all costs, make reasonable profits, service all investors, and also pay the right price to banks we borrow money from.

Everybody is in a win–win situation. If we are able to use this model, then we will be able to channel bigger money into the sector and we'll also be able to increase our scale. We will be able to get into the capital markets, offer IPOs, and so on.

I don't think anybody would have given us those 26 million dollars as a grant...

VIKRAM AKULA: ... I do not feel that the two interests are separate. In our case, we strive to be profitable and increase our investments because it enables us to reach out to more poor; we plough our profits into expansion efforts throughout India. Also, the majority share of SKS is held by members; thus, the interests of our investors and of our clients are aligned. As a response to the concerns that microfinance is not reaching the poorest of the poor, SKS has developed a pilot ultra poor program to target the needs of destitute populations, those too poor to qualify for traditional microfinance.

VIJAY MAHAJAN: Yes, I am concerned about the impact of extreme profit seeking investors on the mission of MFIs. Such investors might say that reaching the poor is not their problem and that they are just investing in a company which is doing microcredit as a commercial service. To such investors I would say, please stay out of this field. The sector has not been built by commercial investors; it has been built by the sweat equity of development workers, by funding from public and philanthropic institutions and accumulation of capital of the poor themselves. Globally perhaps some 3 or 4 billion dollars have been spent to bring the field to where it has reached now. For extreme profit-seeking investors to now cherry pick that part of this field which gives a high return, without any care as to what it does to the poor, is not acceptable. If they still insist on coming in, as they are free to do, they will soon find a rise of popular revulsion against MFIs and political actions to curb interest rates, etc., which will not only kill the extreme profits, but also shut down other MFIs who are trying to be sustainable. Net result, the poor will be back to the clutches of moneylenders and government doles.

MICROFINANCE INSIGHTS: If a decision to move towards commercial funding is taken, what are the key obstacles that MFIs face? How have these changed in recent years?

UDAIA KUMAR: In our case, there are two parts to the fundraising effort: one is equity, the other is debt funds. The debt funds were quite difficult because of the limited capital and surplus we had ... I never thought that we would require such huge investment because of the changes that took place in the banking sector: funding microfinance institutions, stopping partnership arrangements, and so on.

VIJAY MAHAJAN: The key obstacle that an MFI faces in raising commercial equity is what it does to the poor ... For example, let us take the recent case of Compartamos ... Its founders have personally become multimillionaires ... Presumably, this will attract more capital, but on what terms to the ultimate users? Is this what we set up this sector for? ... If this is microfinance, then I repudiate the field: I don't want to be part of this. In BASIX, we don't want to deal with any investor who thinks this is what they are for in microfinance. Instead, we'll raise money from the community, as we did in our sister company Sarvodaya Nano Finance and from development finance institutions and from philanthropic foundations.

MICROFINANCE INSIGHTS: What effect do you think the upcoming microfinance bill will have on the sector? Is there an actual need for stronger regulation?

UDAIA KUMAR: ... The new bill will bring visibility and legitimacy to the sector and ... support from the government as well as from the state governments ... .

VIJAY MAHAJAN: The upcoming bill is a mixed blessing. It is positive in as much as microfinance is being recognized for the first time, but on the down side, it does not extend its scope to NBFC MFIs, which are the main players in the sector ... The problem is that if we leave it to complete self-regulation, opportunism will take off. In Andhra Pradesh last year, this led the government to shut down branches of two MFIs because these institutions were seen to be making excessive profits, charging high rates of interest. Those interest rates were right when they started because they were not breaking even. But when the institutions grew to scale, they did nothing to bring those interest rates down, they just kept raking in those profits until it became an issue. And so they got the treatment that they deserved. The question is: at what stage, do you really expect the regulator to be looking at your quarterly result, and thinking now you are making too much profit? There is a simple way to do it. Look at the Return on Assets. World over, we know that a healthy commercial bank makes ROA of 1.5 to 2.5%, at best. So why do we want a microfinance institution to make 20% ROA? I think we need a sectoral cap. I think something like 4% ROA after tax is the upper limit to ensure that we are providing enough incentive to investors. Even with a 1:5 leveraging, this would mean an ROE of 20%.

Extracts from of an interview by *Microfinance Insights* with three leading Indian microfinance entrepreneurs: Udaia Kumar of Share Microfin, Vikram Akula of SKS, and Vijay Mahajan of BASIX (*Microfinance Insights*, Volume 3, June 2007)

The pressure to maximize returns by the new PE investors is unlikely to result in upward pressure on interest rates, as was the case with Compartamos, although it could dampen the decline of rates that should come with further growth. Public, political, and regulator acceptability will not allow high rates in India. With this option cut off, the pressure to maximize returns is likely to take the form of the desire to reach significant scale. This portends well for financial inclusion and for better regional balance of MFI lending, since the large MFIs are stepping out of their base in Andhra, but it does not portend as well for the quality of growth. The problems in AP in 2006 were caused in part by "the rush to grow." Moreover, since organic growth yields slower increases in scale than mergers and acquisitions, it is widely expected that the sector will witness mergers between MFIs.[25] Further, large investments by private equity are also expected, with the possibility of IPOs.[26]

Recent developments on the equity front have been welcomed by most observers as the only means of meeting the huge equity requirements of a rapidly expanding, but increasingly capital inadequate sector (Chapter 4). The Indian sector is now seen to be attracting the whole spectrum of funding from purely commercial private equity at one end to grants at the other, although the latter are much less important than in other countries. It is too early to say whether the concerns of the pessimists will materialize. There is little doubt that there is considerable interest among new investors in entering the sector, despite declining margins being squeezed by rising costs and limits to acceptable interest rate increases (Chapter 4).[27]

There is no dearth of potential investees either, as more and more non-profit organizations are lining up to transform to NBFCs, a phenomenon driven primarily by capital adequacy concerns, but also by the enhanced sense of vulnerability induced by the AP crisis.[28] The new bill which seeks to confer a modicum of legitimacy to non-profit organizations does not seem to be stemming the flow of non-profit organizations voting with their feet. An active market has developed in NBFC licenses not being used by the original owners which are being brought up for a premium by transforming NGOs.[29] Thus, the chain of consequences set in motion by the Andhra crisis is still playing itself out. By putting an end to partnership lending in the form we knew it, it has increased the demand for term loans, which in turn has increased the demand for equity, and has led to a spate of transformations to NBFC status. The new microfinance bill is out of tune with these developments, as discussed in the following section.

1.7 The new microfinance bill takes a small but important step forward in allowing NGO–MFIs to mobilize savings, but limits savings to "thrift"

The absence of savings services offered by MFIs has distinguished Indian microfinance till now from microfinance in most other countries, and has been likened to "walking on one leg" since without savings microfinance is not microfinance at all but microcredit. There is a widespread misconception that the poor are too poor to save, and that what they need is credit, not savings facilities. On the contrary, as Chapter 9 points out, savings is probably a more widely felt need than credit, and takes place through SHGs and a variety of savings mechanisms and institutions in the informal sector.[30]

Like the rest of us, the poor are looking for savings services which are convenient, safe, liquid, and can preferably be used to leverage loans.

By allowing at least what it calls Microfinance Organizations (MFOs) to organize group savings among their members and use these savings as a source of funds, the draft microfinance bill takes an important step forward. However, ironically, it is this aspect of the bill that has been the most widely misunderstood by critics. India's attitude to savings mobilization by non-banks has been more restrictive than elsewhere, an attitude influenced by exaggerated perceptions of fraud in the informal and cooperative sectors, and strengthened by periodic scams which affect the savings of the urban middle classes and which therefore receive widespread publicity in the press. Most of the countries of South Asia, which share the same legal heritage, now expressly allow savings to registered MFIs in their microfinance legislation. Bangladesh, where conditions are closest to India, and where the MFI model originated, has recently passed the Micro Credit Regulatory Authority (MCRA) Act 2006, which allows the MCRA to allow registered MFIs to offer savings withdrawable on demand.

Unfortunately, the bill limits permissible savings to what it calls thrift, or the small, compulsory savings of uniform size for all members. While the proposal to allow thrift is welcome and long overdue, it is important to note it is only the first small step forward in introducing savings. While many savers welcome the discipline of compulsory savings, they tend to belong to the better-off among the poor, or to the "near-poor" above the poverty line. On the other hand, many of the poorer members of SHGs (and most of the self-excluded non-members), who have highly uncertain and variable incomes, would prefer to *save small variable amounts, with variable frequency*. Several surveys have found that the main reason for why only half the members of SHGs are below the poverty line is the inability of BPL persons to commit themselves to the required mandatory savings amounts and frequencies. Uniform mandatory savings are also the most frequent reason cited by drop-outs for leaving SHGs.

A concomitant of mandatory savings products is their illiquidity. While illiquid savings protect the savings of the poor from daily demands, and are suited to accumulating lumpsums for expected purposes such as life-cycle events or school fees or adding a new room to the hut, they are unsuited to coping with unexpected emergencies including sickness and disease, or consumption smoothening in the lean season, or replacing a leaky roof in the middle of the monsoons. Indeed, recognizing the liquidity preference of the poor for many although not all savings purposes, several MFIs in Bangladesh, and indeed worldwide, who have the requisite accounting systems, are moving to a system of *voluntary savings* in which the saver has some choice over the timing and amount of savings and withdrawals. It is not being suggested that most small Indian NGO–MFIs have developed the requisite systems to be able to offer such a savings product yet, or that mandatory savings do not have their advantages for certain purposes.

However, provision should be made for the day when a larger number of NGO–MFIs have developed the requisite systems and capacity to offer voluntary savings. Also, there is a possibility that the bill may be amended to include NBFCs and S25 companies, who do have such capacities. Since voluntary savings are more conveniently offered as individual savings (because voluntary savings amounts and frequency necessarily vary from individual to individual), it would seem essential to allow the regulator the option to approve individual, voluntary, savings products in appropriate cases after due diligence by the regulator on a case-by-case basis.

Indeed, recognizing the liquidity preference of the poor for many although not all savings purposes, several MFIs in Bangladesh, and indeed worldwide, who have the requisite accounting systems, are moving to a system of voluntary savings in which the saver has some choice over the timing and amount of savings and withdrawals

1.8 Moreover, the microfinance bill excludes the larger and more rapidly growing part of the sector

One of the major omissions in the bill is that it excludes MFIs registered as NBFCs and S25 companies, which account for nearly all the large MFIs, and the larger part of total microcredit in the country. Their number is steadily increasing, as more and more NGO–MFIs transform themselves into companies for the reasons discussed earlier. The argument usually adduced for keeping NBFCs outside the purview of the bill is that they are already regulated by the RBI. However, the argument applies equally to district, state, and urban cooperative banks which are governed by the Banking Regulation Act in respect of banking activities, while conforming to the cooperative law in other respects. Like them, NBFCs would be governed by the microfinance bill in respect of thrift activities, without any dilution of their capital, reserve, or liquidity requirements as NBFCs.

There is understandable reluctance to allow MFIs to mobilize public deposits, without putting in place the necessary safeguards, for sound prudential reasons. But the vast majority of MFI members are net borrowers of the MFI at any one time

The irony is that not only can NBFC-MFIs not accept public deposits, by virtue of being excluded from the bill, but also they will not be able to accept the savings of their own borrower–members either,[31] who will continue to have to rely on less convenient, riskier lower yielding, and often socially less productive savings instruments (such as ornaments). There is understandable reluctance to allow MFIs to mobilize public deposits, without putting in place the necessary safeguards, for sound prudential reasons. But the vast majority of MFI members are *net borrowers* of the MFI at any one time. They borrow to finance their larger investment requirements, but simultaneously save small amounts regularly to finance their liquidity requirements, provide for emergencies, build up a cushion to tide over the lean season when agricultural wage employment is scarce, and aggregate savings into amounts large enough to make useful investments, repair the hut, send a daughter to high school, or a son to the big city to look for work. Since they are net borrowers, prudential concerns are much less pressing.

1.9 So are we missing an important opportunity with the microfinance bill?

In excluding NBFCs and S25 companies, the act will also deprive more than half of borrowers from the protection of the ombudsman envisaged under the bill, and the sector as a whole from the benefits of universal performance standards in respect of microfinance activities, and a much needed database. The bill confers a modicum of legitimacy on the most vulnerable part of the sector, the NGO–MFIs, but is careful not to step on the toes of the states by failing to assert that the principle of cost-recovering interest rates takes precedence over caps on interest rates under state moneylender acts.

The bill violates the spirit and intent of the new MACS acts in reducing the role of government in cooperation. It is true that the registrars under the new acts are not performing supervisory, data gathering, and consumer protection functions any better than the old ones, but will the new regulator be able to do a better job for thousands of thrift cooperatives all over the country? In any case, cooperation is a state subject, and the states will have to sign on, unless the courts take the narrow view that accepting thrift even from one's own member–borrowers constitutes "banking," which is a central subject.

The bill does not provide the sector with a form of registration uniquely suited to microfinance.

It leaves NGO–MFIs with no alternative between remaining NGOs and having to raise enough capital to become NBFCs. Societies and trusts were not designed as vehicles for financial operations, and although NGO–MFIs are non-profit organizations, they have a hard time convincing the local income tax authorities that their surpluses are intended for expansion and leverage of borrowed funds. "Special-window" MFIs, with lower entry capital but higher capital adequacy requirements, as a unique legal form under the act, would have constituted a valuable intermediate stage of incorporation between remaining an NGO and becoming a full-fledged NBFC.

Finally, as Chapter 9 points out, the envisaged Microfinance Development Council will be a government dominated body with a purely advisory role. Given the fact that the microfinance sector, like the IT sector, has grown so rapidly and in many ways creatively, precisely because it was outside the government, one would have thought that sector representation on the council would be higher, and that it would be given much greater autonomy. For all these reasons, discussed at greater length in Chapter 9, the bill, as it presently stands, may be missing an important opportunity.

The envisaged Microfinance … Development Council will be a government dominated body with a purely advisory role. Given the fact that the microfinance sector, like the IT sector, has grown so rapidly and in many ways creatively, precisely because it was outside the government, one would have thought that sector representation on the council would be higher, and that it would be given much greater autonomy

1.10 Why has commercial microfinance been excluded from the bill? Three alternative views of the role of microfinance

The exclusion of MFIs has brought into sharper focus three different visions of the role of MFIs in the sector. The first accords an important place to financial intermediation as a means of offering savings as an essential financial service to the poor, since MFIs under the group lending model meet their borrowers once a week anyway, and therefore enjoy economies of scope in being able to collect savings cheaply and conveniently along with loan repayment installments. Most savers at any one time remain net borrowers of the MFI, which fund the bulk of their on-lending requirement initially from donors and apex financial institutions with access to soft funds, and then from more commercial sources. As NGO–MFIs strengthen their capacity and profitability and transform into for-profit entities they apply for licenses to mobilize the savings also of non-members, or the public. This is essentially the path along which microfinance has developed in most countries where the Grameen bank group lending model is dominant, as it is in Asia and in countries in many other regions.

In India, however, MFIs have not been allowed to mobilize savings even from their borrower–members. They have had to rely exclusively on borrowings to fund their growth, acting as retailers of wholesale funds borrowed from the banks and financial institutions. They have been valued primarily as *retailers of "last-mile" services* in delivering credit to borrowers the banks are not in a position to reach directly. The microfinance bill seeks to allow NGO–MFIs to conduct limited financial intermediation but only in the form of thrift or small, weekly, compulsory savings. By excluding NBFC and S25 companies from the purview of the bill, it denies this limited savings opportunity to their members, as well as cheaper funds to the MFIs themselves, which might enable them to reduce their interest rates.

However, there is a third view of the role of MFIs purely as *facilitators of credit and other financial services and providers of credit-plus services*. The partnership model as noted above has always envisaged the MFI as playing the role of a social intermediary, identifying and monitoring borrowers, and servicing collections for a fee. The major lender to the sector seems to be veering round to the view that new developments in technology have strengthened the suitability of the model to the extent that in the long run it may be able to dispense with the services of MFIs altogether, relying instead on a range of business facilitators and correspondents such as internet kiosks, post offices, merchant vendors (when the guidelines allow it), or even trustworthy local individuals, to provide essential local knowledge and information on borrowers, and enable it, on the basis of credit histories on such borrowers built up through their savings and other behaviour, to eventually lend to them directly (just as MFIs do, with graduates of group lending).

*This third view,
which might be
called the
facilitator or agent
view, is also the
view that the RBI
seems to be
veering around to*

This third view, which might be called the *facilitator* or *agent* view, is also the view that the RBI seems to be veering around to. It was first articulated in the RBI's business facilitator and business correspondent circular of January 2006.[32] The Deputy Governor of the RBI responsible for regulatory issues enunciated it most recently at a Sa-Dhan meeting when she envisaged financial inclusion depending not just on technology but also on the "credit plus services that community-based organizations are able to provide because of enjoying the trust of local persons, having knowledge of the local community and being able to facilitate financial literacy, credit counseling, and garner credit information ..." (Thorat 2007). This view of the role of MFIs was expressed even more explicitly in a recent speech in which she said "... the real value of NGOs and MFIs lies in their role as providing "credit plus" services and not just functioning as an intermediary for on-lending. Banks with their resources and scale have greater cost advantages, but linking with local community-based organizations and local persons/entities would help them get over the information gap and access barriers" (Thorat 2007).

Efforts at extending financial inclusions by the banks in India have focused so far largely on savings products. The greatest progress had been made in opening "no-frills" zero-balance savings accounts which numbered 6 lakhs by March 2007.[33] In mobilizing savings, banks have an advantage over MFIs in that the savings are insured. In her Sa-Dhan speech, the Deputy Governor referred to another advantage bank savings have over MFI savings, that of "being able to obtain access to the national payments systems through bank accounts — or in countries where the regulatory system allows, through electronic accounts facilitated by mobile phones. In South Africa and Brazil, for example, efforts at financial inclusion are targeted at enabling easier and low cost access to payments systems for money transfers, utility payments, and other daily transactions" (Thorat 2006). The financial inclusion movements seeks to remove the disadvantages the banks have traditionally suffered from in respect of access, and the liquidity of their savings for the poor.[34] However, until it succeeds in doing so, it is the regulatory prohibition on MFI savings (proposed to be partially lifted for MFOs) that restricts MFIs in India to contributing to financial inclusion through the remaining three financial services — credit, insurance, and money transfers.

Credit, with the contraction of the partnership model, has reverted for the time being to being provided by MFIs almost entirely as intermediaries retailing funds wholesaled by the banks. Insurance services, however, are being provided mostly in an agency role

(Chapter 7). The provision of remittance services has been rudimentary so far, but for regulatory reasons will also have to be provided in the agency role.[35] An example of a pilot project being implemented by BASIX in partnership with Axis Bank and the technology provider, A Little World, that provides a remittance service using mobile phones, is described in Box 8.3.

MFIs have not succeeded (or shown much interest for that matter) in providing credit under the BC scheme because of the interest rate cap on small loans which has rendered the BC scheme dysfunctional as far as credit is concerned (Chapter 9).[36] Even if there were no cap, however, and even after the full development of the ICT applications discussed above, there is no presumption that the BC role is more suited to MFI credit than the financial intermediary or last-mile retailer role.[37] MFIs will always have a comparative advantage over banks in being able to originate, monitor, and collect microloans. This advantage also derives form technology, but from a technology of a softer kind, the technology of group lending pioneered by the Grameen Bank. While group lending does have well-known disadvantages, and while alternative channels to reach the borrower will and should develop, it is difficult to see how MFIs, with their field presence, will lose their comparative advantage in identifying creditworthy borrowers, providing them with hand-holding support, and dealing with delinquencies. This advantage can be put to use in any of the three roles, but MFIs have shown a distinct preference so far for the first two. This may be for non-financial reasons as much as financial.[38] It is perhaps no coincidence that even in Brazil the services that are being provided by agents (including merchant outlets such as shops, who are not eligible under India's BC scheme) are mostly remittances, bill payments, and savings services, but not credit. The stance the RBI appears to be developing on the other hand is that in the long run, MFIs should function as banking correspondents and agents for all services, including credit, although last-mile retailing will continue to be allowed. It is this vision of the long run role of MFIs that appears to explain the exclusion of NBFCs MFIs from the microfinance bill, even more than concerns about dual regulation of microfinance NBFCs.

MFIs will always have a comparative advantage over banks in being able to originate, monitor, and collect microloans

1.11 Early experience with the new urban microfinance

A major development during the last couple of years has been the upsurge of interest in urban microfinance (Chapter 5). The urban areas have remained virtually uncharted territory, except by a few prominent exceptions such as SEWA Bank, despite the prospects of (i) huge loan demand, (ii) larger average loan size and higher population density making for lower costs, (iii) the need to reach the growing numbers of the urban poor, and (iv) the example of Latin America where microfinance is predominantly urban. The rate of urbanization in India has increased sharply in the 1990s to almost twice the rural population growth rate, the difference being driven by migration from the rural areas.[39] Moreover, while urban poverty is declining in relative terms, it is increasing in absolute terms.[40] India's metros and large towns have some of the most congested slums in the world and are "home" to some of the worst living conditions anywhere.[41]

One of the main reasons why MFIs were reluctant to initiate operations in the urban areas was their apprehension that the Grameen-style group lending model, which was proving so successful in the rural areas, was too dependent on peer-pressure and mutual trust, based on long-standing neighbourhood and kinship ties, to be successful in the urban slums. Also, the one-size-fits-all standardization (of loan size and duration) and the borrower-time requirements (attendance at weekly meetings) of the group-lending model might prove a handicap in the much more heterogenous and time-constrained environment of urban slum-dwellers.

However, mobility and transience have proved to be much less of a problem than was originally feared, and the new urban MFIs are finding that many slum-dwellers have been living in the same location for a generation or more, and that even if they go home to their villages for a couple of months a year they come back to the same area because of proximity to a known livelihood.

More of a problem it turns out is that as many as a third of borrowers have no formal documentation to establish either identity or address. More of a problem, also, than mobility per se, is what might be called "involuntary mobility," caused by the ongoing drive in many cities to demolish slums and relocate them elsewhere, and by the widening of roads, etc. Also, even in slums where a significant proportion of residents are transient, MFIs have to achieve a very high level of penetration before running out of prospective borrower from among permanent residents. The trick, they are learning, is a high success rate in spotting them.

As with many other generalizations, the obstacle posed by mobility and transience depends on which income segment and location one is looking at. Many of the new urban MFIs intend to cater primarily to the vast majority of permanent urban residents who are still unserved by the banks, and depend largely on the informal sector for their financial needs. Reaching the transient poor is not a primary goal, at least initially. For example, while MFIs in Kolkata would like to serve the huge population of mostly day visitors who flood into the middle-class areas of South Kolkata from the rural hinterland as day-labourers, maids, etc., or rickshaw drivers who park by the wayside to sleep in their rickshaws at night, they are unlikely to be able to do so unless they extend their operations to the peripheral rural areas, as many of them are in fact doing.

It is well accepted that microfinance is best suited to reach the economically active poor. It is ill-suited to solve the problem of chronic income deficits. However, it is also the case that there are many potential borrowers whose income deficits could be removed by credit if they were combined with other inputs

It is well accepted that microfinance is best suited to reach the economically active poor. It is ill-suited to solve the problem of chronic income deficits. However, it is also the case that there are many potential borrowers whose income deficits could be removed by credit if they were combined with other inputs.[42] The challenge is to identify such persons, and arrange for the provision of the other inputs by some other agency, if necessary. While urban MFIs are cognizant of the need to offer a full set of financial services including savings, insurance, and remittances, they intend to meet non-financial needs such as health and vocational training through partnerships with NGOs, other civil society organizations, and socially minded corporations.

Some of the recent start-ups in the metros are promoted by professionals who have a proven track record of successful careers in banking and other fields. Their backgrounds have been very successful in attracting lenders and investors. The new urban start-ups are growing particularly strongly in Bangalore and Kolkata, but are still nascent in Mumbai and Delhi. In locations such as Hyderabad and other towns across the country, existing rural MFIs are moving into contiguous urban and peri-urban areas. They are being joined by several NBFCs who have already been operating in the urban areas but are now experimenting with "downscaling" to smaller loans. Banks in India have in effect been excluded from the small loans market by regulatory fiat. They are not allowed to make loans of less than Rs. 200,000 at a rate any higher than their PLR (their lending rate to prime customers) for the loans to qualify as priority sector loans. Despite this cap, Yes Bank is pioneering individual loans in urban microfinance. The Microsate branch of Indian Bank is successfully doing SHG–Bank linkage in Chennai (Chapter 5).

While the MFI human resources challenge – not just training, but attracting and retaining staff – has been engaging the attention of the MFI community generally in the last few years (Chapter 6 of last year's report), its severity in the urban areas has taken the new urban MFIs by surprise. Nearly all of them are finding it difficult to recruit and retain staff in conditions of a tightening job market, especially in cities like Bangalore where attrition rates are as high as 20 to 30 percent a year. The skills field workers acquire are turning out to be in high demand in other parts of the financial sector and in marketing.

1.12 The sector's infrastructure of support services is gradually strengthening

Given its rate of growth, the human resource challenge remains the most important one facing the sector. It has not been possible to include a chapter this year on developments in training and capacity building, but apart from the activities of the older, more established service providers, the year saw several new initiatives, such as *Intellecap's Microfinance Franchise Package* which seeks to incubate start-ups by providing training, manuals, and a complete business plan and financial model combined with operational exposure in group formation, lending processes, and branch and head office management at CASHPOR in Varanasi.[43]

With a view to channeling start-up and capacity building support to MFIs in underserved regions, *MicroSave* relocated itself in the North, with a view to creating a centre of excellence in microfinance at the IIM-Lucknow with links to SIDBI. In line with its plans to create a cadre of 50 to 60 "low cost-high capacity" consultants spread out across India, it continued to impart training in specialized areas such as loan portfolio audits, process mapping, and new product development. Work on running training workshops, and developing action research partnerships and toolkits continued.

The amount of timely information and analysis on the sector is increasing through publications such as Intellecap's quarterly *Microfinance Insights* which devotes each issue to a special topic, and online publications such as the monthly *Microfinance Focus*. Sa-Dhan achieved a major breakthrough by publishing "*Quick Report 2007: A Snapshot of Microfinance Institutions in India,*" within just over 4 months of the closing of the financial year. The report carries core data on the bulk of its membership. Although it based on self-reported data prepared without waiting for audited annual reports, the report greatly enhances the cause of transparency and timely public reporting.

A few, but not enough, extremely educative MFI annual reports are also being prepared which convey more than just the numbers but deal with the nitty-girtty issues facing the sector

A few, but not enough, extremely educative MFI annual reports are also being prepared which convey more than just the numbers but deal with the nitty-girtty issues facing the sector.[44] *The MIX* continues to contribute to the cause of transparency by expanding its reporting on the performance indicators of the larger Indian MFIs in collaboration with M-CRIL. One of the most useful developments in the last year has been UNDP's email-based *Solutions Exchange* service which carries an active, high quality, and widely used exchange of views and information on Indian microfinance.

There is still a need, however, for greater timeliness and coverage in the reports of some of the financial institutions, and for a timely annual statistical compendium, which perhaps the new regulator will bring out. There continues to be a dearth of good case studies, and the research effort remains insufficient to the needs of the sector. Here too, the new regulator will hopefully make a difference.

Finally, although it is not part of the infrastructure of support services, a new product introduced recently by MFIs deserves special mention, and that is participation in *UTI's Retirement Benefit Pension Fund* which accepts monthly contributions of as low as Rs. 50 a month for individual retirement accounts. The fund is approved to invest up to 40 percent of collections in the Indian stock market. SEWA and SHEPHERD (in Trichy, Tamil Nadu) are the first two MFIs to have distributed participation to their members. Subscribers are not required to pay any initiation fees, and are sent monthly statements. Monthly pension payments start at the age of 58, and are paid into bank accounts. In the event of the death of a member accumulated contributions with interest are paid to a nominee.

Endnotes

1   Thirty percent is the estimate of the proportion of new MFI borrowers who are poor, made by the social performance assessment of 12 MFIs conducted by M-CRIL reported in Chapter 6. The proportion of all borrowers who are still poor is likely to be slightly lower, since some of them are likely to have crossed the poverty line after joining. The proportion of currently poor SHG members was found in EDA and APMAS (2006) to be 51 percent. This is learnt to be about the same estimate as that found by the second or endline survey in the 7-year longitudinal study of SIDBI-partnered MFIs undertaken by the Agricultural Finance Corporation (conducted in 2006, but not yet released).

2   Assuming there is slight overlap between SHG and MFI membership, and that in some families more than one member receives microcredit, the 15.8 million persons in Row 8 of Table A.1 can be adjusted downwards to 15 million, which is a fifth of the usually estimated 75 million poor households.

3   For the assumptions see Table A.1.

4   The average size of the first loan received by SHGs members has gone up this year to Rs. 3167 (Table 2.1, assuming 14 members per SHG). However, because the average size of repeat loans is even higher (Rs. 5650, Table 2.1) and because the average tenor of SHG loans is generally 2 years, average loans outstanding may be about the same in the two models. Using the ratio reported in Chapter 2 of loans outstanding being 59% of cumulative bank loans disbursed, one derives a rough estimate of SHG loans outstanding per member of about Rs. 4000 (Table A.1). There is greater uncertainty about the average size of loans outstanding of MFI borrowers. Chapter 4 estimates that because of rapid expansion of out-reach by MFIs, average loans outstanding of sample MFIs is only Rs. 3400. However, Sa-Dhan data yields a higher figure of Rs. 5278. See Table A.1, especially footnote 15.

5   However, see Chapter 4, which estimates that PARs have increased since the last M-CRIL Review, especially sharply for large MFIs, partly because of the deterioration of the credit culture that occurred after the AP crisis. Loan portfolio audits that have been conducted by MicroSave and others often reveal a less rosy picture than the financial statements claim.

6   The average interest rate of the 129 MFIs in the Sa-Dhan Quick Report was 21.1 percent and came down for large MFIs in the sample to 19.7 percent from 20.8 percent last year. Not surprisingly, it was the small MFIs that had the higher rates (22 percent) than the large- and medium-sized MFIs (both 19.7 percent). Chapter 4 reports higher rates of up to 25 percent, probably because it includes fees etc. to the nominal rates to work out the effective interest rate. Although on average, the interest rates of Indian MFIs are slightly higher than that for other South Asian countries. The South Asian region has the lowest average rates of all regions in the world according to MIX data.

7   Thus CASHPOR restricts its lending to BPL families and identifies likely BPL families as those scoring less than 3 points, that is, those living in small houses with mud walls of less than 8 feet in height. These candidates then have to satisfy three further criteria (not less than half of household income from seasonal agricultural labour, no irrigated land, and no large farm animals, or any other significant productive assets) of the assets, and regular savings, before participants join the mainstream credit programme. SKS runs a similar programme for the "ultra-poor" through an associated NGO.

8 Many of them are increasingly describing their target group in such terms as the "the sub-prime market," the "missing middle," "low-income groups," etc. A few others have special projects to target the poorest of the poor. However, these run the risk of becoming niche activities, assigned to special projects.

9 Chapter 7A, last year's report.

10 The issues involved are discussed in Chapter 4 of last year's report.

11 Although KYC norms were motivated internationally mostly by anti-money laundering and anti-terrorism concerns, the KYC guidelines issued by RBI make it clear that they are also designed to serve a risk management and transparency enhancing role. The RBI in November 2006 advised the banks that "they, as principal financiers of MFIs, needed to engage MFIs with regard to their systems, practices, and lending policies with a view to ensuring better transparency and adherence to best practices" (Thorat 2007).

12 Some of them are reported to have suffered declines in their repayment rates, as borrowers were not assured of getting fresh loans on time, and consequent shrinkages in their portfolios. Despite this, however, the sector as a whole has shown surprising resilience, with few reported cases of partners going under.

13 The AP government has distributed smart cards in Warangal district to receive NREGA and pension payments.

14 ICICI Bank is a partner in FINO.

15 Uptake has been slow for several reasons. One of them is the perception that FINO is expensive. Its charges are levied on a per transactions basis with no discount for higher usage, and larger MFIs are concerned that above a certain level of transactions, it would be cheaper for them to go it alone through their own stand-alone systems. Joining FINO or some other core banking solution would seem to be much more attractive for start-ups and small MFIs, and for MFIs functioning as business correspondents, where the front- and back-end are equally important (Chapter 8). Also, some partners are reported to be experiencing problems in customizing FINOs software to their unique requirements, especially as it was developed originally for banking operations.

16 It is also becoming more interested in supporting the livelihoods of its customers by tailoring loan products to the specific size, cash flow, and other requirements of different activities and supporting enterprises that will buy their products.

17 SIDBI is expecting to double its portfolio to about Rs. 1000 crores from Rs. 548 crores in March 2007 (see Table A.3). New players such as Fullerton, a newly set-up finance company could also add to loan supply in a few years. Fullerton has ambitious plans to set up rural branches all over the country and get into both direct and indirect microfinance through intermediaries.

18 Table A.3 contains data on the growth of lending by selected commercial banks, financial institutions, and other bulk lenders to MFIs in 2006–07. Several large loans have been made by banks other than ICICI in the current year, but these include relatively large loans to the newly capital rich MFIs which have received equity investments. One of them is a portfolio buyout of Rs. 180 crores by Citibank (see Section 1.6). Table A.3 is incomplete and contains fewer banks than Table 7.1 in last year's report, because banks are under no obligation to furnish information on their MFI lending, and several of them were unable or unwilling to do so.

19 While arrangements such as this are often referred to as securitizations, they are more correctly regarded as portfolio buyouts, with the purchaser of the loans having the option of securitizing them by pooling them with other assets, getting them rated, and selling them in the capital markets (see Chapter 7B of last year's report).

20 Legatum's financial advisor on the transactions was Intellecap, a microfinance consulting firm and social investment adviser, which is closely associated with Aavishkaar Goodwell.

21 The private shareholders received $150 million for an investment of $6 million, or a return of over 100 percent a year compounded over an 8-year period. They received more than 12 times the book value of their shares, resulting in a valuation of Banco Compartamos of over $1.5 billion (CGAP 2007).

22 It first became a regulated finance company and then in 2006 a full-service bank.

23 See Chapter 7B of last year's report, and Table A.4.

24 The new investors in SKS seek, according to Satterthwaite (2007), to "cash out within 3–5 years," which if true is more aggressive than the stated time horizons of the India-dedicated funds. Dubai-based Legatum Capital has investments of over $1 billion in India's financial sector. Its President, Mark Stoleson is reported as saying "Legatum is a global investor that seems extraordinary opportunities without regard to sector or geography." However, the press note dated 15 May 2007 quotes him as also saying that "...we will seek to support SHARE in setting new standards for best practice and governance..."

25 Another reason to expect mergers is competition from the large MFIs expanding to other states. The borrowers and staff of the smaller existing MFIs may not be able to resist the attraction of switching to a larger, more rapidly expanding MFI. The only reported merger so far has been that between Sonata (one of the start-ups referred to in Chapter 5) and a smaller MFI, also in Uttar Pradesh, but this was reportedly at the behest of a social venture capital company.

26 It is possible also that some existing large MFIs may themselves be acquired by the large corporate houses that have recently made a foray into agri marketing as a means of financing their producers and suppliers. Yet, another possible impact of fresh capital and borrowings may be to accelerate the trend towards increasing the share of the more profitable larger loans in the portfolios of the larger MFIs. The trend towards larger loans could even lead to such MFIs gradually exiting the sector as they move up-market, making room for others. See interview with Ms Padmaja Gangireddy of Spandana in the September 2007 issue of Microfinance Insights in which she refers to a partnership with Mahindra (a tractor manufacturer) and other possibilities for making larger loans. As she points out many borrowers at present take multiple loans from different MFIs because they need larger loans. It would reduce transactions costs if such loans could be serviced by a single lender.

27 Average return of assets in the M-CRIL sample has been reduced to zero. This is not to say some individual MFIs do not offer highly profitable prospects. SKS earned an ROA of 3.3% in 2006 and ROE of 23.9%.

28 For profiles of potential investees, see "Microfinance Marketplace" (ACCESS, CARE, and MIX 2007) a directory produced for the Microfinance Investment Fair held as part of the conference in which this report was presented. The directory contains profiles of the MFIs who prepared "pitchbooks" and participated in "investment readiness trainings" prior to the fair, which was attended also by potential investors.

29   The licenses of thousands of such non-functioning NBFCs are said to be for a sale, at a premium over their net worth given demand by transforming NGO–MFIs, but they still cost much less than raising Rs. 2 crores to seek a new NBFC. The entry capital requirement was earlier Rs. 25 lakhs. Besides, not all MFI applicants have succeeded in getting new NBFC licenses, of which only about five have been issued since 2000.

30   Such as itinerant deposit collectors, small community chit funds, informal credit unions (such as the bishis of Maharashta), investments in livestock or ornaments (which can later be liquefied through the pawnbroker and moneylender), or through "reciprocal finance," that is, lending to a friend in need so that the lender can borrow reciprocally when required. The phenomenal growth of the SHG movement, in which rural women meet with unfailing regularity once a month to save small sums ranging from Rs. 10 to Rs. 50, and the fact that poor urban slum-dwellers, far from earning interest on their savings, are willing to pay to have their deposits collected at the doorstep and stored safely until they amount to a useful sum, and countless other examples, attest to the importance of the almost universal need to save.

31   Quite apart from benefits to members, the cost of funds MFIs will come down. Because Indian MFIs have had to rely exclusively on funds borrowed from the banks, their financial expense ratios (cost of funds as a proportion of total costs) are the highest in the world (see Chapter 4 of last year's report). In Bangladesh, on the other hand, interest rates are slightly lower than in India, because as much as a third of the funds base comes from member savings. Many Bangladeshi MFIs also pay a slightly higher rate to savers than the banks, because of the cost efficiencies that ensue from economies of scope in being able to use existing field staff, who have to meet borrowers once a week anyway to collect loan repayment installments and disburse fresh loans. In fact, Grameen Bank mobilizes more savings than it disburses as credit (as does Bank Rakyat Indonesia, further examples of how savings are as valued by poor clients as credit).

32   For details and a discussion, see Chapter 7A of last year's report.

33   See Ramji (2007) for an account of the campaign to saturate Gulbarga district in AP with no-frills bank accounts as part of the RBI drive to promote 100 percent financial inclusion in at least one district in each state. Nearly, all the accounts were opened in conjunction with the NREGP which would deposit payments in the accounts by cheque. In nearly all cases, the entire amount was withdrawn, with very little subsequent savings activity, on account of the cost of traveling to the banks. SHGs continued to be as widespread a form of savings as the banks, because they cost less. For the banks, the accounts were unprofitable. They were proposed to be followed up in a second phase with the issue of General Purpose Credit Cards.

34   Especially with the use of smart cards, as in the pilots referred to earlier, where the BC's field agent travels to the doorstep to collect savings and dispense withdrawals. The frequency of withdrawals, minimum accounts that can be deposited, etc., are still being worked out. However, smart cards and POS terminals are expensive and will take many years to become widespread.

35   MFIs cannot accept cash for remittances, since these are treated as savings. In the UK, in order to encourage ease of entry and competition among money transfer operators so as to lower the costs of remittances, regulators allow an MTO to hold money for up to 3 days before it is treated as savings. Adhikar (see Chapter 5B of last year's report) is talking to banks to continue its operations as a BC.

36   There are no similar caps on the maximum rate that can be paid on savings or remittance services.

37 The one argument that can be made against the last of these is that it represents an inefficient use of equity.

38 Perhaps, MFIs value the autonomy and psychic satisfactions of being autonomous (the equivalent of "being one's own boss" in preferring self-employment to salaried employment) and do not want to be anyone's agent.

39 The share of the urban population, although still lower than the global and Asian average, had grown to 31 percent by 2001.

40 In the three decades, since 1970 the number of poor went up from 52 to 67 million. Rural poverty is declining both in relative and absolute terms. However, the number of rural poor is still three times higher than that of the urban poor.

41 Thus, the extent of "human poverty" and deprivation is much worse than the "income" poverty measured and reported in the statistics. In cities like Delhi, the income poverty ratio is as low as low as 8.23 percent in 1999.

42 It is important to be able to assess whether the deficit is merely temporary, or likely to remain permanent in the absence of the provision of other inputs. Defining the target group too conservatively finesses this challenges.

43 The package includes periodic visits and hand-holding for 9 months and assistance with the installation of a computerized MIS. Equity can be provided by the sister company Aavishkaar Goodwell and loans by ICICI Bank, which is expected to play the role of lead banker to the institutions. Three start ups have signed on so far. Apart from an upfront fee, partners are charged a part of the margin between their borrowing and lending rates

44 An example is CASHPOR's, from which Box 1.1 is excerpted, and which discusses the problem of the increasing frequency and size of frauds and steps being taken to combat it. Sa-Dhan should institute an annual award for the each of the three most informative annual reports and websites.

References

ACCESS, CARE, and MIX, 2007, "Microfinance Marketplace," Directory prepared for the Microfinance Investment Fair held as part of the Microfinance India Conference, October 9–10, New Delhi

CGAP, 2007, "CGAP Reflections on the Compartamos Initial Public Offering: A Case Study on Microfinance Interest Rates and Profits," Focus Note No. 42, Washington DC

EDA Rural Systems and APMAS, 2006, "Self-Help Groups in India: A Study of the Lights and Shades for CRS, USAID, CARE and GTZ/NABARD," Microfinance India, New Delhi

Ramji, Minakshi, 2007, "Financial Inclusion in Gulbarga: Finding Usage in Access," Paper distributed at Microfinance India Conference, October 9–10, New Delhi, CMF, Chennai and ACCESS, New Delhi

Sa-Dhan, 2007, "Quick Report 2007: A Snapshot of Microfinance Institutions in India," New Delhi

Satterthwaite, David, 2007, "MicroCapital Equity Report: 2007 Starts Strong," *Microfinance Insights*, Vol. 3, June 2007, Intellecap, Mumbai

Thorat, Usha, 2006, "Financial Inclusion for Sustainable Development: Role of IT and Intermediaries," Speech, as circulated at the Annual Bankers' Conference 2006, November 4, Hyderabad

Thorat, Usha, 2007, "Microfinance and financial inclusion," Speech at Sa-Dhan function to release "Quick Report, 2007," Chennai, August 10

World Bank, 2007, "Microfinance in South Asia: Toward Financial Inclusion for the Poor," Washington, DC

CHAPTER 2

Progress Under the SHG–Bank Linkage Programme

2.1 Growth continues to be rapid...

A further 686,408 SHGs were linked during the year, bringing the cumulative number of SHGs that had ever been linked (provided with bank loans) to 2.92 million by March 2007 (Table 2.1). Assuming average group size of 14 members,[1] this translates into coverage during the year of another 9.6 million persons, over 90 percent of them women, and the total number of SHG members who have ever benefited from the programme to about 41 million. Since, some households have more than one member in the programme, the number of families benefited is slightly smaller than these numbers imply.[2] About half of them are below the poverty line. In addition to first loans to new SHGs, 457,410 SHGs received repeat loans.

The number of new SHGs linked this year represents an increase of 31 percent over the cumulative number of SHGs ever linked and an increase of 11 percent over the number of new SHGs linked last year. The latter represents only a slight deceleration of the rate of growth of loans to new SHGs from 15 percent last year. The increase in the number of repeat loans however, was exactly the same, at 33 percent. Lending under the programme grew by Rs. 6643 crores, or an increase of 48 percent over last year's new lending, which had grown by 50 percent over the previous year. The average size of first loans made to new SHGs went up by 18 percent to about Rs. 44,300 per group, or to an average of about Rs. 3200 per member. The average size of repeat loans, on the other hand, grew by 25 percent to almost Rs. 79,000 per group, or Rs. 5650 per member.[3]

2.2 We now have an estimate of the total size of the programme

Reporting under the programme has until now been carried out entirely in terms of disbursements, both annual and cumulative, rather than loans outstanding at the end of the year. The latter is a stock measure of size, as compared to a flow, and provides a better basis for comparison with the size of lending under the MFI model, or with bank lending to other categories of borrowers such as marginal farmers, since it standardizes for loan tenor.[4] In an important study based on a survey of participating banks under the programme conducted

Reporting under the programme has until now been carried out entirely in terms of disbursements both annual and cumulative, rather than loans outstanding at the end of year

Table 2.1 Growth trends in the SBLP

		2001	2002	2003	2004	2005	2006	2007
1	No. of new SHGs provided with bank loans (cumulative)	263,825	461,478	717,360	1,079,091	1,618,456	2,238,565	2,924,973
1a	Of which in Southern region (cumulative)					938,941	1,214,431	1,522,144
1b	Percent in Southern region (percent)					58	54	52
2	No. of new SHGs financed during the year	149,650	197,653	255,882	361,731	539,365	620,109	686,408
2a	Of which in Southern region						275,490	307,713
2b	Percent in Southern region						44	45
2c	Rate of growth of loans to new SHGs (percent)		32	29	41	49	15	11
3	No. of SHGs receiving repeat loans	21,630	41,413	102,391	171,669	258,092	344,502	457,410
3a	Rate of growth of repeat loans		91	147	68	50	33	33
3b	Proportion of repeat loans in total loans		17	29	40	32	36	40
4	Bank loan disbursed cumulative (Rs, crore)	481	1,026	2,049	3,904	6,896	11,398	18,040
4a	Bank loan disbursed during year (Rs, crore)	NA	545	1,023	1,855	2,994	4,499	6,643
4b	Of which, disbursed to new groups (Rs, crore)	290	453	691	1,158	1,727	2,330	3,044
4c	Of which, disbursed as repeat loans (Rs, crore)	NA	92	332	698	1,268	2,169	3,599
4d	Proportion of repeat loans in total disbursed (percent)		17	33	38	42	48	54
5a	Average loan sizes – new	19,379	22,919	27,005	32,013	32,019	37,574	44,343
5b	Repeat		22,215	32,425	40,660	49,130	62,960	78,682

Source: NABARD annual reports and Table 2.3

The RBI has now made it mandatory for all banks to report exposure and NPA figures to it every 6 months, and the NABARD annual report on the programme should be in a position to report at least the former for the year ending March 2008

by GTZ/NABARD in 2005 (Ramakrishna 2006), loans outstanding under the programme as of March 2005 were established for the first time as amounting to 59 percent of cumulative lending till that date. Moreover, of the SHGs that had been linked till that date, 71 percent had loans outstanding.[5] These ratios had been the subject of conjecture until now.

NABARD had been unable to report exposure (loans outstanding) figures under the programme because of the inability of the participating banks to furnish them in a timely fashion. Fortunately, the RBI has now made it mandatory for all banks to report exposure and NPA figures to it every 6 months, and the NABARD annual report on the programme should be in a position to report at least the former for the year ending March 2008. Until then, these estimates are a great step forward in strengthening the statistical base of the programme (and are used in Table A.1).

2.3 ...and of its savings outreach

The GTZ study also carried important new information of savings under the programme, which were reported by the survey participants as amounting to Rs. 2391 crores as of March 2005. RRBs and cooperative banks have a higher share of total savings accounts and savings outstanding than of total loan accounts and loans outstanding. One would like to think, this is because of greater ease of access to these institutions than to the commercial banks, but it turns out that as with loans (discussed in Section 2.5), savings performance is highly concentrated in a few institutions around the country, especially in the case of RRBs.[6]

Since loans outstanding were Rs. 4205 crores, the credit–deposit ratio was 1.76. In other words, a little more than half of linkage loans are financed by the SHGs themselves. However, since 29 percent of SHGs are not currently linked, and the total savings figure includes their savings, the ratio would be higher for those SHGs that are linked.

2.4 Rectifying regional skew

The SBLP expanded by 37 percent in 13 priority states which account for 67 percent of the rural poor (Table 2.2). These states were identified by NABARD in 2005 for special efforts and location-specific strategies. Growth was particularly rapid in Maharashtra (Table 2.3). As a result, the western region experienced the fastest growth (63 percent) of all the regions, and its share in the total number of groups linked is now only 5 percentage points behind its share of the total number of poor (Table 2.4). The two regions which have the most catching up to do are the central and eastern regions, whose share of groups lag behind their share of the poor by 21 and 11 percentage points, respectively. Growth in the East was 33 percent,

The two regions which have the most catching up to do are the central and eastern regions, whose share of groups lag behind their share of the poor by 21 and 11 percentage points, respectively

Table 2.2 Growth of linked SHGs in 13 priority states

State	2003	2004	2005	2006	2007	Percent growth
Assam	3,477	10,706	31,234	56,449	81,454	44
Bihar	8,161	16,246	28,015	46,221	72,339	57
Chhattisgarh	6,763	9,796	18,569	31,291	41,703	33
Gujarat	13,875	15,974	24,712	34,160	43,572	28
Himachal Pradesh	8,875	13,228	17,798	22,920	27,799	21
Jharkhand	7,765	12,647	21,531	30,819	37,317	21
Maharashtra	28,065	38,535	71,146	131,470	225,856	72
Madhya Pradesh	15,271	27,095	45,105	57,125	70,912	24
Orissa	42,272	77,588	123,256	180,896	234,451	30
Rajasthan	22,742	33,846	60,006	98,171	137,837	40
Uttar Pradesh	53,696	79,210	119,648	161,911	198,587	23
Uttaranchal	5,853	10,908	14,043	17,588	21,527	22
West Bengal	32,647	51,685	92,698	136,251	181,563	33
Total	249,462	397,464	667,761	1,005,272	1,374,917	37
Percent increase		59	68	51	37	

Source: NABARD annual reports and Table 2.3

Table 2.3 Growth trends in the SBLP for 2006–07, by state

S. No.	Region/State	Cumulative No. of SHGs provided with bank loan upto 31 March 2006	No. of new SHGs provided with bank loan during 2006-07	No. of existing SHGs provided with repeat bank loan during 2006-07	Cumulative No. of SHGs provided with bank loan upto 31 March 2007 (3+4)	Cumulative bank loan upto 31 March 2006 (Rs million)	Bank Loan during 2006-07 (Rs million)	Of Col.8, repeat bank loan to existing SHGs (Rs million)	Cumulative bank loan upto 31 March 2007 (7+8) (Rs million)
1	2	3	4	5	6	7	8	9	10
A	Northern region								
1	Himachal Pradesh	22,920	4,879	2,282	27,799	863.98	388.27	153.60	1,252.25
2	Rajasthan	98,171	39,666	3,692	137,837	2,447.94	1,447.40	191.53	3,895.34
3	Haryana	4,867	1,966	1,821	6,833	316.01	183.31	69.86	499.32
4	Punjab	4,561	1,893	517	6,454	238.86	117.74	29.24	356.60
5	Jammu & Kashmir	2,354	405	199	2,759	100.48	44.25	15.83	144.73
6	New Delhi	224	112		336	18.58	8.65		27.23
	Total (A)	133,097	48,921	8,511	182,018	3,985.85	2,189.62	460.05	6,175.47
B	North eastern region								
7	Assam	56,449	25,005	160	81,454	1,423.98	794.40	2.91	2,218.38
8	Meghalaya	735	476	0	1,211	16.19	17.40	0.00	33.59
9	Tripura	1,996	910	57	2,906	31.12	18.40	1.48	49.52
10	Sikkim	127	33	0	160	1.86	1.12	0.00	2.98
11	Manipur	1,468	1,215	0	2,683	71.85	40.80	0.00	112.65
12	Arunachal Pradesh	346	101	0	447	13.49	5.72	0.00	19.21
13	Nagaland	422	576	10	998	34.38	33.50	2.97	67.88
14	Mizoram	974	921	0	1,895	64.14	70.56	0.00	134.70
	Total (B)	62,517	29,237	227	91,754	1,657.01	981.89	7.36	2,638.90
C	Eastern region								
15	Orissa	180,896	53,555	28,806	234,451	4,754.65	3,274.27	1,409.33	8,028.92
16	Bihar	46,221	26,118	1,306	72,339	1,052.19	960.28	211.15	2,012.47
17	Jharkhand	30,819	6,498	1,153	37,317	1,114.60	391.96	84.21	1,506.56
18	West Bengal	136,251	45,312	22,014	181,563	2,424.52	2,060.64	888.40	4,485.16
19	UT of A&N Islands	164	47	30	211	8.23	4.58	3.40	12.81
	Total (C)	394,351	131,530	53,309	525,881	9,354.19	6,691.72	2,596.50	16,045.91
D	Central region								
20	Madhya Pradesh	57,125	13,787	1,726	70,912	1,666.86	499.23	65.12	2,166.09
21	Chhattisgarh	31,291	10,412	1,330	41,703	337.81	218.44	27.51	556.25
22	Uttar Pradesh	161,911	36,676	2,873	198,587	5,153.54	1,778.48	192.43	6,932.02
23	Uttarakhand	17,588	3,939	1,288	21,527	891.86	382.69	225.64	1,274.55
	Total (D)	267,915	64,814	7,217	332,729	8,050.07	2,878.84	510.69	10,928.91
E	Western region								
24	Gujarat	34,160	9,412	64	43,572	1,244.51	885.46	4.69	2,129.97
25	Maharashtra	131,470	94,386	19,382	225,856	3,951.67	2,983.86	841.01	6,935.53
26	Goa	624	395	142	1,019	55.21	28.28	9.03	83.49
	Total (E)	166,254	104,193	19,588	270,447	5,251.39	3,897.60	854.72	9,148.99
F	Southern region								
27	Andhra Pradesh	587,238	96,381	262,895	683,619	43,455.18	27,754.55	23,536.74	71,209.73
28	Karnataka	224,928	92,708	56,717	317,636	9,927.53	8,163.89	3,239.26	18,091.42
29	Kerala	86,988	30,925	13,559	117,913	4,821.48	2,889.40	1,067.68	7,710.88
30	Tamil Nadu	312,778	87,699	35,387	400,477	27,121.87	10,984.48	3,721.55	38,106.35
31	UT of Pondicherry	2,499			2,499	350.86			350.86
	Total (F)	1,214,431	307,713	368,558	1,522,144	85,676.92	49,792.32	31,565.24	135,469.24
	Grand Total	2,238,565	686,408	457,410	2,924,973	113,975.43	66,431.99	35,994.56	180,407.42

Source: www.nabard.org

Table 2.4 Growth of linked SHGs in the regions

Region	March 2004	March 2005	March 2006	Percent 2006	March 2007	Percent 2007	Share of population	Share of BPL population
Northern region	52,396	86,018	133,097	6	182,018	6	13%	7%
North-eastern region	12,278	34,238	62,517	3	91,754	3	4%	3%
Eastern region	158,237	265,628	394,351	18	525,881	18	22%	29%
Central region	127,009	197,365	267,915	12	332,729	11	25%	32%
Western region	54,815	96,266	166,254	7	270,447	9	15%	14%
Southern region	674,356	939,941	1,214,431	54	1,522,144	52	21%	15%
All India	1,079,091	1,618,456	2,238,565	100	2,924,973	100	100%	100%

Source: Poverty Estimates for 2004–05, Press Information Bureau, Government of India, New Delhi, March, 2007

about the same as overall national growth of 31 percent, and well below the previous year's growth of 48 percent. Growth in the central region was only 24 percent.

Despite relatively rapid growth in the priority states, the programme continues to remain heavily skewed in favour of the South. While the share of the South in linked groups came down marginally during the year (Table 2.1), lending in the South still accounted for 75 percent of total lending during the year, and an even higher share of repeat lending (88 percent), indicating both higher average initial loan size, and even higher average repeat loan size on account of the seniority of groups in the southern region. In Andhra Pradesh, the number of new loans remained about the same, but the number of repeat loans increased by 31 percent year. Given relatively high loan size in the state, APs share of total and repeat lending during the year constituted as much as 42 and 65 percent, respectively, of that for the country as a whole.

2.5 Operations

Table 2.5 shows the respective share of commercial banks, RRBs, and cooperatives in financing SHGs. The share of commercial banks has gone up in 2006–07, both in respect of number of loans and amounts disbursed, at the expense mostly of the of RRBs in respect of share of number of loans and at the expense of cooperatives in respect of share of loans disbursed. In 2005–06,[7] twenty-seven public sector banks accounted for 93 percent of commercial bank

Table 2.5 Agency-wise share of SHGs financed

Agency	During 2005–06				During 2006–07			
	SHGs		Loans		SHGs		Loans	
	No.	%	Amount	%	No.	%	Amount	%
CBs	34,4567	56	28,284	63	406,707	59	44,101	66
RRBs	176,178	28	12,226	27	170,783	25	17,089	26
Co-operatives	99,364	16	4,481	10	108,878	16	5,242	8
Total	620,109	100	44,991	100	686,368	100	66,432	100

Source: NABARD annual reports

financing and 20 private banks for 7 percent. Among public sector banks, the SBI linked by far the highest number of SHGs during the year (142,034)[8] followed by Indian Bank (30,632) and Canara Bank (18,445). We know from the GTZ/NABARD study that in March 2005, SBI accounted for 40 percent of all active clients (i.e. those in currently linked SHGs) and the top five lenders accounted for more than two-thirds of them.[9] Similarly, 20 out of the 196 participating RRBs served 50 percent of active clients, and cooperative banks in three states (Tamil Nadu, Karnataka, and West Bengal) accounted for 82 percent of those served by the cooperative banks.[10] ICICI accounted for half the SHGs linked by the private banks.

The share of the three models of linkage remained roughly the same, with Model II (SHGs formed by agencies other than banks, mainly NGOs, but also farmer clubs, and individual rural volunteers who are paid a fee) increasing its share from 74 to 75 percent of cumulative linkages at the expense of the share Model I, in which SHGs are formed by the banks themselves. In Model III, NGOs and SHG federations act as credit intermediaries, or in other words as MFIs, borrowing at their own risk to on-lend to SHGs.[11]

An interesting addition to the intermediaries being used under Model III was made during the year through a pilot project in five districts of Tamil Nadu to lend through post offices. Post offices have huge potential outreach, with about 155,000 branches, and have close local knowledge

An interesting addition to the intermediaries being used under Model III was made during the year through a pilot project in five districts of Tamil Nadu to lend through post offices. Post offices have huge potential outreach, with about 155,000 branches, and have close local knowledge. They will borrow at 6 percent from NABARD and on-lend to SHGs at 9 percent. Like the banks, they will use NGOs to form and train groups, and the NGOs will be eligible for the grants NABARD pays NGOs to defray their costs (but only partially).[12]

2.6 SHG lifespans

In perhaps the first rigorous academic study of an aspect of the SHG movement, using sophisticated econometric methods (Baland et al. 2007), welcome confirmation was found for two of the "lights," or reassuring findings, of the SHG "Lights and Shades" Study (LSS) discussed at length in last year's report (EDA and APMAS 2006). These relate to the longevity groups and the dropout rate. In a sample of 1102 PRADAN promoted groups in three tribal districts of Orissa and Chhattisgarh, only 10 percent of groups formed between 1998 and 2006 were found by the survey carried out in early 2007, to be no longer active. This is comparable with the estimated proportion of defunct and broken groups of 7 percent, in groups of average age of 6 years, in the much smaller 214-SHG LSS sample taken across 4 states.

The drop-out rate of individual members was found to be almost identical, at 14 percent.[13] The study found that the factors behind group survival were different from those behind member longevity. The former was strongly associated with the presence of an educated member in the group, perhaps because this facilitates transactions, interaction with bank officials, and the accuracy of book-keeping. A second factor was the presence of other groups in the village. Since PRADAN organizes groups in the same village into clusters, this is the first empirical finding in support of the potential role of higher-level formations such as clusters of SHGs and their federations in enhancing SHG quality and sustainability. On the other hand, a third possible factor, social heterogeneity, measured by the number of different castes represented in the group, does not have systematic effects on group survival.

However, the study found that social heterogeneity does increase the probability of individual member exit from the group (or of dropping out), presumably by increasing the probability of personal conflict with other members, which was the single most important reason for departures in Chhattisgarh, and the second most important one in Orissa, where difficulties in meeting loan repayment and monthly savings obligations were twice as important. This last reason for member departures may also explain the finding of the study that tribal and SC women have shorter SHG lifespans than groups that lie higher in the social hierarchy.

On the other hand, higher levels of education, bigger land-holdings, and more relatives within the groups are associated with a lower probability of exit. The finding about landholdings is interesting, because it is well known that an important use of SHG loans is to finance crop inputs and the other recurrent costs of family agriculture. Since a large proportion of SHG members, both above the below the poverty line, are farmers' wives, the SHG programme, as it expands, is beginning to become increasingly important as a source of crop credit. It already supplies close to one-fifth of total agricultural lending by the banks to marginal farmers with less than 2.5 acres of land.[14]

2.7 Quality remains the major problem, and may be growing: A case study of the programme in a priority state

Another important recent study, "Quality Issues of SHGs in Rajasthan," conducted recently by the Centre for Microfinance, Jaipur and APMAS, gives us a much more differentiated picture of the programme in a particular state than is usually possible in a multi-state study.[15] It provides a useful corrective to any complacency that might be engendered by the impressive macro numbers for the country as a whole. It also serves as a useful reminder that while it is important for the programme to grow in the 13 priority states (Rajasthan is one of them), long-run growth will be much more rapid if it takes place on the basis of strong foundations (Centre for Microfinance and APMAS 2006). The report finds that the "overall quality of groups is low and there are startling inter-district and intra-promoter variations across the groups." The proportion of A groups was 30 percent as against 66 percent found by APMAS (2005) in AP.

The report finds that the "overall quality of groups is low and there are startling inter-district and intra-promoter variations across the groups." The proportion of A groups was 30 percent as against 66 percent found by APMAS (2005) in AP

The study was carried out in five districts based on a sample of 202 SHGs, a little more than half of which were of less than 3 years old given the age of the programme in Rajasthan. However, a third were between 3 and 5 years old. Interestingly, the number of BPL members were almost exactly the same as the number of poor members as defined in LSS (49 percent as against 51 percent, respectively). While the study agrees with other studies that SHGs have a significant impact on *women's empowerment*, a medium impact on *household income*, and that *overdues* and defaults on bank loans are not a serious problem, it found the *drop-out rate* to be considerably higher (30 percent for groups older than 5 years, with a disproportionate share of them being BPL members). Regarding the *quality of governance*, at least a tenth of all groups had held no meetings at all during the year, and more than 20 percent has carried out all transactions outside the meetings.

Savings per member were an average of Rs. 40 a month, but two-thirds of the amount saved had accumulated as idle funds parked in the banks, instead of being lent out to members. The report is critical of the fact that these funds constituted 44 percent of bank loans outstanding to the groups, on which they were paying much higher interest than they received on their savings balances. It is not clear, however, what part of these funds belonged to groups with loans outstanding.[16]

The study observed several other symptoms of weak loan demand, such as the fact that only 59 percent of members borrowed, of which 14 percent were group leaders,[17] and that 12 percent of the groups received first loans of less than Rs. 5000.[18] It also notes some extreme instances of the deleterious effects of targetitis, with cases in one district of small loans being forced on groups who were told to repay within 2 months. Although, on average, groups received 1.6 loans each, the average amount of loans received including repeat loans was only Rs. 27,000.[19]

With two-thirds of sample groups organized by government functionaries, primarily anganwadi workers from the DWCD,[20] which is also the nodal coordinating agency, as it is in many other states, the Rajasthan programme is particularly vulnerable to the distortions introduced by targets. The study proposes that monitoring of the programme should henceforth be in terms of the respective numbers of A, B, and C grade groups, as well as in respect of repeat loans and size of loans, which is a useful suggestion for the programme at the national level too. It suggests that the 50 percent of groups in the B grade need to brought up to the A grade with extra inputs of training, hand-holding support, and exposure visits. The DCWD, which receives inadequate funds as the main SHPI, needs to enhance its own capacity in order to accomplish this.

The study proposes that monitoring of the programme should henceforth be in terms of the respective numbers of A, B, and C grade groups, as well as in respect of repeat loans and size of loans, which is a useful suggestion for the programme at the national level too

The report makes the important point that although it is claimed that the programme has achieved an important paradigm shift from a loan-centred to a savings-centred strategy, "the sample groups, by and large, are functioning around loans if not subsidies.[21] Savings are nominal at times."[22] But because they are compulsory they exclude a large number of the poor, whose incomes fluctuate. Several other studies have shown that reluctance to commit themselves to fixed monthly savings in the face of uncertain and fluctuating incomes is the single most important reason for why only half the membership of the movement is poor, and for dropping out. The report recommends introducing therefore some flexibility in savings and repayments to overcome the effects, which are particularly strong in Rajasthan, both because of seasonality in agriculture,[23] and of migration. Second, it proposes distribution of at least part of the accumulated corpus of groups from time to time as "dividends," both as an incentive to save, and so as to ensure that the accounting is timely and accurate enough to ensure allocability of the corpus between members. It recommends that at the very least, all groups prepare, discuss and approve the balance sheet of the group once a year, which is yet another reminder of the importance of good bookkeeping (and training for it) in the programme.

All in all, the study provides a much more nuanced view of how the programme actually operates in one priority state, and draws attention to the urgency of tackling quality related issues if the programme is to grow sustainably. We need many more state-level studies before deciding how representative the problems identified are, but anecdotal experience suggests they are widespread, and a "vision document" prepared by the Government of Orissa itself says the "mushrooming growth of groups in the state and lack of adequate monitoring has resulted in irregular savings, irregular meetings, improper book-keeping, lack of solidarity and peer pressure in the groups..." (Government of Orissa 2005).[24]

As the Rajasthan study points out, the programme suffers from several "structural" constraints which are particularly acute in Rajasthan, with its low population density and widely dispersed habitats,[25] high female illiteracy,[26] cultural tradition of female seclusion,[27] predominance of agriculture, and high incidence of migration.[28] One suspects however, that the most important factor explaining differences in programme quality across states is the quality of grass-roots governance in a state. It is also important that such studies be carried out by neutral observers such as state level resource agencies whose independence is not fettered by any assistance they may receive from the state government or interested donors.

2.8 Statistics

As noted earlier, the biggest gap in the statistical foundations of the programme, the lack of exposure (loans outstanding) data, is about to be filled. But the others identified in last year's report remain: (i) the lack of disaggregated data on repeat loans (separating them into second, third and subsequent loans) so that loan size progression can be observed, (ii) data on savings balances and CD ratios (although we now have an estimate for March 2005), and (iii) reported data on institution- and state-wise NPAs under the programme, although, again, we do have one-time information on NPAs as of March 2005 from the GTZ report. A further suggestion, as noted above, is a tabulation of the quality of the groups in terms of the mix of their A, B, and C grades.

Since NABARD is likely to become the regulator under the new microfinance bill pending in parliament, a major objective of which is to improve the national database, it needs to set a good example by presenting timely and comprehensive data on the programme under its own direct oversight.

Since NABARD is likely to become the regulator under the new microfinance bill pending in parliament, a major objective of which is to improve the national database, it needs to set a good example by presenting timely and comprehensive data on the programme under its own direct oversight

Endnotes

1   *This is the average size for the overall sample reported in the most recent large scale survey of SHGs, "Self-Help Groups in India: A Study of the Lights and Shades" (EDA and APMAS 2006), discussed in last year's State of the Sector report, and hereafter referred to as LSS. For a national average, this is probably on the lower side, given that the average age of the groups was 6 years, and the drop-out rate 10 percent. In its annual reports on the programme, NABARD uses a higher figure (15 percent in 2004–05 and 14.7 percent in 2005–06).*

2   *A recent estimate of the percentage of members who have at least one relative in the group is about 10 percent (Baland et al. 2007). If they had only one relative each, the number of families benefited would have to be adjusted downwards by 5 percent.*

3   *The corresponding increases last year were 17 and 28 percent, respectively. Data on repeat loans are for an unreported, and probably unknown, mix of second, third, and further loans.*

4   *Thus two six monthly seasonal crop loans will show twice the disbursement level of a 1 year loan of the same size.*

5   *See Table 1 of Ramakrishna (2006). Responses were received from all the 27 public sector commercial banks participating in the programme, 192 out of the 196 RRBs, and 114 cooperative credit institutions from the five major states who hold 95 percent of the share of the cooperative banks in the SHG programme.*

6   *Thus, in terms of savings outstanding, 10 percent of RRBs in the country account for 83 percent of total savings outstanding. The situation is better with the DCCBs where 20 percent of the institutions account for 45 percent of total savings outstanding.*

7   *NABARD's annual report on the SBLP, and hence, the corresponding data for 2006–07, were not available at the time of writing this chapter in late September 2007.*

8   *The SBI has announced a goal of linking 1 million SHGs by March 2008.*

9   *These are the State Bank of India, Andhra Bank, State Bank of Hyderabad, Indian Overseas Bank, and Indian Bank (Table 1 in Ramakrishna, 2006). Most of AP's programme is served by the second two.*

10   *See Tables 6 and 7 in Ramakrishna (2006).*

11   *The share of Model I declined from 20 to 17 percent, unlike last year when it increased, and that of Model III increased from 6 to 8 percent, after declining steadily for the last few years.*

12   *Thus, the post offices under the pilot are in a sense being given special treatment since intermediaries under Model III are expected to defray the costs of group promotion through the margin. The most common estimate used for the actual cost of forming and "hand-holding" groups is Rs. 10,000, incurred over the few years necessary, but NABARD treats the incentive as an add-on, meant to supplement grants from other sources. See last year's report for a detailed discussion. An increase in the incentive*

from Rs. 3000 to Rs. 4000 is reportedly under consideration. (The incentive is already higher in the Northeast, where it is Rs. 5000 per SHG.)

13 The rate in LSS was 10 percent, but some of the drop-outs among the 14 percent went on to join other groups. Overall, the study estimated that about 20 percent of SHG members who had joined a group had left the SHG network within the 8-year period.

14 Commercial bank loans outstanding in 2003–04 to marginal farmers were Rs. 7953 crores according to Table 59 of the RBI Handbook of Statistics on the Indian Economy (on short- and long-term direct commercial bank finance to farmers in various land-holding classes) as compared with Rs. 4068 crores of SHG loans outstanding (estimated, as discussed above, by assuming they constituted 59 percent of cumulative lending in that year). Commercial bank lending to marginal farmers is of course lower than cooperative and RRB lending.

15 Although LSS provided extensive tabulation and analysis on state-wise performance in the four states it studied (AP, Karnataka, Orissa, and Rajasthan), it looked at 214 SHGs in the four states as against the 202 in a single state in this study. The state that has been studied the most extensively is AP, largely because of the presence in that state of the first and largest SHG resource institution, APMAS. Last year's Report carries in Chapter 2 a section describing the findings of APMAS (2005), a comprehensive summary of several studies on SHGs in AP, conducted by APMAS since 2003.

16 To the extent they were, one reason could be mismanagement by group leaders, made possible by the fact that many members had no clear picture of "where the savings is, how it is being used and for what purpose..." Another reason could be the reported practice by the banks of impounding the savings of the group as collateral, against both the letter and spirit of the linkage programme. Impounding of part of the loan amount is also reported to have been in vogue, with no interest paid on the deducted amount. To the extent savings belonged to surplus groups with no bank loans outstanding, the "balancing" of funds between surplus and deficit groups is one of the functions proposed for federations performing financial intermediation, as discussed in Chapter 3.

17 In this sense loan distribution was less equitable than in LSS. On the other hand, need-based borrowing is clearly preferable to loans being distributed between all group members equally, which is another symptom of weak loan demand (and in some cases also lack of trust within a group) and happened in the case of 13 percent of all loans, with another 16 percent being distributed on the basis of "need plus equal basis."

18 The banks lend at between 8 and 12 percent as in other parts of the country, but on-lending rates range from as low as 8 percent (the rate at which funds are borrowed) to 36 percent. The on-lending rate is the lowest in the district in which the leaders receive the highest proportion of loans.

19 Instances were noted of first loans of Rs. 1000, a second loan of Rs. 2000, and third loans of Rs. 5000. Evidence of the emergence of a significant loan absorption constraint has been found in many other studies. However, the solution lies not within the SHG programme, but enhancing the effectiveness of the general development programme in increasing the productive opportunities open to the poor.

20 These are the Anganwadi Worker (AWW) and Assistant Anganwadi Worker (AWA), who not only organized groups, but in most groups promoted by them also became the leaders of the groups, and sometimes of more than one group. The report notes that groups have failed to internalize the norms of the programme, and tend to be perpetually dependent on SHG staff for their day-to-day activities. Also, meeting dates, venues, and timing tend to be fixed at the convenience of SHPI field staff and leaders.

Thus, group meetings are fixed in the afternoons, which is a convenient time for the AWW and field staff of NGOs, but not for members, who are free only by late evening.

21   *The reference to subsidies is to the 10 SGSY groups. Apart from subsidies, these groups had received average loans of Rs. 300,000, which is 10 times higher than the average received by the 151 groups linked under the regular programme. Fifty-one groups in the sample of 202 groups had not yet been linked.*

22   *Although average savings were Rs. 40 a month, about 50 percent of groups had saving of Rs. 20 or less a month.*

23   *Over 85 percent of the female work force is employed in agriculture, either as cultivators or labourers.*

24   *Orissa, along with Rajasthan, is one of the 13 priority states where the programme is growing relatively rapidly. With the assistance of CARE India, Orissa prepared a "vision" document released by the Chief Minister for Mission Shakti, which lays down the goal of forming 300,000 groups by the end of 2008, of which 80 percent would be credit linked, and would be of grade A. Repeat linkage would be ensured in the case of 50 percent of the groups and average lending per group would be Rs. 40,000. Every revenue village in the state would have at least one SHG. Top priority would be given to the formation of cluster and block level federations in every panchayat and block, respectively, as well as "activity based federations" and cooperatives (see Chapter 3). The government would facilitate the setting up of a Capacity Building Institute to meet the capacity building demands of stakeholders (Government of Orissa 2005).*
Unfortunately, the Department of Women and Child Development does not publish statistics on progress towards these goals, although the target for credit-linked groups is likely to be 90 percent reached as can be seen from Table 2.2. Also, 6065 panchayat level clusters and 208 block level federations had been formed by March 2007, a coverage of 95 percent of the goal, although mostly only on paper. According to NABARD statistics, the proportion of repeat loans was only 12 percent by March 2007 (Table 2.3). Since a capacity building and resource institute for the programme has not been set up yet, no quality assessment study exists yet similar to the present one being discussed for Rajasthan, although a rating exercise was carried out in 2003 which found that the number of A, B, and C groups constituted 29, 14, and 57 percent of the total, respectively.

25   *These partly explain relatively low average group size of 12 and irregularities in meetings and attendance.*

26   *At about 75 percent, one of the lowest in the country.*

27   *Rajasthan is one of the most conservative states in the country, with high discrimination against women. A high proportion of members are elderly women who are subjected to less seclusion.*

28   *Migration is one of the most important livelihood strategies in the state. Those women who are left behind are unable to participate in meetings, because of heavier workloads caused by the absence of the male family members.*

References

APMAS, 2005, "A Study on SHG–Bank Linkage in Andhra Pradesh," Hyderabad

Baland, J-M, R Somanathan and L Vandewalle, 2007, "Micro-finance Lifespans: A Study of Attrition and Exlusion in Self-Help Groups in India," Paper prepared for presentation at the Brookings–NCAER India Policy Forum 2007, July 17–18, New Delhi

EDA Rural Systems and APMAS, 2006, "Self-Help Groups in India: A Study of the Lights and Shades for CRS, USAID, CARE and GTZ/NABARD," Microfinance India, New Delhi

Government of Orissa, 2005, "Empowered Woman: A Vision Document for Micro-Finance in Orissa," Women and Child Development Department, Bhubaneshwar

Centre for Microfinance and APMAS, 2006, "Quality Issues of SHGs in Rajasthan," CMF, Jaipur

Ramakrishna, RV, 2006, "Management Information System (MIS): SHG–Bank Linkage Programme," Mimeo, GTZ, New Delhi

CHAPTER 3

SHG Federations: Financiers or Nurturers?[1]

A few years ago, a chapter such as this might have started with the question "are federations necessary?" but today, whatever the answer to that question, federations seem to be a fait accompli, with a 2005 estimate of at least 66,000 in the country as a whole (Reddy et al. 2007). This number has increased since then,[2] propelled both by a variety of push factors, with donors, governments, and several banks supporting them for various reasons, as well as by the pull factor of the demand for credit that remains unsatisfied by the SBLP. Several multilateral and bilateral donor-sponsored projects have included federations as an important component of their SHG-based livelihoods projects, primarily as a means of ensuring the long run institutional sustainability of the SHG programme.[3] More communitarian-minded donors, mainly international and local NGOs, have promoted federations for the stronger organized identity, and greater possibilities for collective action, they offer SHG women, much stronger than a single SHG could ever do.[4]

A number of state governments, AP being the most important of them, accounting for almost half the federations in the country through the IKP programme, are attracted by federations as a convenient means of offering a variety of economic and social services in the rural areas, as well as for their empowerment and potential political advantages. West Bengal, for instance, has a minister for SHGs, who is reported to oversee 13,600 panchayat level federations and 350 block level federations, and Kerala implements the Kudumbasree programme consisting of about 15,000 federations through local bodies.[5] Banks are interested in the federations for the economies of scale they promise, and SHGs are attracted by the greater sense of efficacy they experience through belonging to a larger fraternity, referred to often as "being able to walk into the Collector's office." Finally, in areas or pockets where credit demand is high, many of them are impatient with the quantum and timeliness of credit available under the SBLP, despite rapid expansion of the programme in recent years.[6]

A number of state governments, AP being the most important of them, accounting for almost half the federations in the country through the IKP programme, are attracted by federations as a convenient means of offering a variety of economic and social services in the rural areas, as well as for their empowerment and potential political advantages

While the estimate of 66,000 federations needs to be updated, it is important to note that the numbers come mostly from a few states in which government-sponsored programmes have set up federations in every panchayat or block. Except in AP and Kerala, many of these have yet to be registered, and the vast majority are still inactive. The number of federations set up by NGOs and NGO-networks is much smaller, and probably below 2 to 3 thousand.[7] Even for them, details on distribution by level (whether cluster or higher), size, type, major programme under which promoted, etc. are lacking. The sheer heterogeneity of federations,[8] the fact that many of them are still nascent and inchoate, and the dearth of case studies all complicate the effort of coming up with a satisfactory typology, a necessary step in building a meaningfully differentiated database.[9]

It is important to note also, that despite their obvious appeal, the "are they necessary?" question is still being asked by the main actor in the SHG movement – NABARD[10] – and by others who argue that in a situation of limited promotional resources (promoter capacity and the long-term commitment required), it is more efficient to devote these scarce resources to improving the quality of SHGs and, therefore, the flow of resources from the banks to SHGs directly, which after all is likely to remain by far the larger source of funds to SHGs than bulk funding through federations. Thus although many federations have already been formed, this argument goes, they are not entirely a "sunk cost" in the context of the further huge growth of the SBLP envisaged.

The tentative hypothesis put forward in this chapter is that we should still be very interested in federations primarily as a cost effective means (but not the only one) of enhancing the prospects of sustainability of the SBLP and individual SHG quality

The tentative hypothesis put forward in this chapter is that we should still be very interested in federations primarily as a cost-effective means (but not the only one) of enhancing the prospects of sustainability of the SBLP and individual SHG quality.[11] We need a greatly stepped up programme of coordinated action research to fully investigate the potential of federations in this respect. Moreover, as discussed below, there appear to be situations where they are needed for their financial services too, as in bridge financing, as DHAN Foundation seems to have concluded, or where federations have become so strong and efficient that lenders are genuinely persuaded about the scale advantages of lending to them directly, adding a third channel to the two main existing channels of microfinance in the country, or what have been called Community-based MFIs (CBMFIs). Third, federations offer the prospect of very real empowerment benefits. Ultimately, and quite apart from their benefits as aggregators of services, it is these benefits, of experiencing a sense of efficacy through advocacy and collective action, that drives SHGs and many promoters to federate. It is this aspect of the SHG "revolution" that attracts many observers the most. As Jairam Ramesh points out, financial services are only part of the success story. "More fundamental has been voice, identity, and empowerment" (Box 3.1).

Box 3.1   "The SHG Revolution: What next?"

"Today, in some parts of the country, SHGs are taking on new roles and responsibilities that lie at the very core of livelihood security for the poor. Indeed, as institutions of social capital, they offer great potential... The SHG network in Andhra has gone beyond credit...

First, it has taken up the marketing of commodities like maize, neem, soybean, coffee, lac, and red gram. Last year, the value of procurement in the region was of Rs. 130 crores. The big challenge here is to go beyond traditional marketing and get into value-addition in meaningful measure and develop linkages with exporters and processors directly.

Second, it is being used to distribute old-age pensions in 2006–07, over Rs. 700 crores was distributed to around 3 million beneficiaries through the SHGs. Timely disbursement of pensions and disbursements without a "consideration" are the hallmark of SHG involvement.

Third, the elements of a community-based food security system are being put in place. At the moment, it consists almost entirely of a rice credit line, but the goal seems to be paddy purchase and milling by the SHG network at the village and mandal level itself.

Fourth, dairy interventions have started with livestock being purchased through SHG–Bank linkages and with the SHG network setting up bulk milk coolers and milk procurement centres. My own involvement has been to try and ensure that there are links established between the network of SHGs and the traditional NDDB procurement network... Dairying is very important as an income-augmenting occupation to crop agriculture.

There is one more somewhat unusual intervention through the SHG network. This relates to non-pesticide management in agriculture, particularly cotton... Cotton lies at the heart of the suicide tragedies that have stalked the state over the past decade and so this particular initiative has great significance. So far, something like 2 lakh acres have been covered and by the end of the decade about 10 percent of the net sown area in the state will be covered.

In my capacity as Minister of State of Commerce, I am particularly interested in exports of spices. Today, about 25 percent of the $600 million of spice exports is accounted for by chillies that are grown predominantly in Andhra Pradesh. We have discovered that chillies without pesticide residue command a premium in world markets. I will distinguish here between non-pesticide agriculture where fertilizers are still used and organic farming where yields may turn out to be lower but net returns to farmers could actually increase. NPM agriculture is, in my view, the first step to organic farming that has relevance in certain situations and niche regions.

I want to mention another important initiative... About 2 million hectares of government land has been assigned to the landless poor in Andhra Pradesh over the past decades. But as is well known, the productivity of these assigned lands is very low — perhaps, that is why they were "assigned" in the first place. Against this background, the state government has launched a comprehensive land development project that takes up about 10 percent of this area to be brought under productive use in four years time.

The Andhra SHG story has undoubtedly been government-driven.... What it shows is that government can innovate, that government can demonstrate commitment and concern. Efficiency is not the monopoly of the private sector nor is sensitivity the preserve of civil society. Within the government system, there are people who are motivated and who, given political support, can and will deliver...

To be sure, over time the SHG network must become self-sustaining. Indeed, that is the true test of whether the government has succeeded or not. When will this happen? I have been asking this question of my colleagues in Andhra Pradesh and the answer they have come up is the following. A Mandal Samakhya will have the capacity to be on its own feet when it has a monthly net income of Rs. 50,000. Today, while a detailed financial analysis is still being done, it appears that of the 1000 Mandal Samakhyas, perhaps just about 10 to 15 percent meet this criteria. Clearly, there is a long way to go yet. Further, even in these 100-odd Mandal Samakhyas, the bulk of the monthly income — around three-fourths — is really interest income. This proportion has to reduce.

.it is critical to see SHGs not as just networks for confidence-building and empowerment, but also as networks that must have access to new economic opportunities. One of the initiatives taken by the Ministry of Commerce in recent months is to link export promotion councils with SHGs so that the benefits of export expansion can accrue directly to the poor where they have skills. A beginning has been made in leather in Tamil Nadu and in shellac in Andhra Pradesh. The export promotion councils are working with SHGs to provide design and marketing assistance, while the SHGs are responsible for production. Another example is how the SHG-run lace export park in Narsapur in West Godavari district of Andhra Pradesh is being facilitated to establish global linkages. A recent breakthrough has been obtained with Ikea.

... it is critical to see SHGs not as just networks for confidence-building and empowerment but also as networks that must have access to new economic opportunities

...SHGs are not panaceas for every situation. In India, there have been many instances of innovative initiatives have been taken and pretty soon these initiatives degenerating into "solutions in search of problems" ...Since the state administrative machinery has collapsed in so many areas, there is a temptation to give the SHG network an ever expanding role.

...Proponents of SHGs have raised the possibility of SHGs managing PHCs, for instance. When there is a good thing going, exaggerated expectations can and do set in, especially when there is political mileage to be derived as well. Drawing a *Lakshman Rekha* around the SHG network, so that it does not spread itself very thin is very essential. At the same time, I do recognize that there has to be some room for responding to new challenges. For instance, now that

Andhra Pradesh has emerged as number 1 in HIV/AIDS prevalence in the country, public health planners should use the extensive SHG network for combating this scourge.

I had alluded to MFIs earlier... I believe that both have important roles to play. The separation of the social organization to be performed by the IKP and capital mobilization and disbursement to be performed by the MFIs is the starting point of a cooperative approach. In such an approach, the regulation of the industry will be driven by the market and community, rather than by legislation.

...the panchayat revolution...has swept India, thanks to the 73rd Amendment to the Constitution. While much remains to be done, over 30 lakh elected representatives now all over rural India with over 12 lakh of them being women is a visible manifestation of this momentous change.

...Simultaneously, there has been the SHG upsurge, an upsurge that is uniquely Indian. Over 3 crore women are now linked to banks through over 22 lakh SHGs and as I have shown, financial services is only a small part of their success story. More fundamental has been voice, identity, and empowerment.

...The relationship between SHG institutions and panchayat bodies needs greater attention... There is really no conflict between the two. SHG institutions can and must play a supporting role in social mobilization and in social audit, like, for instance, in the NREGA.

...Over time, as SHG members gain in voice and self-confidence, they can be expected to contest panchayat elections on their own. In the recent local body elections, about 9 to 10 percent of those elected to mandal and zilla panchayats were "SHG women," something that was unheard of before.

...For inclusive growth which has become the mantra these days, India needs not just globalization as traditionally understood but actually *globalization* which ensures that economic growth is more broad-based, equitable and sustainable than it has been so far. Panchayats are institutions of representation. SHGs are institutions of participation. These are the twin pillars on which India's glocalization strategy should rest."

Excerpts from Silver Jubilee Lecture at the Society for the Promotion of Wastelands Development, New Delhi, May 5, 2007 by Jairam Ramesh, Minister of State for Commerce (with a shortened version in the *Economic and Political Weekly*, September 8–14, 2007)

The separation of the social organization to be performed by the IKP and capital mobilization and disbursement to be performed by the MFIs is the starting point of a cooperative approach

3.1 Non-financial support services to SHGs

It is useful to discuss the experience with federations according to three broad sets of objectives they could serve. These are (i) non-financial support services designed to strengthen the quality of member SHGs, (ii) financial services, and (iii) non-credit related economic and social activities.

Between the first two of these at any rate, most observers would regard the first as more important. While credit can be accessed through direct linkages, and that too relatively easily judging by the pace of expansion of the SBLP, studies show that the long-run health of SHGs and the very sustainability of the programme depends crucially on strengthening SHG capacity.[12] Federations are an important means of doing so, although it is important to note that they are not the only ones.

Other approaches are (i) institutions such as MYRADA's Community Managed Resource Centres (CMRCs) (Box 3.2), (ii) accounting system innovations such as Computer Munshi, (iii) greater capacity building of the capacity builders themselves, strengthening SHPAs to provide more effective and longer-term hand-holding of SHGs directly, financed if necessary by higher and longer-term promotional assistance from government, (iv) bank branches insisting on better account keeping and playing a stronger role in capacity building of linked SHGs, either directly or though outsourcing (as SBI is doing), (v) DRDAs and government programmes eschewing targets, and preferably direct group formation by government functionaries altogether, or at least improving their own capacity building efforts, and (vi) induction of technology.[13]

Box 3.2   MYRADA's Community Managed Resource Centres

MYRADA had set up 89 CMRCs with 303 full-time workers by December 2006, each covering 100 to 200 SHGs, watershed institutions, and other CBOs to provide training, support, and information on a variety of government schemes, insurance and legal matters, and equipped with telephone and internet facilities to access information, download forms, etc. The major activity is training (about 6000 trainings a year) not just on SHG related skills such as book-keeping, but in other areas too such as awareness of health, veterinary care, disability, and legal issues. Eye, blood-donation, and animal health camps are also organized. All services are paid for. Fifteen CMRCs had reached self-sufficiency by September 2005, including payment for the services of the Manager and other staff, both full-time and community volunteers.

CMRCs play a key role in MYRADA's withdrawal strategy after 6 to 8 years in an area. The centres are strictly speaking not representative organizations (and are unlike federations in this respect), but are run by management committees comprising representatives of member CBOs. MYRADA also has federations through which representatives to the CMRCs are chosen, but these are cluster level groups of only 10 to 15 SHGs, kept small so as to maximize participation, and are paid for by one-time admission fees and monthly membership fees from the SHGs. Unlike in many other parts of the country, the availability of local book-keepers does not seem to be a major issue in MYRADA's areas, and book-keeping is handled by the SHGs themselves, with the assistance of training offered by the CMRCs. Facilitation in availing of linkage loans from the bank branches, and in getting loans from Sanghamitra, is offered by the CMRCs and not by the federations, whose task is essentially to offer audit services, review the functioning of member SHGs, resolve any conflicts, and organize trainings and exposure visits through the CMRC.

Based on discussions with Al Fernandez, MYRADA

However, these approaches are not alternatives to federations,[14] or to each other. The main non-financial services federations can provide to develop capacity are (i) training and hand-holding in book-keeping and accounting, (ii) direct provision of accounting services, (iii) ongoing quality monitoring, (iv) periodic grading or quality assessment, and (v) annual auditing. Other non-financial services they can provide, although not directly related to capacity-building are (i) conflict resolution and problem solving within and between groups, (ii) promoting new groups, (iii) awareness building and advocacy of social issues, and (iv) livelihood promotion activities if the funding is available.

We need much more action research to get a feel of how federations can provide such services effectively and sustainably. APMAS's (2006) quality assessment report found that the provision of services to be the weakest aspect of federation performance across the six indicators in GRADES.[15] One of the best-known cases of a federation providing non-financial services along with limited financial intermediation (but no bulk borrowing[16] from external sources) is that of Sakhi Samiti in Alwar district, Rajasthan, which was promoted by PRADAN. After supporting it for about 10 years PRADAN exited Sakhi Samiti 6 years ago. Since then Sakhi Samiti has been successfully providing book-keeping services to about 250 SHGs on its own, through a small staff of field workers at the federation level, and one munshi (accountant) based at each of the three clusters. Sakhi Samiti charges member SHGs Rs. 2 per Rs. 1000 of cumulative group savings a month, so that a typical group pays about Rs. 200 a month. It also facilitates linkages of new groups with the local banks, for which it charges half a percent of the loan amount. A third source of revenue is lending from an associated fund called Sakhi Suvidha, to which each group makes a one-time contribution or Rs. 1000, and each group member Rs. 50. Loans from the fund are meant to tide groups over periods when they are waiting for loans from the banks, and the fund lends much less than the banks. It seems these sources of income[17] are insufficient to recover costs fully, which are met through cross-subsidization from other activities. It is not known how much higher fees (and interest on Sakhi Suvidha loans, or its scale of operations) would have to be for Sakhi Samiti as a whole to achieve self-sufficiency.[18]

Anecdotal evidence suggests that once federations get into the business of accessing bulk funds, the preoccupation with sustainability leads to a neglect of non-financial services

A question that often arises is whether it helps to separate non-financial from financial service provision (i.e. for federations to do one or the other). Anecdotal evidence suggests that once federations get into the business of accessing bulk funds, the preoccupation with sustainability leads to a neglect of non-financial services, given limitations on field worker time and managerial energy and attention-span. Also, it has been pointed out that the balance of power within federations tends to shift away from the primaries towards the higher tiers, with the former becoming more dependent on the latter, and the federation becoming less responsive to the primaries and their non-financial needs and interests. Shashi Rajagopalan in particular has in various writings described the dynamics involved.[19]

It could be argued, on the other hand, that a bulk funder would itself be expected to exercise pressure for maintaining group quality out of prudential self-interest. However, there is little evidence to support this hypothesis. One district level federation visited by the author that was borrowing from the banks to on-lend to its middle-tier secondaries, widely referred to as MACS in AP after their form of incorporation, relied for its high recoveries by the MACS from their groups more on the informal personal responsibility each MACS member took for the geographical set of SHGs she represented in the MACS, than on the inherent good quality of the groups. Moreover, the accounting assistance that the MACS level accountants provided to the groups was restricted to the loan ledgers relating to the MACS loan and not to the rest of the group's books. (The groups were free to borrow also from the large government-sponsored SHG federation programme, IKP, formerly called Velugu.) In this respect, the federation was functioning more as an MFI than a federation set up to strengthen its primaries.[20] Indeed APMAS (2006) and a number of other studies point out that recoveries within groups are much poorer than those from groups to the secondaries, so that each level is drawing at least temporarily on its own funds (savings deposits and accumulated surpluses from operations), a process which in the long run is not sustainable. It would be useful to gather empirical material on how real these concerns are, and the other dynamics involved.

If the case studies were to show that the fee-for-service concept has not usually worked in purely non-financial federations, then one argument against separating financial from non-financial service provision is that the former might be able to pay for the latter. An example of a federation that has been successful in doing so is KVK sponsored by the DHAN Foundation. KVK is one of the few federations that have been studied carefully through a case-study (Srinivasan 2005). KVK offered credit through bulk borrowing and on-lending services, apart from providing non-financial services to its members, and the margin of 3 percent added on by both the apex level as well as the cluster level sufficed to pay not just for accounting assistance costs, but for total operating costs including all staff. From 2002–03, however, KVK switched from financing support costs from lending margins to a system of sharing total costs determined once a year (at the AGM) by all SHG members equally. The switch to this system was made to ensure greater accountability to the SHGs, and was in keeping with DHAN Foundation's new policy of moving away from bulk borrowing for all its federations as discussed in Box 3.3.

If the case studies were to show that the fee-for-service concept has not usually worked in purely non-financial federations, then one argument against separating financial from non-financial service provision is that the former might be able to pay for the latter

---

Box 3.3   DHAN Foundation Federations: Changing with the Times

DHAN Foundation's policy towards bulk borrowing by federations has evolved through several stages. In the first stage, as an increasing number of SHGs were formed under the Kalanjiam banking programme, the demand for linkage loans could not keep pace with supply from the SBLP, which was still gathering pace. In order to increase the quantum of credit available to SHGs, capture scale economies, and earn much needed revenue to support non-financial services to the clusters and groups through the spread, several federations initiated bulk borrowing from the banks and financial institutions. SPMS and KVK are prominent examples, the former being located, unusually, in an urban area (Tirupati). Cumulatively, 25 federations are reported to have mobilized 24 crores from this source, as against Rs. 134 crores through linkage lending (Vasimalai and Narender 2007).

However, as it became apparent that building up truly member controlled federations with the specialized financial skills to manage bulk borrowing was going to take an unacceptably long time, the Kalanjiam community banking programme decided to centralize bulk borrowing in a S25 company, the Kalanjiam Development and Financial Services (KDFS), which was registered in 2001 and had borrowed Rs. 14 crores from SIDBI, ABN-AMRO and others by March 2004 (DHAN Foundation 2004). The company is owned by the federations, but professionally managed by employees. Direct bulk borrowing by the federations was increasingly restricted thereafter to specialized purposes such as housing, where the lending institutions were themselves wholesale institutions without branches, such as HUDCO, HDFC, and NHB, and could not make small loans to individual SHGs. It is important to note that for the same capacity-related reasons affecting bulk borrowing (with a few prominent exceptions such as KVK and SPMS) KDFS decided to lend directly to the groups and not to the federations.

According to the booklet "Catalysing Linkages: SHGs and Banks: The KDFS Experience 2001–2004" (DHAN Foundation 2004), the demonstration effect of KDFS lending has been partly responsible for growth of direct linkage lending from the banks and the improvement in the overall proportion of groups linked (to 75 percent) and the leverage ratio, or loan amount to own savings (to about 1:1). The booklet is very clear that "KDFS needs to maintain its role and identity as an enabler and for bridging the gap. It should guard against becoming another microfinance agency providing credit services."

Of the 130 odd locations in which DF currently has operations, it has so far registered federations in about 80 (20 in AP, 10 in Karnataka, 2 to 3 in Orissa, 1 in MP and the rest in Tamil Nadu). Several of these are in urban areas such as Madurai, Vishakapatnam, and Salem. Federations are registered as societies and trusts so that SHGs can become primary members. Of the 80 federations only about 10 are currently involved in bulk borrowing, and that too at a reducing level. The primary mode of group financing is through direct linkages with the federation acting as facilitator for a fee (as in Karnataka where the SBI pays the federations 1 percent of the interest rate charged the groups).

Even SPMS, which is possibly the first SHG federation registered in the country, in 1992, as a society, and which relied primarily on bulk borrowing in the first few years after receiving loans from SIDBI, HUDCO, and HDFC in the mid-1990s, has with the growth of the SBLP for the last few years been encouraging direct linkages. These increased rapidly after 2002 and finally overtook bulk borrowing in 2005. One of the major lenders was the Venkateshwara Grameen Bank, with SHG lending accounting for 10 percent of its business. Unlike institutions in cities, those in towns can operated in the surrounding peri-urban areas with access to public sector branch banks. Apart from a major emphasis on housing, which it shares with urban microfinance generally, SPMS has like other DF federations branched increasingly into economic and social initiatives such as insurance, health programmes, slum improvement, reproductive and child heath, and even consumer stores (DHAN Foundation 2005). This is in accordance with DF's philosophy of seeking to provide critical missing services, based on core competencies at each level.

Contrary to the hypothesis that bulk borrowing would increase self-sufficiency, federations that have not got into financing (as noted above, the majority now) are more often cost recovering than those which do bulk borrow. Roughly 35 to 40 of DHAN's 80 federations are reported to be fully cost recovering.

Based on discussion with K. Narender, DHAN Foundation

It has been pointed out that one factor driving federations towards provision of financial services is precisely this scope for cross-subsidization, and if grant funds were more readily available to finance their non-financial services, federations would more often resist the temptation to get into bulk funding

It has been pointed out that one factor driving federations towards provision of financial services is precisely this scope for cross-subsidization, and if grant funds were more readily available to finance their non-financial services, federations would more often resist the temptation to get into bulk funding. Another issue that arises, therefore, is whether there is a case for greater use of grant money to enable federations to undertake non-financial services without getting into bulk funding.[21]

However, too much should not be made of the cross-subsidization benefits of bulk financing. Data contained in comments on this chapter received from PRADAN (Box 3.4) show how viability might be achieved without bulk borrowing but with assistance from economic activities. Some federations such as Shramik Bharti in UP have actually got out of bulk borrowing because they felt they were losing sight of their objectives as peoples organizations, and are now facilitating direct linkages through the local banks.[22] Several SHPAs promoting federations at a recent Sa-Dhan consultation on federations said that revenues from fees manage to pay for a substantial part of expenditures on training, accounting assistance, auditing, and other support services offered by their federations.[23]

Box 3.4   Making Non-Financial Federations Viable: PRADAN's Experience

Federations are needed to provide support to SHGs in maintaining quality by providing appropriate services. Groups are complicated phenomena, however small they are. It is not wise to expect them to survive on their own without support from some mechanism external to the group. That is where the peerage created through clusters and the federation comes into play. But then, clusters and federations are also groups. So we have to create an integrated prototype, with SHGs, clusters and the federation as the different levels, and a set of community resource persons housed in it. It has to be a financially sustainable model, the revenue being generated by different services that the different levels provide.

The clusters and federation also need to evolve as independent entities of their own, each with a clear vision and agenda of its own. This evolves over a period of time. The clusters are for peer monitoring and learning, collective action at the local level and sharing resources at the local level when needed, such as a cluster accountant. The federation provides identity to the women, plays the role of a people's organization dealing with poor peoples' agenda, and provides a set of services relevant to the SHGs — hosting the Computer Munshi, the MIS system, as many livelihood support services as can be managed, and building solidarity and empowerment. Clusters and federations have to be built around the skills and resources of the SHG women and not on that of the NGO professional.

If there are 200 SHGs and 3000 members in a federation, the income and expenditure will look like this

12 staff @ Rs. 1500 per month — 12 months	216,000
Computer Munshi — 2000 pm	24,000
Federation manager — 2000 pm	24,000
Stationery — 2000 pm	24,000
Admin — rent electricity, computer maintenance etc., — Rs. 3000 pm	36,000
Local travel @ Rs. 2000 pm (board meeting monthly)	24,000
Contingencies	10,000
Total	**358,000**

This works out to about Rs. 120 per member per year, which is on the high side. Thus the federation will have to get into livelihood support activities such as collective purchase of inputs or collective marketing which can earn it a surplus of about Rs. 50 to 60 thousand, and can help maintain the member contribution at about Rs. 100 per member per year. In Kerala, last year the federation mobilized a surplus of Rs. 70,000 by trading in agri inputs. So it is possible. We can further reduce the member contribution by mobilizing grant funds if available, or building up a corpus from start up grants.

The services that the member gets are regular group monitoring support, in situ training, periodic audit, MIS, and problem solving support. In addition to the Rs. 100 contribution made to the federation by each member, the group pays the group accountant Rs. 30 to 50 every month for writing accounts, from their interest surplus. We need to do more action research on this before we surmise anything... What we need are inputs from the behavioural sciences. They are the ones to can tell us about groups, group dynamics, institutions, etc. Action research is required with inputs not just from bankers and economists, and NGO-wallahs, but from people who understand groups from the most basic psychological, human processes point of view. Institutions are after not about services but about people.

One of the reasons PRADAN is against financial services by federations is because it requires a lot of sophistication to run a MFI especially when volumes are large, and it has to be done by professionals, which introduces its own kind of information asymmetry. When finances are made available though the SBLP it does not make the women dependent on the professionals. At the same time, the women have other kinds of skills — political skills, skills of mobilizing, human skills, leadership skills, etc. That is what needs to be used and nurtured, we are unnecessarily burdening the women by making them run MFIs.

I would even go so far as to say that even if financial and non-financial services are unviable or ineffective, the empowerment benefits still make federations worthwhile. I think it is even possible to have a viable organization only involved in empowerment related issues. The question is — will people pay for empowerment and dignity? Intuitively yes. If people are willing to give up lives for such issues, surely they would pay Rs. 100 a year to have an organization of their own which gives them an enhanced sense of dignity! But how do we bring it to life? There might be need to really look around, for example, there is a need to document

Federations are needed to provide support to SHGs in maintaining quality by providing appropriate services. Groups are complicated phenomena, however, small they are. It is not wise to expect them to survive on their own without support from some mechanism external to the group

3.2 Financial services

3.2.1 Bulk funding

Bulk funding (of a truly commercial nature) is driven by the prospect of scale economies for the lender and greater access to funds by the borrower

Among financial services, the most important one is clearly bulk funding.[24] Bulk funding (of a truly commercial nature)[25] is driven by the prospect of scale economies for the lender and greater access to funds by the borrower. Private banks (such as ICICI, HDFC, ABN-AMRO, UTI), wholesale lenders (HUDCO, FWWB, SIDBI, NABARD), public commercial banks (SBI, Canara Bank, Bank of India, Indian Bank, Bank of Maharashtra), RRBs, and BASIX (through both its NBFC and LAB) are all current or erstwhile lenders.[26] The most recent phase of bulk lending to federations took place by *private banks to NGO-promoted federations,* mostly in AP. Lending by the *public commercial banks* took place mostly in Tamil Nadu to DHAN Foundation promoted federations when DHAN Foundation was actively encouraging its federations to borrow. It has since changed its policy as discussed below, and has set up a S25 company to centralize bulk borrowing, but only to supplement direct linkages in a "bridge financing" role. This is because the SBLP is now judged to have reached the stage where the argument for bulk borrowing (credit stringency) is no longer valid. Several other NGOs have recently set up similar S25 companies to play the same role. Finally, there has been *some nascent RRB lending to Village Organizations,* the second-level tier in the IKP programme in AP, propelled largely by moral suasion from the state government.

A documented example of bulk borrowing is an ICICI loan for SHGs in 19 MACS organized by *Pragati Seva Samiti,* an MFI in Warangal district, AP (described in Harper and Kirsten 2006). The loans to the SHGs, while more expensive than the loans the SHGs received when sourced from the local RRB, were for a larger amount, and part of the difference in price was offset by lower borrower transactions costs.[27] The case does not provide information on the relative importance of the bulk funder as a source of loans as against direct linkages, if any. Some federations discourage or even prohibit constituent groups from borrowing directly from the banks, which are usually cheaper despite higher transactions costs. What should the policy be here?

Another issue is the distribution of functions between various levels. Although many federations have three levels, in some cases the apex or intermediate level performs only non-financial or economic and social activities so that the intermediating tiers are in effect only two. The distribution of the total spread between the various levels depends largely on the distribution of functions, respective staff complements, and which level pays for them. Thus, in *MARI,* also in Warangal district and also a former CASHE partner, the MACS managers are paid for by the apex level and are transferable.[28]

MARI borrows in bulk from ICICI, on behalf of a district level apex, Sangatitha. A UTI loan was borrowed by Sangatitha directly. Accessed funds are on-lent at 16 percent to the MACS which on-lend to the SHGs at 19 percent. Kakatia Grameen Bank has made housing loans to the MACS directly. Total membership is expected to grow to about 50,000 borrowers by March 2008, with loans outstanding of Rs. 35 to 40 crores. The MACS are graded monthly according to certain parameters, have all been rated by APMAS, are audited annually, and there is an incentive component to field and HO staff pay. The average Operational Self-Sufficiency (OSS) of all the MACSs was 149 percent in August 2006, and that of the Sangatitha, the district level apex, 118 percent. An urgent need (in this as in other federations) is the induction of one or more professionals at the apex level, for which the federation will have to be willing to pay the going market rate.[29] MACS promoted by the AP NGO, GRAM, are reported to be even larger than MARI's. *Indur MACS* promoted by GRAM has received convertible debt from Bellwether, the social venture capital fund.[30]

A third AP federation, *Ankuram Sanghamam Poram (ASP)*, which borrows from the commercial banks[31] constitutes in a sense a unique model for federations in AP because it is a state level federation, and was not promoted by any particular NGO, but grew out of the Dalit movement.[32] ASP is the subject of a detailed case study, which is full of insights into the relationship between the three levels by Rewa Misra, who refers to it as "a massive combination of a trade union movement, a Dalit movement, and an NGO" (Misra 2007). Now, ASP has about 150,000 members at the base level and has received considerable grant funding from donors in view of its uniqueness. The case shows that while ASP absorbed the initial risks and costs associated with outreach to remote areas and marginalized communities, it is facing competition from new entrants at the primary level, and further growth will have to depend less on member loyalty than the ability to deliver timely and adequate loans. The sample SHGs in the case now have a choice of borrowing not just from the banks and IKP's Village Organizations, but some of them even belong to more than one federation (other than IKP).[33]

Bulk funding as we have seen has come so far mostly from the private banks, who in the absence of extensive rural branch networks have an incentive to lend to SHGs through federations in order to meet their priority sector targets. Indeed, banks like HDFC have also been lending to urban SHGs through their federations, such as Roshan Vikas (Box 3.5) for the same reason. Seven private banks currently have loans outstanding to the largest bulk borrowing federation in the country, *Sarvodaya Nano Finance Corporation*.[34] In a sense, the real test (for the economies of scale argument) is whether banks with rural branch networks such as SBI see it as cheaper to make bulk loans to federations rather than conduct direct linkages, and whether scale economies will ever offset the perception of higher risk in making say one Rs. 50 lakh loan rather than 50 Rs. one lakh loans. This test has not really been met yet, although there continue to be cases of public sector banks lending to federations, such as the recent cash-credit loan extended by the Bank of Maharashtra to Chaitanya in Maharashtra.

In a sense, the real test (for the economies of scale argument) is whether banks with rural branch networks such as SBI see it as cheaper to make bulk loans to federations rather than conduct direct linkages

As noted earlier, there has also been *sporadic RRB lending to VOs* in AP, especially in Mahbubnagar district where a concerted effort was made in 2005 at the urging of the IKP programme, to lend to VOs in accordance with guidelines issued few years ago by the Hyderabad office of NABARD. It was reported at a recent workshop on financing federations in AP that about 150 VOs have been financed in the district by several banks to the extent of about Rs. 10 crores. While the workshop favoured the concept of lending to VOs, bankers urged the need to proceed cautiously as several VOs had been defaulting for more than a year. Among the prior steps necessary was a clear strategy for training raters, bankers, SHPI staff, and federation leaders especially in VO financial management.

The dominant trend currently is for mostly public sector banks to *lend to S25 companies being* set up by SHPIs such as MYRADA, DHAN Foundation, and several others, which lend directly to SHGs rather than to their federations. The first of these was Sanghamitra Rural Financial Services incorporated by MYRADA in 1995 (see Fernandez 2007) followed by KDFS, which was registered by DHAN in 2001. More recently CYSD has promoted Swayanshree Micro Credit Services in Orissa, with loans outstanding to SHGs of Rs. 7.5 crores in July 2007, borrowings from SBI and HDFC, and quasi-equity from Bellwether, and SEARCH has set up KOPSA in Tamil Nadu.[35]

It is important to note that DHAN Foundation's rationale for centralizing bulk borrowing and on-lending into a community owned but professionally managed S25 company was that building up truly member controlled federations with the specialized financial skills to manage bulk borrowing was turning out to be more difficult than was originally anticipated and was taking an unacceptably long time. For the same capacity-related reasons, KDFS decided to lend directly to the groups and not to the federations. DHAN Foundation is very clear that "KDFS needs to maintain its role and identity as an enabler, and for bridging the gap (in direct linkage loans). It should guard against becoming another microfinance agency providing credit services" (DHAN Foundation 2004).

An important issue for both types of federations (non-financial as well as financial) is how high are promotional costs, and who is to bear them? Promotional costs have been borne so far (and continue to be borne)[36] largely by donors, including international NGOs with an ideological leaning towards federations. One of the few estimates we have for promotion cost per SHG is for the DHAN foundation in Srinivasan (2005) ($150 to $200) and Nair (2005) (also about $150).[37]

3.2.2 Insurance

A second increasingly important financial service is insurance.[38] According to EDA's evaluation of 20 SIDBI MFIs (EDA 2005), insurance is less extensive among SHG members than MFI members. If this is because individual SHGs are too small to access insurance, federations would seem to offer an opportunity to rectify the situation. Insurance is one service where large government-sponsored federation programs should have an advantage, since they can aggregate huge numbers. IKP is reported to have 1.8 million of its members insured.[39] Banks too can play a useful role. Some banks such as Andhra Bank is reported to insist that 15 percent of its linkage loans be used to avail of insurance.[40] An area calling for field investigation is how extensive insurance is through federations, how it is organized, and how it could be increased. It should be noted though insurance can be provided just as well by non-financial federations.

Insurance is less extensive among SHG members than MFI members. If this is because individual SHGs are too small to access insurance, federations would seem to offer an opportunity to rectify the situation. Insurance is one service where large government-sponsored federation programs should have an advantage, since they can aggregate huge numbers

3.2.3 Rotating liquidity between groups

A third financial service is the movement of surplus funds from surplus to deficit SHGs, or what is commonly referred to by practitioners as the "balancing" role. This liquidity balancing role seems to be fairly common. At least two promoters in the Sa-Dhan consultation, Roshan

Vikas (Box 3.5) and Chaitanya said their federations "balance" funds, as does ASP.[41] To the extent the option of depositing surplus funds in a higher tier increases choice, and SHGs and MACS remain free to deposit them in the banks instead, the balancing role could be extremely useful in well-managed federations. Idle funds with SHGs crop up as a concern in many APMAS studies, but they seem to be a problem at the federation level too. It would be useful to investigate why this is, if they can be routed to deficit SHGs.

To the extent the option of depositing surplus funds in a higher tier increases choice, and SHGs and MACS remain free to deposit them in the banks instead, the balancing role could be extremely useful in well managed federations

---

Box 3.5   Roshan Vikas: An Urban SHG Federation

Roshan Vikas is an urban cooperative SHG federation operating in Hyderabad's old city with plans to expand into roughly a third of the city's 40 to 50 municipal wards by 2010. It started off as a two-tier structure (SHGs federated into a ward level MACS) in the late 1990s, with an emphasis on linking its SHGs to health and other government programmes, but as its groups started accumulating idle funds, it commenced the activity of inter-lending, or "balancing" funds, by paying surplus groups 12 percent on their deposits and lending them to deficit groups at 18 percent, at a 5:1 ratio on their savings (only those deposited with the federation or on total savings?). There was also a requirement that the SHGs, whether surplus or not, would pool 25 percent of their savings in RV for lending to deficit groups.

In 2006, Roshan Vikas (RV) decided to augment the supply of loans to its groups by linking them to the banks, starting with a 3-year term loan of Rs. 2.5 crores from HDFC Bank. To prepare for the large planned expansion into a number of new wards, it also decided to decentralize to a three-tier structure, with ward-level federations, also registered as MACS, taking on the accounting functions handled till now by RV. The HDFC loan, at 8 percent, which can be used for IG purposes only, reaches the SHGs at 14 percent, with each of RV and the ward federations taking a margin of 3 percent. Although documentation is prepared by the federation, the loan documents are signed directly with the groups at a gearing of 6 to 8 times of the group's surpluses.

The groups (who on-lend at 24 percent) decide on the allocation of loans among members. Only about a fifth of the total membership have taken bank or federation loans, the rest being happy to take positions as net savers (the savings requirement is Rs. 30 a month). Maximum loan size is Rs. 50,000. Each accountant employed at the ward level visits up to 35 group meetings a month to help with the book-keeping, and returns with an audit report showing the group's latest position at the next monthly meeting. Group share capital in the ward level MACS is Rs. 100 per member, and membership fees Rs. 10 per member. The system of banking a minimum of 25 percent of savings with the higher tiers continues, with three-quarters going to the ward MACS and one-quarter going to RV. Group surpluses above this can be parked with RV in savings accounts, fixed deposits, or recurring deposits.

To meet the heavy demand for funds, and to have the flexibility to introduce new products such as housing and gold loans, RV is negotiating with several private banks to lend to RV directly. As a prelude to housing loans, RV is planning to assist members in registering their homes, with the cost being recovered as a loan.

RV is functioning as a truly representative structure, and at the bottom level the SHGs are genuine autonomous SHGs. The loan is a single loan to the group with the SHG deciding who the loan should be given to, for what purposes, on what terms and with what schedule of recovery (bank loans are typically recovered in less than 36 months and recycled). As in the rural areas, an SHG federation is less likely to reach down to the poorest of the urban poor as compared to an MFI that can target the poor actively it wants to (SHGs are in theory at least self-selected). Members would seem to enjoy more empowerment than in urban MFIs using JLGs, however, through opportunities to participate in the federation structure.

Based on discussion with Mohd Kareem, Roshan Vikas

3.2.4 Facilitating linkages

While we have already counted this service as non-financial, it could be regarded as financial if it is backed by guarantees from the higher tier. Federations often render assistance to new groups by helping banks appraise loan applications, and setting up counters at a bank on a fixed day of the week to assist groups with repayments and new applications. Federations and SHPI staff seek to improve their leverage with banks by promising exclusive banking relationships with them, and making deposits of their own idle/surplus funds. Again, except for providing guarantees, all these services can be provided by non-financial federations too.

3.2.5 Savings services

These too need to be studied and described in greater detail. Many federations require SHGs to share their monthly savings with the higher tier compulsorily (an example being Swayanshree described in Box 3.6) and many offer voluntary savings too (for instance, Roshan Vikas as described in Box 3.5).[42] Security deposits or margin money payments are also often required to be placed in the higher level on receipt of a loan, as in the case of MARI above. On the face of it a federation should be able to offer a higher rate on savings than a bank if it is intermediating to deficit units at lower cost or higher interest than the banks. An issue here is how much incremental savings take place as a result of a federation's savings service and how much of it represents diversion from bank savings. Another issue (discussed in Section 3.4) is that of appropriate regulation and supervision to ensure the safety of savings. Finally, some federations are reported to be offering pensions, such as some of those promoted by DHAN Foundation, although for most others this would seem a bit futuristic.

Box 3.6   Swayanshree at the Crossroads: To Borrow or to Facilitate Direct Linkages?

Swayanshree, a member owned and controlled but professionally managed urban federation serving the slums of Cuttack, has grown steadily over the last 12 years to attain its present size of almost 9000 members distributed over 670 SHGs and 80 JLGs. The primary groups are clustered into zonal bodies each of which elects a director to the governing body. On joining the federation an SHG pays Rs. 100 per member as share capital, Rs. 10 as membership fees, and Rs. 20 to go into a fund to provide legal services to members in cases of domestic violence, dowry deaths, and other forms of gender discrimination. SHG members save an average of Rs. 40 a month, Rs. 30 of which goes to the federation to fund various loan products and Rs. 10 of which remains in the SHG to fund emergency loans. Until 2006, the federation had idle funds, partly on account of grant funds received to subsidize operational funds from the CASHE project. But by 2007, with the general process of urban growth, the termination of CASHE, an increase in the maximum loans granted for various purposes and a decrease in the interest rate on loans from 24 to 18 percent, loan demand began to exceed the supply. In response to increasing loan demand from non-members Swayanshree also started organizing 5 member JLGs, whose members have to save only Rs. 10 per month and can start borrowing immediately (although at a higher interest than older SHG members) without going through the mandatory 6 months savings requirement for SHGs.

Swayanshree is faced with an important strategic decision. Should it meet growing loan demand by encouraging member SHGs to borrow from the banks, and facilitating the process by assisting in loan appraisal and monitoring for a fee, or should it start bulk borrowing on its own account to on-lend to member SHGs and JLGs. The banks have become much more interested in the last year or so in lending to urban SHGs (although not to JLGs). Thus SBI recently made loans to four SHGs, and like some other private banks HDFC Bank is willing to lend to them along the same lines it lends to Roshan Vikas in Hyderabad (see Box 3.3). HDFC is willing to share 3 percent with Swayanshree out of the 12 percent loans it proposes to charge SHGs. However, it does want a letter of comfort from Swayanshree backing the loans.

Swayanshree is inclined to prefer the alternative of borrowing itself from the banks and organizations like Swayanshree MCS, the S25 company, since it stands to earn more from the intermediation margin (of about 6 percent) in on-lending to SHGs, and more in the case of JLGs. It will be interesting to see which way it goes, and why.

Based on discussion with Nayana Mohanty, Swayanshree

3.3 Social and economic activities

A seemingly huge variety of social and economic activities and services are being undertaken by federations in AP, some of them described in Box 3.1, and increasingly in other states, and it would be useful to categorize them meaningfully and identify issues with respect to each of them that need to be looked into further. Among *economic activities and services* being undertaken by federations (some of them as agents, others on own behalf) are foodgrain procurement, marketing, input supply, ration shops, other retailing, food security activities such as grain banks, works under the watershed programme, and preparing mid-day meals. Second, potentially at least, federations provide a forum for viably aggregating *business development services* for livelihood promotion and microfinance plus activities (such as veterinary care, skills training, marketing support, milk chilling plants, design upgradation in, for example, crafts activities, etc.).

Social services include distribution of pensions and payments under the rural employment guarantee scheme, running crèches, supervising the implementation of social programmes, participating in health education, sanitation, drinking water, nutrition and family planning activities, and serving as a conduit for development information generally. A fourth set of activities relates to *social causes and advocacy* relating to domestic violence, alcoholism, child labour, gender sensitization, etc. A fifth entails *political participation and representation* activities, both formally through the gram panchayat and higher level echelon elections, and informally by constituting a pro-poor pressure group for rights and entitlements.

The processes and dynamics through which "empowerment" accrues through participation in these activities is still only hazily understood and needs to be researched further. However, SHG federations constitute an important vehicle for promoting grass-roots democracy and participation and for the women themselves a vehicle for experiencing and asserting a much stronger collective identity and solidarity. They have led to the emergence a new kind of elite in rural Andhra Pradesh, who have been given an opportunity "to elect, be elected, make policies and take decisions" (Misra 2007).[43] A less benign political effect of federations is that they have become a potential vote bloc and an attractive target of "capture" by political parties through inducements and subsidies, including credit subsidies as in AP's pavla vaddi scheme. It would be interesting to look at the effects these are having, quite apart from their cost.[44] Thus, there is anecdotal evidence that hitherto defunct groups of the non-poor are getting revived in order to avail of the pavla vadi scheme.[45]

The processes and dynamics through which "empowerment" accrues through participation in these activities is still only hazily understood and needs to be researched further. However, SHG federations constitute an important vehicle for promoting grass-roots democracy and participation, and for the women themselves a vehicle for experiencing and asserting a much stronger collective identity and solidarity

Another issue is the interplay between this third category of functions of federations (economic and social activities) and the first two. It has been pointed out that they can pre-empt scarce managerial talent and energy to the detriment of the first two functions (the provision of financial and non-financial services). Is this true, or do they more often enhance the skills and sense of ownership that strengthens those functions too, increasing credit absorption capacity and repayment discipline? Also, activities like bulk purchase have in cases contributed revenue to pay for non-financial support services (an example of which is contained in Box 3.4). On the other hand, unless all the groups in a federation participate in an economic activity equally, losses can put non-participating (or reluctantly participating) groups at risk. A related issue is whether federations should first focus on achieving institutional and financial viability before branching into economic activities?[46]

3.4 Regulation and supervision

SHG federations registered as MACS have become important players in the sector in AP, where the two tiers of SHG federations at the mandal and village level, have either already been, or are slated to be, registered as MACS (Chapter 9). In Orissa, panchayat level federations are being registered under the Orissa Self-Help Cooperatives Act (the equivalent of the MACS act in the state).[47] Tamil Nadu does not have a parallel cooperative law, where panchayat and block level federations are being registered as societies.

The MACS Act was a major step towards building more member owned and accountable institutions. However, the new microfinance bill is proposing to supplant the registrars of cooperative societies, whether under the new or old acts, by a new regulator, NABARD, for the regulation of thrift services. There is some question whether federations (the two tiers above the SHG level) fall within the purview of the bill. Chapter 9 argues that it would seem more practicable (and certainly more in accordance with the spirit of cooperation) for the bill to leave out cooperatives altogether, whether thrift cooperatives at the primary level or their federations. If the bill is amended accordingly, and even it is not, if it is clarified that federations do not fall under its purview, it will become all the more important for the states to energize their state registrars, and ensure that they carry out their supervisory obligations towards cooperative thrift societies, whether primary or higher level, much more diligently. At present, according to one observer, the relationship of most federations with the MACS act ends as soon as they have been registered, and they simply exist in the books of the district registrar.[48]

...it will become all the more important for the states to energize their state registrars, and ensure that they carry out their supervisory obligations towards cooperative thrift societies, whether primary or higher level, much more diligently

A second alternative is for MACS conducting microfinance to set up a system of self-regulation, a possible solution being studied by APMAS, with the right to suspend, merge, or close non-compliant federations to be vested in a state-level body. A third solution is much stronger self-supervision by federations themselves. However, this requires a foundation of strong management and record keeping. Some of the difficulties that stand in the way of relying entirely on more effective self-supervision especially in large state-wide federations such as ASP are (i) the high cost of on-site supervision, (ii) the lack of stringent standards, (iii) relatively weak staff capacity, (iv) the lack of regular rating, and (v) good book-keeping. The difficulties may be a little less intractable for smaller federations, but are still formidable. A combination of all three alternatives (energizing the registrars, self-regulation by the microfinance MACS community, and stronger self-supervision) is likely to be required.[49]

3.5 Conclusion

In stating a preference for the non-financial over the financial role of federations, it is not the intention of this chapter to be prescriptive. Despite the expansion of the SBLP, there may well be circumstances and areas where financial federations are called for, and not just because the SHG women themselves "want their own bank" as is often claimed by promoters. Such areas will generally have a higher demand for credit than the SBLP can satisfy, unlike areas where the absorptive capacity of the community is low, as in tribal belts, dry and rain fed farming areas. They could also be areas where the demand for credit is high but bank branches are sparsely distributed, as in the northern hill states.

Also, in using a three fold classification of functions for analytical reasons it is not being implied that federations must choose between one and the other. Thus non-financial support services aimed at enhancing SHG quality can, and usually are, combined with activities from the third category from very inception, such as addressing gender and other social issues, accessing and seeking convergence for members of ongoing government programmes, and perhaps providing what are referred to in the jargon as "business development services" or BDS.

As Girija Srinivasan points out[50], federation building needs to be carefully sequenced, with each phase responding to a real need, and carefully monitored. The first stage is social mobilization of groups, providing non-financial services, and institutionalizing the fee-for-services concept. After 3 or 4 years, the federation could intensify the provision of BDS in order to improve credit absorption capacity, as well as introduce specialized bulk loans for housing, etc., which are not catered to by SBLP. Finally, after 5 or 6 years it could start providing financial services if they are a critical missing link. Each phase should respond to the growth and changing needs of SHGs and their members, and will require the promoter to re-engineer its own role. "Promoting a federation requires long hand holding and perpetuates dependence on external assistance. One of the most empowering aspects of (the evolving financial landscape) is the way it allows SHG members to pick and choose between financial service providers. Federations can demand loyalty, the price of which is essentially a loss of freedom. Overall, there are more issues and questions on the financial intermediation role of the federations than clear answers even after 10 years of federating experience in India."

Endnotes

1   The purpose of this chapter is to raise issues, stimulate discussion, and suggest further field work and case studies. Given limitations of space, the issues discussed are mainly policy issues centering on the problem of financial sustainability, since there is some existing literature on institutional sustainability issues (governance, representative structure, systems, training, number of levels, the distribution of functions between levels, etc.) as well as what were referred to as "non-negotiables" at two workshops held in December 2002 and June 2003, based on an extensive Sa-Dhan study of 27 federations. Examples of these are (i) promotion of federations should be process rather than blue-print oriented, (ii) it should be undertaken only after strong primaries are in place, and (iii) should add value without competing with the primaries (Sa-Dhan 2004). The study categorized federations into four quadrants depending on the whether they were member of promoter controlled, and whether they offered only microfinance or microfinance "plus", that is, also social and livelihood interventions. The consensus was that federations with an internal locus of control and microfinance plus had the best chance of developing into true institutions of the poor. A financial analysis of 7 out of the 27 federations in a study by Ramesh Arunachalam presented at the seminar found that from the point of view of financial sustainability, however, federations with high member control but offering microfinance only had the highest sustainability (because they relied primarily on member savings, a low cost source capital, had lean organizational structures, good asset quality, and minimal idle cash). Unfortunately, this was the last nationwide empirical study based on extensive field work. More recent documents include Sa-Dhan (2004) and several APMAS's quality assessment reports, the latest being APMAS (2006). One of the best shorter studies on federations remains that Nair (2005) and for a highly readable account of the history and rationale of the federation movement in Tamil Nadu, full of practical programmatic detail, Gariyali (2007). Finally, simultaneously with the presentation of this report at the Microfinance India conference in October 2007, APMAS released a comprehensive report (APMAS 2007), which contains considerable additional information on federations in India, on the basis of which a few additional footnotes included here were added to the conference version. I am grateful to CS Reddy, LB Prakash, Girija Srinivasan, and the participants at the Sa-Dhan consultation in Delhi on 30 May 2007 for useful discussions and comments.

2   APMAS (2007) contains an update.

3   Thus, IFAD, UNDP, and the World Bank have all promoted federations, as have bilateral donors such as DFID though the CASHE project. The World Bank is reported to be preparing further projects containing federations for Bihar, Jharkhand, and the Northeast.

4   Some donors and international NGOs with an interest in federations are NOVIB, HIVOS, Christian Aid, and CRS.

5   More than the programme in other states, Kudumbashree emphasizes collective as well as individual activities, and convergence with government services.

6   These areas, ironically, tend to be those where the SBLP is longest established, since the demand for credit is probably correlated with the presence of good promoting NGOs, both of them being associated with the general state of development, and largely explaining the regional skew of the SBLP.

7   Some of the leading NGO federation promoters have been PRADAN, DHAN Foundation, MYRADA, CDS, SEWA, PREM, Chaitanya, Gram Vikas, ASA, and YCO.

8   As a further example, the Tamil Nadu Corporation for the Development of Women (TNCDW) sponsors urban federations at the ward level, and AP is piloting them too (for an example see Box 3.5).

9   Thus, in AP most of the 29,000 federations (estimated at the time) belong to the World Bank-assisted IKP programme's three-tier federation structure. Tamil Nadu's 14,104 federations consist mostly of the 12,527 panchayat level federations that were formed under the leadership of the TN Corporation for the Development of Women (TNCDW) in accordance with orders issued by the state government in 2002. Till 2000, there were only 645 cluster level federations in Tamil Nadu that had been set up under an IFAD sponsored project (Gariyali 2007). Similarly, the 5429 federations reported from Orissa in the estimate consist of panchayat and block level federations set up under Mission Shakti. Their number has now gone up to 6278 (March 2007) or 95 percent of the total number of panchayats and blocks. As in Tamil Nadu, most of these have yet to be registered, and are still inactive. The numbers for two other states, Kerala and West Bengal have already been mentioned above.

10 This is no longer strictly true. APMAS (2007) contains an abstract of a NABARD circular dated 14 September 2007 saying that NABARD had decided to support federations "on a model-neutral basis." However, it adds that federations should not "normally involve themselves in managing financial resources of SHGs and in on-lending to groups."

11 There is consensus that the focus should be on the constituent SHGs, whose interests the federations should always serve rather than the other way round, although best practice towards the goal of federation systems being self-managed is still evolving. The situation is one of a thousand flowers blooming, which is what makes the field particularly fascinating, but also challenging to document and distill lessons from.

12 Many of these are discussed in Chapter 2 of last year's report. APMAS (2005) finds a disquieting tendency for SHGs to deteriorate with age. Of concern is the apparent tendency of the doctor to succumb to the same disease – APMAS (2006) finds that federations too generally weaken with age.

13 Such as data transmission by mobile phones to a centralized MIS being developed by Ekgaon Technologies (Chapter 8), etc.

14 Indeed, CMRCs provide representation to federations in their area along with other CBOs, and the Computer Munshi system uses cluster level federations to discuss monthly trial balances of member groups (see Box 2.1 of last year's report).

15 G stands for governance, R for resources, A for asset quality, D for design of systems, E for efficiency and profitability, and S for services to member SHGs and their performance. Only 3.6 percent of the federations assessed were providing quality services overall, of which only 17 percent were providing quality support services as against 93 percent providing quality financial services (APMAS 2006).

16 We use the term bulk borrowing in this chapter to distinguish outside borrowing from collecting and lending out savings within the federation, although the latter term is usually used as a generic term that covers both.

17 A fourth source of income is Rs. 500 charged from numerous visitors from nearby Delhi!

18 Sakhi Suvidha is reported to be the most profitable of the four federations studied in Part I of CGAP (2007).

19 See Rajagopalan (2004), but she has written many other discussion papers available unfortunately only in mimeo form.

20 For semantic purposes, the distinction between an MFI lending through SHGs on one the one hand, and a federation accessing bulk funds on the other, would seem to lie in whether the institution has at least one layer of autonomous organizations above the SHG. If the institution accesses bulk funds to lend directly to SHGs it should be regarded as an MFI, but if it has autonomous secondaries even if they provide only support services or undertake social and economic activities, the institution should be regarded as a federation, even if loan funds flow directly from the apex to the SHGs as is sometimes the case. On this definition SNFL would be defined as a federation rather than an MFI.

21 Some questions of interest are how much grant money is already available under the major programmes (state womens' development corporations, DRDAs, Velugu, Swashakti, etc.) and how well is the money being used? NGO-promoted SHGs in AP used to pay for accounting services directly. Now that many of them have joined Velugu, and their accountants have become "government" employees, are the latter as conscientious?

22 It has paid off its former bulk lenders such as SIDBI, HUDCO, and RMK (Rakesh Kumar Pandey at the Sa-Dhan consultation, see endnote 1). It is hopeful that its federations will be able to recover their accounting-support, auditing and account-book costs through fees, and is planning to introduce the Computer Munshi system, and get into livelihood support once the federations have been strengthened further. Many federations have scaled down the financial intermediation role. Other federations that are reported to have scaled down financial intermediation are those that have been promoted by SSP in Mahrashtra, and by CCD in Tamil Nadu.

23 PRADAN said that in Jharkhand, its federations manage to recover the entire cost (approximately Rs. 75 per member a year) either through a once-a-year contribution per member or in installments over the year. Box 3.4 contains a slightly higher estimate. Participants pointed out, however, that grant money played a crucial role initially, although it was often inherited from previous programme activities, such as grants for revolving funds, watershed development, and health.

24 We use the term bulk funding to distinguish it from the broader term financial intermediation because the latter includes borrowing from members. Bulk funding is of course indirectly intermediating the savings of savers in the formal sector. Of the 129 MFIs covered by Sa-Dhan's Quick Report, 21 were MACS with 1.6 percent of the total number of borrowers, and 4 of them cooperatives not registered as MACS (such as Sewa Bank), with 3.9 percent. In addition, many federations are registered as societies rather than cooperatives, such as those in Tamil Nadu. The Quick Report contains data on borrowings for each MFI.

25 Commercial, as opposed to donor funding of on-lending funds such as Velugu's Community Investment Fund, or CASHE's revolving fund, which has now been inherited by ACCESS to support their incubation of new MFIs.

26 However, there is no estimate of total lending to federations.

27 In the case of direct linkages, all the SHG members had to travel to the Kakatiya Grameen Bank to collect their loans, costing them bus fares as well as lost wages. The Grameen Bank also conducted bulk lending to the groups, and the groups received these loans at 18 percent. The case does not include information on margins retained by the MACS and PSS, or say whether any deposits had to be made by the SHGs in the MACS and by the MACS in PSS to fund the deposit of 15 percent of the loan amount PSS had to make as an FLDG deposit with ICICI earning 5.5 percent interest.

28 The pros and cons of this arrangement – better control over possible malfeasance at the MACS level but less autonomy for the MACS – also need to be analyzed.

29 A topic that generates much heat in sector conclaves is the need to manage the relationship between professionals and the representative governance structure sensitively. The following comment received on this chapter is frequently heard. "Another very frustrating observation I have made during my field visits and interactions with promoting agencies' staff and federation leaders is that most of the time professionals who manage the entire show on behalf of federations are too intimidating, over-powering, and lack sensitivity and patience. They are unable to understand the limitations and unique strengths of these women. As a result, the vibrant leaders of federations are reduced to good accountants and obedient workers of promoting agencies. Given a choice, federation leaders would not like to go through that route... in most cases it is the promoting agencies' agenda that push federations into a provider role. Given a choice, women would like to keep out of this game. Federations might have proved their utility for the promoting agency, but we need to check whether the same applies when it comes to SHGs." The view taken here is that if the relationship is successfully managed (and it can be) a community based institution can be community or member owned without necessarily having to be entirely community managed. The best known example is AMUL, and among federations, SIFFS, a federation of fishermen's cooperatives, and SNFL, both in Tamil Nadu.

30 This is something of a first. An equity investment is ruled out, however, by the cooperative principle of one man one vote.

31 Currently, Syndicate Bank, ICICI, Canara Bank, and the State Bank of Hyderabad.

32 Apart from NGO-promoted federations and ASP, the third federation model in AP is the ubiquitous IKP, which does not borrow from the banks but does on-lend Community Investment Funds (CIF) it has received from the World Bank. These funds are on-lent down the three-tier structure with each tier earning a margin. Finally, there is the well-known fourth model in AP of the two-tier federations of thrift cooperatives, also in Warangal district, promoted by CDF (Chapter 9). This, however, is a special case since the primaries here are not SHGs but much larger thrift cooperatives or in effect credit unions, with credit activities funded almost entirely by savings and with little outside borrowing as a matter of philosophy.

33 ASP's operational sustainability is only 25 percent, partly because of the relatively large staff required to support state wide operations, and also because in keeping with its respect for the autonomy of each level, ASP's relationship with member MACS is loosely defined. Its strategic plan lays down that "the standardization of systems and procedures that are required for taking advantages of economies of scale will be realized through processes of consensus building" (Misra 2007).

34 SNFL is in a sense a unique case, since it is an NBFC at the apex level which on-lends to federations registered as mutual benefit trusts at the secondary level. Although the CEO and two board members of each MBT are appointed by the apex, they otherwise enjoy substantial autonomy, and the apex itself is owned by the MBTs. Thus, SNFL is professionally managed but community owned. It is the largest federation in India, with loans outstanding of Rs. 64 crores in March 2007 and an outreach of 126,000 SHG members organized in 25,140 SHGs belonging to 108 MBTs in six states.

35 KOPSA, in three districts of Tamil Nadu, borrows from SBI at 8 percent and on-lends at 12 percent, directly to SHG groups. It also has a loan from ING Vysya Bank.

36 For instance in the new World Bank IKP-type project in Bihar.

37 Presumably, this includes the historical costs that were incurred on promoting the individual SHGs. Ultimately, it is the total promotional cost at both levels that is relevant. Federations, once formed, offer the prospect of bringing down the average cost per SHG formed as they get into the business of promoting new SHGs themselves.

38 It is usually provided by the federation as an agent for an insurance company, but sometimes also through the in-house model, as with life and health insurance in DHAN, although DHAN Kalanjiams are reported to be switching to the former model, at least for life insurance (Chapter 5A of last year's report).

39 APMAS (2007) describes how the zilla (district) federation under IKP in Chittoor district sold 1.9 lakh LIC policies in 2006. DHAN Foundation federations cover 163,000 members.

40 The commission payment of 20 percent of the premium payable to the agent is an incentive to the banks.

41 However, it is only the apex that balances the surpluses of its MACS, since SHG prefer the safety of depositing their funds in the banks or leaving them idle.

42 The distinction between the liquidity balancing and savings services role can be thought of as the former applying only to group as opposed to individual savings, and being shorter term.

43 She points out also that new elites can fall into old habits, leading to issues of elite domination at the second tier, dominating the agenda at general assemblies, "deciding which entitlements and schemes to opt for, which members to pull up for non-repayment and which loans to sanction without any form of active engagement even with the SHG leaders."

44 Assuming an interest subsidy of 9 percent (the bank rate minus the pavla vadi rate of 3 percent) on about Rs. 3500 crores of loans outstanding in AP in March 2007 (or 60 percent of cumulative disbursements of Rs. 5889 crores using the assumptions discussed in Chapter 2), the bill to the state government could come to Rs. 300 crores at current levels of lending.

45 At the Microfinance India conference in October 2006, a Rajya Sabha member from Orissa credited the SHG programme for getting his party re-elected in the last elections.

46 Economic, because social activities do not pre-empt scarce skills to the same extent.

47 The Orissa act allows membership to the primaries or SHGs unlike the AP MACS Act which only allows membership to individuals or cooperatives, so that SHGs have to be represented by representatives acting formally in an individual capacity. This is the reason DHAN Foundation prefers to register federations as societies or trusts.

48 As Rama Reddy points out "Neither the SHG Federation, nor the promoting GO, nor the promoting NGO, nor the registering DCO is interested in the functioning of the village organization as a MACS cooperative. They do not need any supervision and/or regulation since they themselves are part and parcel of the governmental organizations or of the non-governmental organizations. On the one hand, as a policy, the State Government is interested in getting village organizations registered as MACS cooperatives and on the other hand, again as a matter of policy, the same government puts a ban on the registration of citizen-promoted genuine thrift cooperatives and dairy cooperatives under the MACS Act" (Personal communication).

49 APMAS (2007) describes examples of the first two approaches: A pilot project being developed by APMAS in Nizamabad district in collaboration with DGRV of Germany, and the network set up the DHAN Foundation for its federations called INFOS.

50 This paragraph is based on comments received from Girija Srinivasan.

References

APMAS, 2005, "A Study of Self-Help Group (SHG)—Bank Linkage in Andhra Pradesh," Hyderabad

APMAS, 2006, "Status of SHG Federations in Andhra Pradesh: Quality Assessment: 2nd Report," Hyderabad

APMAS, 2007, "SHG Federations in India: A Perspective," Report presented at Microfinance India conference, October 9–10, New Delhi

Christen, Bob, and Guatam Ivatury, 2005, "A Systemic View of the SHG—Bank Linkage System: Four Sustainable Models," Paper presented at World Bank conference in New Delhi, December

CGAP, 2007, "Sustainability of Self-Help Groups in India: Two Analyses," Occasional Paper, World Bank, DC

DHAN Foundation, 2004, "Catalysing Linkages: SHGs and Banks: the KDFS Experience 2001–2004."

DHAN Foundation, 2005, "Impacting Urban Poverty Through Microfinance: The SPMS Experience," DHAN Foundation, Madurai

EDA Rural Systems, 2005, "The Maturing of Indian Microfinance," Study done for SIDBI, Gurgaon

Fernandez, Aloysius, 2007, "A Microfinance Institution with a Difference," *Economic and Political Weekly*, March 31, Mumbai

Gariyali, CK, 2007, "Climbing Higher: Federations of Women Self-Help Groups at the Panchayat Level," Vetri Publications, New Delhi

Harper, Malcolm, and Marie Kirsten, 2006, "ICICI Bank and microfinance linkages in India," *Small Enterprise Development*, Volume 17, Number 1, March.

Misra, Rewa, 2007, "Case of Mutually Aided Cooperative Societies, India: SHG federations as a model for remote outreach of financial services," Study commissioned by Ford Foundation, Coady International Institute, Antigonish, NS

Nair, Ajay, 2005, "Sustainability of Microfinance Self-Help Groups in India: Would Federating Help," Policy Working Research Paper 3516, South Asia Region, Finance and Private Sector Development Unit, World Bank, DC

Rajagopalan, Shashi, 2004, "Do federations have a role in financial intermediation?" Paper written for "Microfinance India 2008" conference, February 24–26, New Delhi

Ramesh, Jairam, 2007, "The SHG Revolution: What Next?" Silver Jubilee Lecture at the Society for the Promotion of Wastelands Development, May 5, New Delhi .

Reddy, CS, N Tirupathaiah, and S Ramalakshmi, 2007, "Emerging SHG Federations and Challenges," International Conference on Andhra Pradesh Experience with Member-Based Organizations of the Poor, Mimeo, CESS, June 5–6, Hyderabad

Sa-Dhan, 2004, "SHG Federations in India: Emerging Structures and Practices"

Srinivasan, R, 2005, "Canara Bank, Allanganallur branch, Madurai district, Tamil Nadu, India," in Harper and Arora, eds. "Small Customers, Big Markets:Commercial Banks in Microfinance," Practical Action Group, London

Vasimalai, MP, and K Narender, 2007, "Microfinance for Poverty Reduction: the Kalanjiam Way," *Economic and Political Weekly*, 31 March 2007

CHAPTER 4

MFI Performance: Efficiency with Growth

Sanjay Sinha[1]

4.1 Overview

The past 2 years have seen a series of critical developments in the Indian MFI sector. These are both positive and negative. On the positive side, MFIs have started to leverage their new found management expertise to achieve scale and to spread their operations well beyond their traditional operational areas. Thus, rating data from a large sample of the leading MFIs shows that these have recorded high growth rates of the order of 80 percent per annum in terms of numbers of borrowers and around 40 percent per annum in terms of portfolio reaching from 300,000 to one million clients each. Also positive is that a significant part of that expansion has been either to less developed areas of the country — Orissa, Jharkhand, Rajasthan, Madhya Pradesh, Tripura, Assam — or to areas such as Maharashtra that also have substantial numbers of low income families in some regions even if their overall development indicators are not as low as those for the other states.

The past 2 years have seen a series of critical developments in the Indian MFI sector. These are both positive and negative. On the positive side, MFIs have started to leverage their new found management expertise to achieve scale and to spread their operations well beyond their traditional operational areas

On the negative side, MFIs have been under attack from politicians and bureaucrats in some of their traditional operational areas in Andhra Pradesh and Karnataka (with questions even being asked in Orissa). Their loan recovery practices have been questioned and their interest rates described as exorbitant. The related publicity has vitiated the credit culture in the traditional microfinance states forcing a lowering of interest rates and increasing the necessary level of loan loss reserves and provisioning. Operationally, the increase in costs has been compounded by the spread of the operations of individual MFIs simultaneously (and inorganically) to a number of non-traditional states. This has put pressure on operating efficiency and resulted in slowing the trend to lowering unit costs.

The growth of the microfinance sector has been fuelled by continuing interest from banks in increasing their exposure to microfinance resulting in a highly leveraged industry with capital adequacy ratios down below 10 percent and debt-to-equity ratios of the order of 11:1. Given the pressure on margins (which has already reduced the collective return on assets of the sector to negligible, if still positive, levels), it is unclear for how long such high leverage ratios can be sustained.

The increased coverage of clients made possible by the high growth rates of Indian MFIs is laudable. Even as it increases outreach, the industry continues to be amongst the most efficient in the world. But, high growth brings with it possible dangers of mission drift as many MFIs emphasize commercial behaviour and may not strategically balance this with their original social mission, or with social values expected in microfinance. As the discussion in this chapter and that on social rating shows, it is apparent that while MFIs have learnt much in terms of operational efficiency, a substantial effort is required in the areas of clarifying social objectives, poverty targeting, product development, and client orientation. The challenge for MFIs over the next few years is to achieve growth with equity as well as efficiency.

This chapter presents a summary analysis of the information obtained by M-CRIL during its ratings of 58 Indian MFIs over the 18-month period, January 2006 to June 2007. The overview of the performance of Indian MFIs emerging from this analysis is placed in perspective by a comparison with the benchmarks emerging from the database of the MIX's latest set of 37 reporting MFIs (for March 2007). The India Microfinance Review, published separately by M-CRIL and the MIX, presents the detailed analysis.

4.2 Characteristics of MFIs covered by this analysis

Regionally, this analysis provides a comprehensive picture of microfinance in India. The samples used contain a large number of MFIs from South India.

This is de facto recognition of the fact that South Indian MFIs provide a substantial portion of client coverage in Indian microfinance. Table 4.1 presents a broad regional analysis of the samples.

Table 4.1 Regional distribution of Indian MFIs rated by M-CRIL

Regions	M-CRIL MFIs			Update sample	MIX dataset	
	Rated	Sample	% of sample		2005–06	2006–07
South	27	24	24	18 (62%)	28	24 (64.9%)
East & NE	24	20	20	8 (28%)	8	10 (27%.0%)
West	10	6	6	1 (3%)	0	1 (2.7%)
North	11	8	8	2 (7%)	2	2 (5.4%)
India	**72**	**58**	**58**	**29 (100%)**	**38**	**37 (100.0%)**

There are many SHG-based microfinance programmes but, in recent years, most of the new MFIs have been established using the Grameen model. There has been a tendency for MFIs increasingly to adopt the Grameen model, since this is seen by many as a means of accelerating their growth and progress towards sustainability. By and large, however, Indian MFIs have been innovating, experimenting with and growing out of the conventional mould of SHG and Grameen operations, to cater to the needs of their markets more effectively. The distribution of sample Indian MFIs based on microfinance models is shown in Table 4.2. This distribution is a broad reflection of the pattern of microfinance undertaken through MFIs (as opposed to the SBLP) in India.

By and large, however, Indian ·MFIs have been innovating, experimenting with and growing out of the conventional mould of SHG and Grameen operations, to cater to the needs of their markets more effectively

Though there is a trend, India-wide, towards for-profit and formal registration of MFIs as finance companies, not-for-profit institutions continue to dominate by numbers of organizations in the provision of microfinance services. Table 4.3 shows the distribution of sample MFIs across legal forms. The 15 for-profit companies in the M-CRIL sample of 58 includes

Table 4.2 Distribution of sample Indian MFIs by microfinance model

Models	M-CRIL sample			Updates	MIX dataset	
	2005	2007	Top 10		2005–06	2006–07
G	19	23	7	16	19	21
IB	15	8	1	6	14	15
SHG	50	27	2	10	25	21
Total MFIs	**84**	**58**	**10**	**32**	**38**	**37**

Table 4.3 Distribution of sample MFIs by legal form

Form of registration	M-CRIL	Top 10	MIX, 2006
Not-for-profit			
Societies & trusts	34	1	22
Cooperatives	4		1
S25 companies	5		2
Non-bank finance companies/bank	15	9	12
Total MFIs	**58**	**10**	**37**

5 institutions that were still registered as not-for-profit institutions (when rated) but are either in the process of transforming or have already transformed to companies (at the time of writing).

Of the 10 best institutions selected for the purpose of comparison with the overall sample, just two in this group have been replaced since the last review. However, while earlier 6 of the 10 were Non-Bank Finance Companies (NBFCs), all but one of the top 10 MFIs in India is now legally registered as such.

4.3 Client outreach and services

The microfinance outreach of sample MFIs amounts to some 5.6 million clients (M-CRIL, September 2006) to 6.6 million clients (for the MIX dataset, March 2007). Around three-quarters of these are based in South India and another 20 percent in the East. Most of the remainder MFIs are in North India. There are relatively few MFIs in the West. Grameen MFIs with over 130,000 clients each are the largest in the country and together serve over 50 percent of the total number of clients covered. Though, extensive government support for SHG programmes has resulted in the establishment of a large number of MFIs using the SHG methodology, these are around half the size of Grameen MFIs and, as a result, provide outreach to only about one-third of the total number of clients covered (Figure 4.1). From the perspective of the legal framework, the proposed new microfinance law does not cover nearly 80 percent of these clients since 73 percent are served by NBFCs (or MFIs on the verge of transformation to NBFCs) and another 6 percent by S25 (not-for-profit) companies. Such institutions fall outside the ambit of the proposed law.

There are relatively few MFIs in the West. Grameen MFIs with over 130,000 clients each are the largest in the country and together serve over 50 percent of the total number of clients covered

Indian MFIs have minuscule outstanding Rs. 3400 ($82) compared to the international average Rs. 19,200 ($468) and has not grown over the past couple of years. The Grameen clients have the smallest loan balances Rs. 2700 ($65). This has happened despite a high growth rate

Figure 4.1 Membership of sample MFIs

(a) ... by microfinance methodology

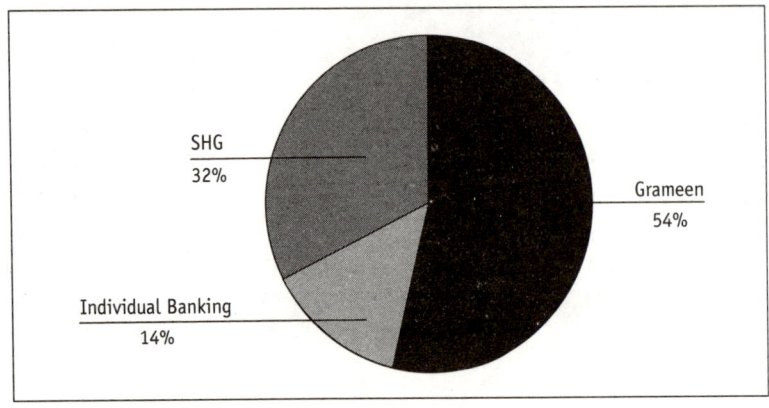

(b) ... by legal form

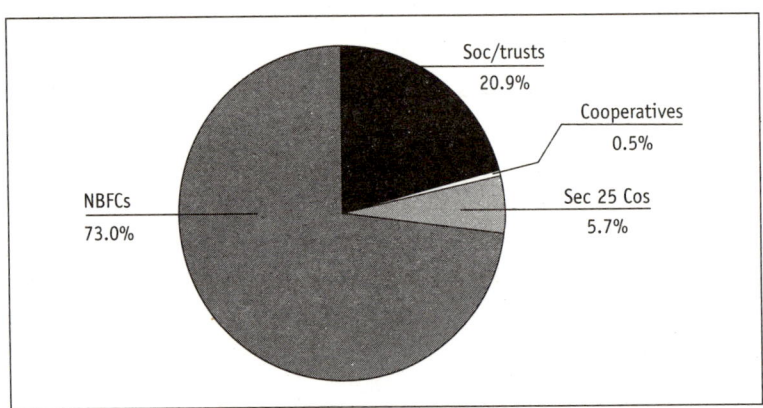

of MFI portfolios (40 percent) because client outreach has expanded even faster (84 percent). Large numbers of new MFI clients inevitably means small loan sizes.

At an average loan balance that is just 9.9 percent of GNI per capita, depth of outreach is apparently substantial. However, field experience shows that significant numbers of not-so-poor women join microfinance groups — often for social reasons — so the loan balance-GNI ratio is not a good indicator of poverty outreach (at least for India).

A highly restrictive legal framework for deposit taking has severely constrained the offering of thrift services, so client savings form just 8.1 percent of outstanding loan balances. As Figure 4.2 indicates, all the methodologies have low average savings per member except for the individual banking model. Each of the bars reflects the nature of the methodologies and the legal framework in which the organizations operate.

Usually, SHG programmes have voluntary deposit schemes in which the members themselves determine the amount of the recurring savings deposit. Since disposition of this amount is determined by the group rather than by the individual saver, this often results in minimalist norms and leads to deposits that are far lower than the members' savings

Figure 4.2 Average savings per member by model (Rs)

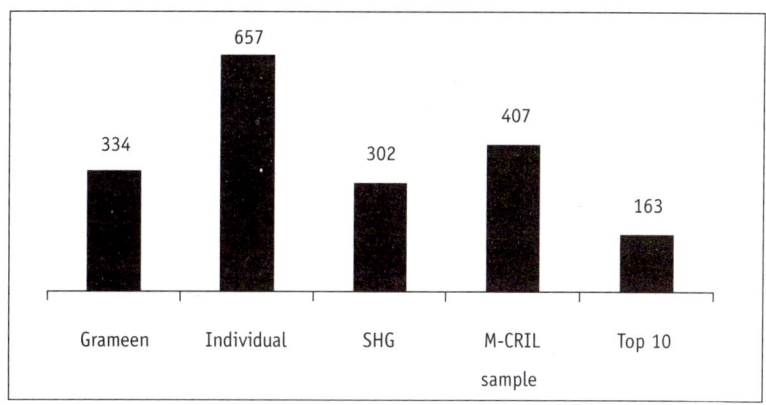

potential. Deposits form just 4.0 percent of the average SHG MFIs' portfolio, though (as indicated earlier) this excludes the far larger amounts revolved internally by SHG members.[2]

4.4 Operating efficiency and portfolio quality

Staff productivity in India is now higher than in any other major region offering microfinance. Some 326 staff members per MFI serve over 230 borrowers each while the leading MFIs average 275 borrowers per member of staff. This results in some of the lowest servicing costs for MFIs anywhere in the world. Both Grameen and SHG MFIs record average servicing costs of the order of Rs. 400 ($10) per borrower, lower than the MIX median even for Bangladesh. As MFIs have grown and staff productivity has increased over the years, servicing costs have come down even in nominal terms. With an inflation rate averaging 5 percent per annum in the mid-2000s, this has resulted in a decline of around 9 percent per annum in the cost of servicing borrowers.

Indian MFIs are now amongst the most efficient internationally. At 15.9 percent, the average operating expense ratio (Table 4.4) has not changed much since the M-CRIL Microfinance

Staff productivity in India is now higher than in any other major region offering microfinance. Some 326 staff members per MFI serve over 230 borrowers each while the leading MFIs average 275 borrowers per member of staff. This results in some of the lowest servicing costs for MFIs anywhere in the world

Table 4.4 Operating expense ratios of Indian MFIs

Model	Weighted average (%)	Typical MFI (%)	Operating expense ratio				Total no. of MFIs
			<10%	10–15%	15–25%	>25%	
G	16.7	16.4	4	8	6	3	21
IB	20.5	24.5	2	1	4	1	8
SHG	11.2	23.2	7	4	7	7	25
M-CRIL							
2007	15.9	20.7	13	13	17	11	54
2005	15.6	18.5	25	19	23	16	83
2003	20.1	36.6		23	21	46	90
Top 10	13.1	11.6	4	4	2	0	10
MIX*	India	Bangladesh	Nepal	South Asia	MIX global	MIX Asia	
	10.4	14.2	11.2	14.3	20.1	17.2	

*Operating expense as a proportion of Gross Loan Portfolio (GLP)

Review 2005 as growth focussed MFIs have accepted higher travel and other costs, while productivity gains have also been neutralized by lower loan balances, hence smaller portfolios serviced per member of staff, in real terms. OERs reported by Indian MFIs are, nevertheless, lower than those of MFIs in Bangladesh and significantly lower than the medians for Asian and other MFIs worldwide.

Analysis of operating expense ratios by size of MFI, its age, microfinance methodology, and loan size shows that it is the last factor that is the major determinant of operating efficiency. As the size of loans disbursed increases from Rs. 3000 ($75) to Rs. 10,000 ($250), the operating expense ratio declines from 25 percent down to an average of around 12 percent (Figure 4.3)

Figure 4.3 OER by loan size (Rs)

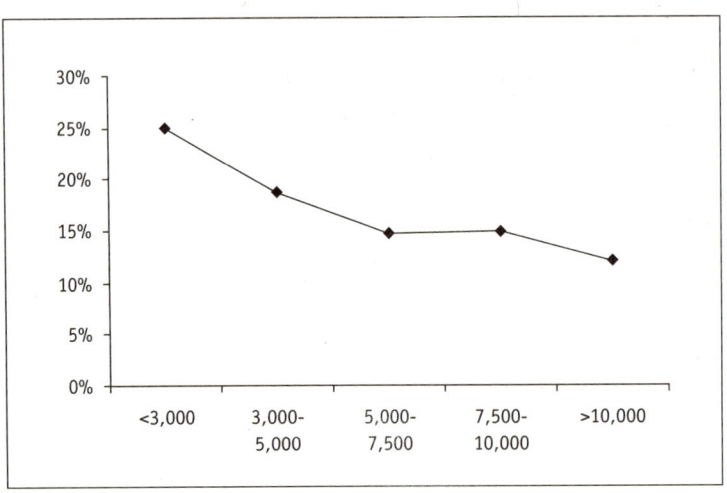

The effective interest rate paid by the average Indian microfinance borrower is no more than 25 percent – not significantly different from the ~24 percent usually charged even by commercial banks on consumer finance. By and large, new institutions have low yields and high OERs but, as expansion takes place, and economies of scale set in, yields improve and OERs decline to acceptable levels. There are significant economies of scale up to a portfolio size of Rs. 2.5 crores ($600,000) (Figure 4.4.).

Official action against MFIs in Andhra Pradesh and elsewhere has resulted in a significant deterioration in the credit culture, having an adverse effect on microfinance operations. Portfolio quality has deteriorated since the 2005 Review with the weighted average PAR60 has declined from 4.7 percent in 2005 to 6.0 percent now. Particularly affected are the leading MFIs whose PAR has declined from 1.4 percent for the 2005 sample to 4.6 percent now. This is also much higher than the MIX benchmarks for Asia. The implications of this for the long-term performance of the microfinance sector are yet to emerge.

Figure 4.4 Relationship of portfolio size with efficiency

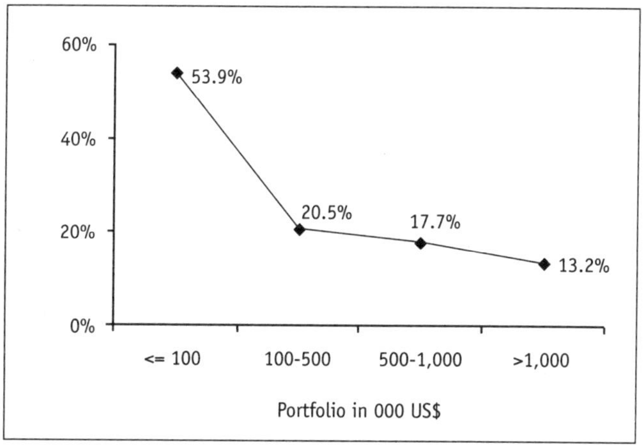

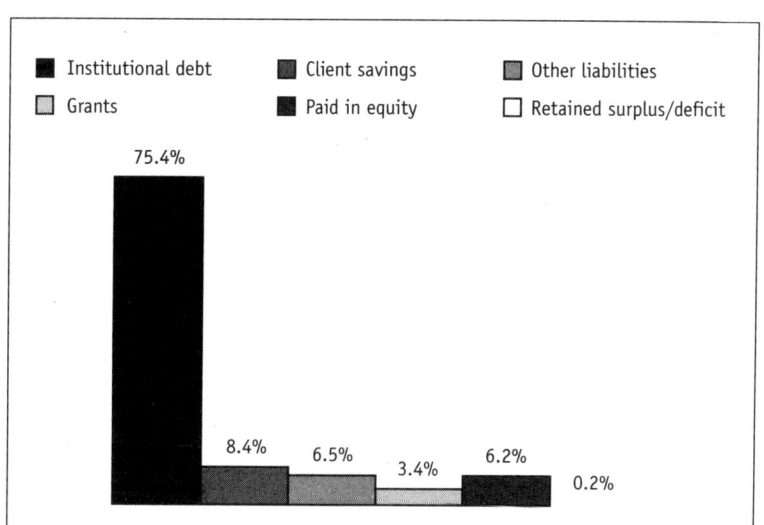

4.5 Portfolio financing

The structural shift indicated by an increase in debt financing among Indian MFIs has continued while net worth as a proportion of the total has been reduced as current surpluses and a very limited flow of grants have failed to keep pace with growth. Borrowings have reached three-quarters of total liabilities on MFI balance sheets as funds have been readily available from both private and public commercial banks (Figure 4.5). Even small institutions with relatively low exposure to financial markets have succeeded in sourcing half of their liabilities through bank borrowings, bringing over 60 percent of MFIs under the 15 percent suggested capital adequacy ratio.

Until now, with substantial historical grant funding and more recent operating surpluses accompanied by relatively small portfolios, the Indian microfinance sector has been well provided for in terms of owned funds. Now, the growth aspirations of MFI managements,

Figure 4.5 Sources of funds for microfinance operations

competition and the relative paucity of grant funds, on the one hand, and the availability of liberal commercial debt funds, on the other, have taken their toll. The aggregate figures suggest that capital adequacy is now an issue as even the top 10 MFIs fail to register the 15 percent norm suggested above, though it is not alarming yet (Table 4.5).

Table 4.5 Capital adequacy ratios of Indian MFIs

Models	Weighted CAR (%)	Typical MFIs (%)
Grameen	11.3	13.6
IB	22.3	15.6
SHG	8.4	12.5
	12.7	13.4
Top 10	11.1	9.4
Debt-equity ratios		
M-CRIL sample	7.2	14.2
Top 10	8.6	10.5
MIX India median		11.9

The trend towards commercialization becomes even stronger in the context of off-balance sheet financing under the partnership model, which accounts for an additional 44 percent of the overall portfolio in the sector. When managed loans are added back to the balance sheets of a subset of leading Indian MFIs, the leverage ratio jumps from 10.7 to 11.9, far exceeding the regional median of 5:1. While a limited amount of debt continues to be available at concessional rates, much of it is contracted at commercial rates in the range of 10 to 14 percent per annum. With such financing and accounting for four-fifths of the portfolio of leading MFIs, the commercialization of the Indian sector far exceeds that of other important markets in the region, such as Bangladesh, where institutions source less than one-tenth of their portfolios from commercial funds.

When managed loans are added back to the balance sheets of a subset of leading Indian MFIs, the leverage ratio jumps from 10.7 to 11.9, far exceeding the regional median of 5:1.

Indeed, Indian MFIs are increasingly turning to the banking sector as their access to grants and customer deposits continues to diminish. The share of grants dropped from one-third of the balance sheet in 2003 to just 3 percent in 2006, barely covering cumulative losses among smaller institutions. With the ability to raise equity capital limited to just a few legal entities, reliance on net worth fell to 10 percent, less than one-third of that in 2003. Bank borrowings have also had to fill in for customer deposits, which amounted to one-fourth of MFI resources in 2003 and are now under one-tenth of the balance sheet. Concerns over the legality of savings mobilization combined with increasing transformation to NBFCs have phased savings out of MFI balance sheets and mostly confined these to community-based institutions such as SHGs and cooperatives.

Indian financing patterns, however, could look quite different in the next few years. Under proposed legislation, societies, trusts, and cooperatives will be able to offer thrift services. While companies are excluded from this proposed regulatory regime, a number of these have recently announced large investments by private equity funds. With the top 10 accounting for two-thirds of the financing, debt may be ceding some of its share to equity capital.

4.6 Financial performance

The financial viability of MFIs in India is under threat, despite improvements in the yield gap. The 2.1 percent weighted return on assets of the 2005 sample has been reduced to zero, while typical MFI returns are −9.8 percent, well behind Bangladeshi institutions reporting to the MIX, which lead the region in profitability. Low portfolio yields, combined with poor portfolio quality and rising financial costs have reduced Indian MFI surpluses, though improvements in collection measures have boosted portfolio yields to 93 percent of the expected figure, up from 85 percent in 2005 (Table 4.6). Yields, however, remain low, with 43 percent of Indian MFIs earning less than 24 percent on their portfolios. In comparison with 36 to 50 percent real costs of bank loans and moneylender interest rates ranging from 36 to 120 percent, MFI average yields represent a substantial benefit for low income clients.

The financial viability of microfinance institutions in India is under threat, despite improvements in the yield gap. The 2.1 percent weighted return on assets of the 2005 sample has been reduced to zero while typical MFI returns are -9.8 percent, well behind Bangladeshi institutions reporting to the MIX, which lead the region in profitability

Table 4.6 Portfolio yield relative to APR

Model	Yield (%)	APR (%)	Yield/APR (%)
Grameen	27.6	27.6	100
Indl Banking	26.1	32.3	80.7
SHG	13.8	16.9	81.5
M-CRIL India	24.2	26.1	92.8
Top 10	23.5	24.8	95.0
M-CRIL 2005	25.0	29.3	85.2
Top 10, 2005	23.9	27.8	86.0

Nonetheless, these are not sufficient to cover rising costs brought on by ambitious growth plans, deteriorating portfolio quality, and hardening of domestic interest rates on borrowings. Benchmarks for profitable Indian MFIs indicate that they charge more sustainable rates than their unprofitable peers and earn 24.8 percent on their portfolios as compared to 19.5 percent, but they also maintain tighter cost control. While both groups face similar financial costs, sustainable institutions benefit from lower provisioning expenses because of their superior portfolio quality. Moreover, they benefit from economies of scale as the typical sustainable MFI manages a much larger portfolio than an unsustainable institution. Indeed, the sample of 58 institutions shows a concentration of portfolio and borrowers among institutions that are at or near sustainability. As Table 4.7 shows, nearly 50 percent of borrowers are served by MFIs with operational self-sufficiency in excess of 90 percent. Since outreach has grown dramatically, the absolute numbers of clients served by sustainable institutions has actually increased by 35 percent over the past 2 years.

Table 4.7 Outreach of efficient MFIs

OSS(%)	Number	Proportion (%)
>100	1,696,447	39.5
90–100	440,107	10.3
80–90	824,990	19.2
<80	1,330,527	31.0
Total	4,292,071	100

Despite the sobering events of the past 2 years, the overall impression of an efficient MFI sector that is growing strongly remains unchanged. As the discussion in this chapter and that on social rating shows, it is apparent that while MFIs have learnt much in terms of operational efficiency a substantial effort is required in the areas of clarifying social objectives, poverty targeting, product development, and client orientation. The challenge for MFIs over the next few years is to achieve growth with equity as well as efficiency.

Endnotes

1   *Sanjay Sinha is Managing Director of M-CRIL.*

2   *Issues of deposit orientation of MFI models and their relationship with regulation and resource mobilization are discussed in Section 4.5.*

Reference

M-CRIL, 2006, "M-CRIL Microfinance Review 2005," Micor-Credit Ratings International Limited, Gurgaon

CHAPTER 5

Urban Microfinance

5.1 The new urban microfinance[1]

There has been an upsurge of interest in urban microfinance with several recent start-ups in the metros, promoted by professionals who have a proven track record of successful careers in banking and other fields.[2] Other start-ups are being promoted by microfinance professionals who already have some experience in rural microfinance, but feel challenged by the relatively unfamiliar territory of large-scale urban microfinance.[3] Both sets of entrants are part of what have been referred to as a "generational change"[4] in Indian microfinance.

A third set of entrants are many of the well-established, primarily rural MFIs expanding increasingly into small towns and peri-urban areas as they grow.[5] Fourth, an increasing number of NBFCs and banks already operating in the urban areas are experimenting with "down-scaling" through smaller, individual, loan products.[6] A possible fifth, although still very small category consists of the new urban MFIs being incubated by ACCESS Development Services in Kolkata.[7] Finally, there is a renewed interest in the pioneers of urban microfinance such as SEWA, WWF, and SPMS, whose experience over the years is being reexamined by the new comers for the valuable lessons they offer.

Although the "new generation" urban MFIs exhibit considerable diversity, they are distinguished by the following broad features. First, in contrast to the pioneers they have much greater ambitions in respect of scale. Several of them intend to grow rapidly to become national institutions with branches in several metros and large cities as well as in the surrounding rural hinterland.[8] In keeping with this ambition, they intend to achieve sustainability as soon as possible so as to be able to attract the huge volume of on-lending funds required, as well as the investments with which to support them. They have been very successful in attracting funds so far, largely because of the backgrounds of their promoters.

They intend to cater primarily to the vast majority of urban residents who are still unserved by the banks and depend largely on the informal sector for their financial needs. Reaching the poorest of the poor is not a primary goal, at least initially. Phrases like sub-prime borrowers, the missing middle, and lower income groups are frequently used in descriptions of their target clientele. Some of them are experimenting with new lending models more suited to urban microfinance, and they intend to induct the latest offerings of technology, wherever cost effective, to enhance scale and efficiency. They are cognizant of the need to offer a full set of financial services including savings, insurance, and remittances, over and above a range

There has been an upsurge of interest in urban micro-finance with several recent start-ups in the metros, promoted by professionals who have a proven track record of successful careers in banking and other fields

of credit products to suit the greater heterogeneity of urban financial markets. However, they intend to meet non-financial needs such as health and vocational training through partnerships with NGOs and other civil society organizations and socially minded corporations.

Some of them are treating their first couple of years as pilot projects, which they are using to stabilize delivery technology and product design, and learn the lessons of large-scale urban microfinance first hand. In this, they are being assisted by at least three service providers who also in a sense belong to this new generation, the Michael and Susan Dell Foundation, which sees its mission in India to catalyze urban MFIs by providing grant support for capacity building, and risk capital; ACCION, an international NGO with considerable experience worldwide in the introduction of individual lending and downscaling, and Unitus (Table A.4).

The third set of entrants, the Rural Converts, are mostly moving into urban microfinance from the contiguous rural areas and are operating mostly in the smaller towns and peri-urban areas.[9] Initial and average loan size is higher than in their rural operations, and this is where they are also introducing larger, individual loans to microentrepreneurs, both of which are advantageous from the point of view of profitability.

The fourth set, the increasing number of existing NBFCs and banks getting interested in downscaling, are an extremely heterogeneous bunch. Among the former are Satin Creditcare in West Delhi, which is best known for its system of doorstep daily collections, even though average loans size is currently as high as Rs. 27,000.

Banks in India have been excluded from the small loans market partly by regulatory fiat. They are not allowed to make loans of less than Rs. 200,000 at a rate any higher than their PLR (their lending rate to prime customers), if they want the loans to count towards their priority sector targets

Banks in India have been excluded from the small loans market partly by regulatory fiat. They are not allowed to make loans of less than Rs. 200,000 at a rate any higher than their PLR (their lending rate to, prime customers), if they want the loans to count towards their priority sector targets. Despite this disincentive, Yes Bank has decided to get into the microfinance market by introducing a personal loan product, ranging in size from Rs. 8000 to Rs. 25,000 repayable in 3 to 6 months, with technical assistance from ACCION. The area surrounding the bank's headquarters in Worli has been divided into 8 zones not more than 45 minutes' walking distance away. Each has been placed under a Relationship Manager who identifies borrowers and remains responsible for them, but with all cash transactions being handled out of an office at bank headquarters itself.[10]

Indian Bank's Microsate branch in Chennai is unusual in being a bank branch in an urban area which only makes loans to SHGs.[11] It is in effect doing SHG—Bank linkage in an urban area. With the assistance of about 51 registered NGOs, it is currently lending to about 4000 active groups out of an estimated 14,000 spread over about 140 slums in Chennai. Average group size is 17, and the main member activities are retailing, trading, and handicrafts. Microsate branch[12] had a portfolio of Rs. 7 crores in March 2007, which is expected to go up to about Rs. 20 crores by March 2008. This is its third year, and it has become profitable. Indian Bank has already set up another Microsate branch in Patna, and plans to open one in South Chennai, apart from branches in several cities all over the country. The main challenge it will face will be the availability of good NGOs with the capacity to form good SHGs. Tamil Nadu is unusual in having a very strong women's development corporation with an important urban component in its SHG programme, and with a policy to form SHGs only through NGOs (as distinct from the government agencies commonly used in other states). It ensures quality control through a system of accreditation of NGOs and provides training and other forms of assistance to them.

Experience with SHGs in some other urban microfinance programmes has been mixed, as discussed below. However, if the Microsate experience can be replicated it will be a significant breakthrough.

The Pioneers have stayed relatively small. In contrast with the more minimalist, financial services approach, of their successors, and in keeping with the more holistic view of the nature of poverty and powerlessness they espouse, many of them have placed equal emphasis on organizational inputs and collective action in pursuit of working women's rights and other social goals.[13] This meant accepting a much lower rate of growth, although in response to member needs, SEWA Bank, in particular (Box 5.6) has expanded much more rapidly in respect of savings and insurance than on the credit side. Generally, its experience in respect of savings and insurance services in an urban context as well as on credit products such as housing loans and individual loans are of great interest. Sri Padmavathy Mahila Abyudaya Sangh (SPMS) is unusual in several respects, which combine to make it unique. It may be the country's first SHG federation. Not only is it one of the few federations located in an urban area, it relies only for technical and strategic inputs on its promoters, and has become self-sufficient in respect of financial activities, although it receives grants for a variety of economic development activities, including participation in urban infrastructure activities such as housing, environmental sanitation, and even road building (DHAN Foundation 2005 and Box 3.3).

5.2 The Context

5.2.1 Urbanization and urban poverty

Some of the salient facts on India's urbanization and urban poverty are as follows:[14]

(i)   The rate of urbanization increased sharply in the 1990s to almost twice the rural population growth rate. The share of the urban population, although still lower than the global and Asian average, had grown to 31 percent by 2001. Much of the growth is being driven by migration from the rural areas.

(ii) While urban poverty is declining in relative terms, it is increasing in absolute terms. In the three decades since 1970 the number of poor went up from 52 to 67 million.[15] However, in some cities like Delhi the poverty ratio was as low as 8 percent in 1999 (Mukherjee 2004).

(iii) India's metros and large towns have some of the most congested slums in the world and are "home" to some of the worst living conditions anywhere. Thus, the extent of "human poverty" and deprivation is much worse than the "income" poverty measured and reported in the statistics.

5.2.2 The urban informal financial sector

In our use of the term financial inclusion (or inclusion into the formal and semi-formal or MFI sector), there is a danger of forgetting that the "excluded" are in fact served by a huge informal financial sector. The challenge is not to fill a supposed credit vacuum, but to improve on

In our use of the term financial inclusion (or inclusion into the formal and semi-formal or MFI sector) there is a danger of forgetting that the "excluded" are in fact served by a huge informal financial sector. The challenge is not to fill a supposed credit vacuum, but to improve on the terms of the informal sector

the terms of the informal sector. This will have two benefits. First, there is a direct benefit to those "included," and second, there is an indirect benefit to those left behind in the informal sector (likely the great majority). The terms on which the latter receive financial services will improve because of the competition offered by MFIs, just as they have in pockets in the rural areas where MFIs have achieved significant penetration.

There is a huge literature on the variety of informal sector lenders, and lending and savings devices and mechanisms, including moneylenders, pawnbrokers, chit funds, informal finance companies, employers, and pygmy deposit collectors, etc.[16] In Kalibasti, a squatter settlement in West Delhi, Ruthven (2001) mentions (i) interest-free loans from friends, neighbours, and relatives,[17] (ii) wage advances, (iii) groceries on credit, (iv) goods on credit, (v) private loans taken on interest from ex-neighbours, relatives, etc. at rates lower than moneylenders, and (vi) loans from professional moneylenders. It is important for MFIs to understand each of these sources, but particularly moneylenders, because they are the main competition, both with respect to serving the poor and the excluded non-poor. In Kalibasti, of the various sources, moneylenders had the highest share of poor users, or 40 percent, as Box 5.1 (excerpted from Ruthven 2001) describes. For households with monthly income bracket one-notch higher, who constitute Ujjivan's target group, they are ubiquitous, as described in Box 5.2 (from Ujjivan 2006).

Box 5.1   The uses and abuses of moneylenders

While 18 percent of respondents used (or admitted to using) professional moneylenders, close to half of these (40 percent) were categorized as poor. The operations and role of moneylenders in Kalibasti has been documents elsewhere (see Patole and Ruthven 2001). It is our observation that moneylenders hold a special place in the financial portfolio of poorer residents for two main reason. First, their convenience and reliability is unbeatable, an attribute particularly valuable for poor people who are short of time and money to negotiate deals and whose needs are most urgent. Second, they are unique within the informal sector, in being commercial (or "professional") and incur no wider social obligations on the part of the borrower. In other words, there is no dignity at stake in dealing with a professional moneylender — it is just a straight commercial deal. This makes them attractive to those who require discretion, who do not wish to strain social relations with financial concerns, or who simply do not have such relations to lean on. As one respondent put it, "When I go to the moneylender, it's between him and me. I give my relatives no reason to talk."

While the users of professional moneylenders are a mixed group (mostly Muslims and OBCs), the circumstances in which people borrow fall broadly in to two types: (i) those facing income shortfalls for whom other borrowing options are limited or non-existent (Box 5.1.1), and (ii) those managing a mixed credit portfolio, within which moneylenders have a niche of convenience and instant access (Box 5.1.2). Both types frequently drag repayment, but those of the first type — unless their income increases — find it increasingly difficult to raise money as they are refused in turn by each moneylender who recognizes their cash-flow inadequacy to repay.

Box 5.1.1 The uses and abuses of moneylenders

Surender (27) and Anita (24) have been in Delhi for most of their lives. Surender is a painter, taking contracts through a local hardware store, and has an erratic income due to the seasonal nature of his work. Anita stopped working recently following pregnancy. This is the couple's seventh year in Kalibasti and over the years they have become acquainted with several of the local moneylenders. Usually they go to those who take daily installments since this suits Surender's income pattern. A month ago they took one such loan of Rs. 1500 from a Tamil moneylender and passed the money on to a friend who had just given birth. Handing them Rs. 1350, he informed them they'd need to pay Rs. 35 for 50 days (a monthly rate of about 50 percent). They agreed, as they had in the past. But when Surender's income dried up they started facing repayment problems. Anita informed us she was planning a visit to a Rajasthani lender well known to her mother. Since he collects monthly rather than daily, his terms are more suited to the couple at this time of year. She'll try for Rs. 2000 at 3 percent per month. She'll repay the Tamil moneylender with this loan and use the balance to pay the house rent which is already two month overdue.

Box 5.1.2 The USP of the professional moneylender

At first glance one would have thought Santosh (42) and Roshan Lal (45, B), would have no use for moneylenders and their high interest rates. They've both got permanent jobs from which they can take advances, only one son to look after, an array of friends to borrow from when the need arises, they have a bank savings account, and Roshan sits in a Rosca at the office. Nonetheless, when they heard 5 years ago about a cheap deal going for a plot in Kalibasti they went straight to the moneylender and borrowed Rs. 5000 to make the offer. Over the next 4 months they repaid the loan at 5 percent per month. It was — they say — the only way they could raise money quickly enough.

Adapted from Ruthven (2001)

Box 5.2   The ubiquity of moneylenders in Bangalore

The unorganized sector is dominated by a vast assortment of virtually nameless, faceless financiers. They are present in market and non-market locations, and undertake their business very quietly and unobtrusively. The relationship between moneylenders and borrowers is symbiotic. With poor access to any formal funding, borrowers work to maintain a good relationship with their only source of credit, i.e., the non-formal individual moneylender. Additionally, there is a sense of loyalty towards him as he is considered to be his saviour in times of need. As for the moneylender, the borrower is his market. He services good borrowers with relatively easier repayment terms.

Generally, the interest rates levied by moneylenders are higher than those charged in the organized sector. Moneylenders charge between 2 and 10 percent per month on a loan amount. There are exceptions where the interest rates are lower or higher then these rates. In spite of the high interest rates that they charge, moneylenders are the most popular source of finance. This is probably because they offer unsecured loan that are tailored to the income cycle of customers.

Based on Ujjivan (2006)

Finally, it is worth reminding ourselves that the burden of exclusion falls most heavily on the poor, because it is the poor who are most likely to be excluded also by moneylenders and other informal sector lenders, for essentially the same reasons. So at the bottom of the pyramid, there may indeed be a credit vacuum. Second, to the extent rural microfinance reduces rural–urban migration, it reduces the inclusion task for urban microfinance. On the other hand, it could on balance fuel it, by financing it.[18]

5.3 The particular challenges of urban informal finance

Why was urban microfinance left unexplored territory for so long, despite the prospects of huge loan demand, larger average loan size, and higher population density making for lower costs, the need to reach the growing numbers of the urban poor, and the example of Latin America where microfinance is predominantly urban?

Why was urban microfinance left unexplored territory for so long, despite the prospects of huge loan demand, larger average loan size and higher population density making for lower-costs, the need to reach the growing numbers of the urban poor, and the example of Latin America where microfinance is predominantly urban? Some of the reasons have to do with institutional factors, such as the lack of a structured programme similar to the SBLP promoted by a single apex agency such as NABARD, which enjoyed the visibility the SBLP gave it. Similar programmes in the urban areas such as the Jawahar Shahari Rozgar Yojana failed to attain anywhere near the same prominence, although this was largely due to the same inherent difficulties that beset urban MFIs discussed in this chapter.

As regards the MFI model, the inspiration and delivery technology were derived from the Grameen Bank, which was almost exclusively rural, and whose model was proving as successful in the densely populated parts of rural India as in Bangladesh. Why jeopardize high growth and expend scarce managerial energy on venturing into unchartered territory, especially when the *standardization and borrower-time requirements* of the group-lending model might prove a handicap in the much more heterogeneous and time-constrained urban environment? Even more frequently mentioned as a difficulty for group lending with its *reliance on peer-pressure and mutual trust based on long-standing neighbourhood and kinship ties* was the supposed much greater mobility and lack of social cohesion, even atomization, of urban slum-dwellers.

5.3.1 Mobility and transience

As urban microfinance expands, some of these constraints and apprehensions are beginning to come into clearer focus (although only just, we are looking at the tip of the iceberg in terms of what we need to learn through patient rigorous field work, an example of which is contained in the boxes included here from Ruthven, 2001). As with most generalizations, the validity of that relating to the obstacle posed by mobility and transience depends on which income segment and location one is looking at. It certainly seems to the case that mobility has proved less of a problem than was originally feared. Fairly typical is Veena Mankar's observation that many slum-dwellers have been living in the same location for a generation or more, and that even if they go home to their villages for a couple of months a year they come back to the same area because of proximity to a known livelihood.[19] More of a problem in these areas, as Swadhaar finds, is that as many as 30 to 35 percent of its borrowers have no formal documentation to establish either identity or address. More of a problem, also, than mobility per se is what might be called "involuntary mobility," caused by the ongoing drive in Mumbai (and elsewhere) to demolish slums and relocate them elsewhere, which has affected 10 percent of her clients already.[20]

More of a problem in these areas, as Swadhaar finds, is that as many as 30 to 35 percent of its borrowers have no formal documentation to establish either identity or address. More of a problem, also, than mobility per se is what might be called "involuntary mobility"

On the other hand, in her research in Kalibasti, an unauthorized squatter settlement in West Delhi, Ruthven (2001) found that 16 percent of her sample had been resident for less than a year, and 35 percent for 2 years (Box 5.3 from Ruthven 2001). There is no doubt that much of the growth of India's urban slums is being fed by accelerating migration.[21] However, it is not in-migration we are concerned with, so much as the intention to stay, and here she reminds us that a good proportion of recent arrivals are planning to move on within a year or two

Box 5.3   Mobility in a Delhi slum

If we take the World Bank's global poverty line of US $1 (equivalent in Rupee purchasing power parity) of income per day per family member, just under a third of our sample emerge as below the poverty line. There is only a partial correspondence, however, between this group, ranked by current income, and the "poor" group ranked by our wider range of criteria during wealth ranking exercises. Current income after all is not able to reflect the changing dynamic of livelihoods over time and the wider context of assets and security which people experience (or not) independently of immediate income sources.

A large proportion of Kalibasti residents are on the move. Sixteen percent of our sample had been in Kalibasti for less than a year, 35 percent for 2 years or less. Clearly this challenges assumptions of slums as inhabited by permanent squatters since a good proportion of those who come are moving on within 1 or 2 years. Almost half of residents were experiencing a "dynamic trajectory" – improving their circumstances quite rapidly, or conversely in the midst of hard times or a crisis which sees them impoverished. Most of the others were facing some turbulence and hotly engaged in avoiding economic decline, making themselves less vulnerable to shocks, paying off past debts, and securing higher and more regular income. A minority of respondents (20 percent) could be seen as "cruising," not moving in any direction having secured a comfortable niche in Delhi and without much ambition...

...we can divide respondents into five broad categories in respect of their history and the circumstances which led to their arrival in Kalibasti. This is important because – even after several years in the colony – it informs their money management strategy. The following table describes these five categories.

Reasons for respondents moving to Delhi ($n = 27$)

Reason	Percentage
Gradual rural impoverishment: Shrinking, unviable landholdings are not compensated by availability of alternative employment, over generations	29
City hoppers hunt for opportunity: Business/self-employed families from regional cities try their luck in the capital	29
Young members of secure rural families hunt for opportunity: Unmarried male members of families with land (especially from Western UP) take time out before settling down to marriage and village responsibilities	21
Refugees from a crisis in the village: The death of the male bread winner, a severe health problem or an accident forces people to the city where they seek work to repay debts, rebuild assets, or start a new life	13
Long-term Delhi residents in financial crisis: Lower middle-class families downshift their lifestyle after being cheated, robbed, or imprisoned	17
Total	**100**

The table highlights the misconception that slum-dwellers are necessarily impoverished economic refuges from the countryside permanently flowing to the city. Nearly, half (44 percent) of our respondents are from relatively secure backgrounds, already urbanized or with a strong asset base in the village. Even among the balance, while most have come to Delhi in response to economic hardship of some kind, it cannot be assumed that most will stay. Many are using city earning power to build a more viable life in the countryside.

Based on Ruthven (2001)

(mostly back to their villages, in this case).[22] Aajivika in Delhi has been affected by mobility not directly, but indirectly, in that it is located in a resettlement colony in Northwest Delhi where more than 10,000 households have been located in the last 5 years. Aditi Mehta (2007) talks of the "almost complete lack of mutual trust within the community," which affected operations initially.

The main response so far to the problem of mobility in areas where it is acute is exclusion. Thus, Arohan in Kolkata would like very much to serve the huge population of mostly day visitors who flood into the middle-class areas of South Kolkata from the rural hinterland as day labourers, maids, etc., but has for very understandable reasons been unable to do so. Likewise, they have been forced to exclude the large population of rickshaw drivers who park by the wayside to sleep at night. If there is any successful experience of reaching Mumbai's pavement dwellers through microfinance on a significant scale, it has not yet been documented. Although Ujjivan defines its target group as those with a household income of between Rs. 2000 to Rs. 8000 a month, 98 percent of its clientele were above the Rs. 3000 line in March 2007.[23] Mehta is explicit in recognizing that Aajivika's participation comes so far from the "economically active poor, validating the opinion that microfinance may not be the most suitable instrument to target the poorest households. In the urban context this leaves unanswered the question of how the livelihoods of this segment might be addressed" (Mehta 2007).[24]

In locations where they do operate, most urban MFIs do, however, appear to have found ways of providing themselves with enough comfort to establish that the borrower has a fixed abode locally, despite lack of formal documentation.[25] Thus, Swadhaar and others establish veracity of information through cross checks with neighbours and using whatever documents are available, even wedding photographs. While joint liability groups may not be able to ensure repayments above a certain level of loan size (which most urban practitioners put at Rs. 15,000 to Rs. 20,000),[26] they do serve as a screening mechanism in respect of residence. Another screening mechanism, which has been used by BASIX and others, is to require prospective borrowers to save regularly for a period before becoming eligible for borrowing.[27]

A final point to be made is that even if a significant proportion of residents in a slum are transient, MFIs would have to achieve a very high level of penetration before running out of prospective borrower from among permanent residents for group membership, especially for the smaller, JLG groups, as discussed below. The trick would seem to lie in achieving a high success rate in spotting them.

5.3.2 Urban heterogeneity

There are several cross-cutting ways in which we can view urban heterogeneity. It can be viewed in terms of financial needs, or purposes for which money is raised, as in Box 5.4 excerpted from Ruthven (2001) describing "spending sets" in Kalibasti. It can also be viewed in relation to loan types designed to serve those needs, such as the informal sector business and personal loans taken by persons in the MHI class that constitutes Ujjivan's target group (as described Ujjivan 2006). Again it can be described in terms of occupational segments (an example of which, from Mumbai, is given in Box 5.4) or in terms of modes of employment (self versus wage employment).

Box 5.4   Segmentation by loan purpose

What do Kalibasti residents need financial services for? The spending behavior of residents (and the concomitant way in which they raise significant sums of money towards such expenses) can be divided into six "spending sets" as:

i.   Life-cycle costs: Overwhelmingly towards the marriage of daughters.

ii. Income shortfalls: Chronic or intermittent.

iii. Dependents outside Delhi: Relatives in the village but also children in school.

iv. Health crisis, chronic health problems and the stresses associated with these.

v.   Investment: In fixed assets or a job opportunity, in Delhi or the village.

vi. House construction in Delhi or the village.

The following table illustrates the purposes for which significant sums of money ("lump sums") were raised (whether through savings, advances or loans) by residents in the months running up to our survey. It shows the proportion of residents who had recently raised a lump sum for each of the purposes described and – among these residents – how many were ranked as poor.

Use of lump sums among Kalibasti residents (%)	% of sample	Of which ranked as poor(%)
Lifecycle cost	39	25
Income shortfalls in Delhi	27	57
Dependents outside Delhi*	31	25
Health & mental stress	24	58
Investment	24	0
House construction	24	33

*This is not equivalent to all those remitting money to the village since it includes only those who raised a significant sum for a trip or to send resources to the Village. Remittances have been examined separately.

As we might expect, the poor face disproportionately high expenses for health as well as to cover periodic or regular income deficits. No respondents ranked as poor had recently raised lump sums for investment. On the other hand, a proportionate number of this group was making investments in houses, mostly in their home towns or villages. This highlights the role of urban livelihoods in making possible the acquisition of rural assets.

Based on Ruthven (2001)

To take the last of these dimensions first, quite apart from the much greater importance of wage employment in the urban areas, self-employment itself, whether in manufacture or services, is likely to exhibit a much greater diversity than in the rural areas where a much smaller

...quite apart from the much greater importance of wage employment in the urban areas, self-employment itself, whether in manufacture or services, is likely to exhibit a much greater diversity than in the rural areas where a much smaller group of activities such as livestock and petty trading often account for the majority of loans

group of activities such as livestock and petty trading often account for the majority of loans. The proportion of wage and self-employed among MFI borrowers is likely to vary according to income group targeted, the urban area concerned, and MFI policy. As many as half of Ujjivan borrowers are wage-employed in occupations such as domestic help, garment factory workers, sweepers in the municipal corporation or are helpers in shops, schools, and hospitals. Many of them, however, have secondary self-employment activities. The self-employed are flower or vegetable vendors, or pushcart vendors of food and snacks, or run tea shops, or retail saris out of their homes, etc. Piece-rated job-work, which accounts for 10 percent of customers is an intermediate form of employment, is common in agarbatti making and beedi rolling and tends to be the worst remunerated, absorbing the most recent arrivals. In the case of Swadhaar and SWAWS, the proportion among borrowers is the reverse, largely for reasons of policy.[28] But, clearly there is plenty of scope for lending to both sets of borrowers in India's metros. In Mumbai, one estimate places the number of workers in various occupational segments (offering both self and wage employment), which engage a high proportion of women, as 700,000 household workers, of which 95 percent are women (maids); 200,000 hawkers (25 percent women); 100,000 each of sweepers and rag pickers (40 percent women and children); and 50,000 zari workers (35 percent women and children).[29]

The numbers engaged in the more male-dominated occupational segments such as taxi drivers, auto drivers, loom workers, leather industry workers, and mathedi and hamali workers were estimated in the same study.[30] At least, one urban MFI would like, at some stage, to lend to men too. As with rural microfinance, and contrary to the enduring fiction that "95 percent" of microfinance borrowers are women, a large share of the loans are used by men anyway, and not just husbands (Chapter 6).

Also, there is no clear-cut correspondence between mode of employment and use of loans. As many as 30 percent of Swadhaar's borrowers, who are running businesses, borrow for non-business purposes. Retirement of high-cost existing debt to moneylenders and others tends to be one of the commonest uses of the first and second loans for both sets of borrowers (as may be the case in the rural areas too). Given the shortage and dilapidated condition of housing in the urban areas, the demand for housing loans is extremely high, as is that for products designed to cater to life-cycle events, education, and health expenditures (given the high income elasticities of demand of all these services, and higher incomes in the urban areas). All this has implications for the range of products offered and their design, as well as for lending procedures.

Given the shortage and dilapidated condition of housing in the urban areas, the demand for housing loans is extremely high, as is that for products designed to cater to life-cycle events, education, and health expenditures (given the high income elasticities of demand of all these services, and higher incomes in the urban areas)

5.4 Responses

5.4.1 Products

Several MFIs have conducted careful market research and are in the process of developing products based on it. Ujjivan's research into the market for housing loans revealed the lifetime progression of the typical customer from renting to "leasing" (in which the tenant pays in lieu of rent a relatively large interest-free lump sum to the owner), to buying a house site, to building a house, to extending and repairing it. For good customers who have established a track-record, Ujjivan has started offering loans of up to Rs. 30,000 for any of these purposes using a loan from HDFC which should suffice for 1700 customers. (Box 5.5). It is looking also at educational loans required specially at the beginning of the school year, and loans for higher education. These products are in addition to Ujjivan's standard family-needs (or personal) loans, business loans, top-up loans, emergency loans, and festival loans. SWAWS and VWS also have educational loans.[31] SEWA's products have evolved over 30 years to result in the diversity described in Box 5.6.

Box 5.5 Ujjivan's approach to urban housing microfinance: Helping customers climb the housing ladder

Driven by the heavy migration into the city and a booming economy, Bangalore faces a critical housing shortage, boosting the price of housing ever higher. For the urban poor, bearing the burden of rising housing costs requires substantial financing. To date, this has been supplied by Bangalore's highly developed yet costly informal financial sector, with little presence of urban MFIs. Ujjivan recognized the opportunity for affordable housing finance, and recently began a pilot urban housing microfinance scheme.

The pilot process commenced with a study designed to provide an understanding of urban housing needs. The study revealed three types of urban residents: renters, Leasers, and homeowners, who each correspond to a progressive rung on what Ujjivan terms the "Housing Ladder." The first rung is renting, which typically requires a monthly rent of Rs.1000 to Rs. 2000 and a refundable deposit of 10 times the monthly rent. The second rung is leasing, which typically requires a lump sum between Rs. 50,000 and Rs.100,000 in lieu of a monthly rent for 3 to 5 years. Leases are desirable because the lump sum is returned at the lease end, albeit without interest, allowing customers to reinvest the amount in a larger lease, land site, or other purposes. The third rung is owning a home, which typically occurs in three phases: buying a land site, constructing a simple home, and later progressively improving the house.

The study revealed three types of urban residents: renters, leasers and homeowners, who each correspond to a progressive rung on what Ujjivan terms the "Housing Ladder"

To climb each rung, the urban poor are dependent on access to affordable financing. For example, Sunita, an Ujjivan customer, is renting a house for Rs. 2000 per month with a deposit of Rs. 20,000. She says, "I want a lease because they are better than renting because you do not have to pay every month, and you can save your money. But I need Rs. 30,000 more to afford a lease in my area, and moneylenders are too expensive." The need for housing financing was echoed by Uma, also an Ujjivan customer, who says "I own my house and I am very happy because I can stay here forever now. But now I need money to build one more room because my children are older now and we don't have enough space." The presence of renters and leasers in the urban housing landscape marks the key difference between urban and rural settings, as nearly 60 percent of Ujjivan's customers rent or lease while just 40 percent own, in contrast to 80 to 90 percent home ownership rates in rural areas.

The study also demolished several myths about urban housing microfinance. *Myth 1: Housing loans must be large with long tenors and are unsuitable for MFIs.* The Housing Ladder reveals that, in fact, the poor need loans as small as Rs. 10,000 to reach subsequent rungs in the Housing Ladder, for example, a move from a Rs. 50,000 to a Rs. 60,000 lease. Smaller, incremental loans are actually better suited for both customers and MFIs, because they are more affordable for customers, and offer lower risk and returning customers for MFIs. *Myth 2: The urban poor are too mobile for MFIs to give loans to them.* Despite this perception, urban families are highly rooted to their communities and often live in the same area for generations. In fact, because the pressure to move is often created by an inability to afford rising costs, microfinance may have a stabilizing effect on the mobility of urban low-income families. *Myth 3: The poor do not have proper documentation for their homes.* While the majority of renters and leasers do not have documentation for current contracts, MFIs can influence new documentation, because customers will be entering into new agreements with the loans they receive. MFIs can require customers to submit proper documentation, putting pressure on them to demand documentation from landlords. For home owners, the study found that over 90 percent of urban customers did have legal land titles. Although MFIs must develop

---

methodologies to screen for forged documents, Ujjivan found that documentation is not in fact a major barrier.

Ujjivan's housing loans have attempted to address each rung in the Housing Ladder and are currently being tested in a pilot phase. The products offered include rental deposit, lease amounts and house improvement loans, ranging in size from Rs. 10,000 to Rs. 30,000 with tenors of up to 3 years. Original documentation is not required, and customers can avail of the loan after completing one full year with an excellent repayment record, and with center and group recommendation. Ujjivan plans to roll out the loans nationwide in 2008, and in the future will offer value-added housing products, larger loan sizes and individual housing loans.

Anjali Banthia, Product Manager, Ujjivan Financial Services

Box 5.6 Individual loans and product diversification at SEWA Bank

Recognizing that the diversity of occupational, economic, and social backgrounds of SEWA Bank members, with their very different financial requirements, made group lending suboptimal in the urban context, SEWA was one of the first MFIs to take the more challenging path of individual lending. Starting in 1974 with a simple savings and a simple loan account, SEWA Bank has evolved into a composite financial institution offering a variety of savings and recurring deposit accounts, fixed deposits and secured and unsecured loans. Unsecured loans have to be backed only by two guarantors, one of who can be a family member. About a fifth of its roughly 150,000 members are borrowers, of which three-fourths have unsecured loans of up to Rs. 50,000 repayable in 35 months at an interest rate of 18 percent. Slightly better off clients with urgent cash requirements can avail of secured loans at 12 percent, backed by a personal asset, usually jewelry. In 1998, the Bank introduced longer term housing loans in partnership with HUDCO, linked to a requirement to save Rs. 20,000 through a 5-year recurring deposit scheme for housing. Finally, in 2001, SEWA introduced daily collection loans to extend outreach to poorer clients with a daily income cycle such as vegetable and flower vendors. This product mimics the money-lender, although at a much lower rate of interest, through bank "sathis," a team of former client with good financial literacy skills, who work on a commission basis, and visit clients daily not only to collect daily loan repayments, but to offer also daily savings collection and other recurring deposit schemes.

By introducing various specialized recurring deposit schemes each tailored to a specific life-cycle need (including, now, pensions for old-age), SEWA has greatly reduced the cost of predictable expenditures for life-cycle needs. For unexpected shocks (death, accidents, sickness), it has made insurance compulsory through its insurance wing VIMO SEWA. Based on close studies of its clients' needs, today SEWA offers more than 40 differentiated products. Jayshreeben Vyas describes the process "We looked at their life-cycle needs and have come up with various savings products to mirror those needs — various recurring accounts, savings for buying gold, for education, for marriage, for old age, etc. Similarly, we have developed a range of products within credit."

Based on Pasheva and Desai in CMF (2006)

5.4.2 Processes

As regards processes, one response to urban mobility and heterogeneity has been to do away with center meetings altogether, and experiment with smaller sized JLGs, more suited to accommodating the diversity of occupations, loan sizes requirements, and time availabilities.

As Veena Mankar points out, a maid and a hawker are unlikely to be free at the same time to attend a group meeting (assuming they have any free time at all). Both Ujjivan and Swadhaar have introduced monthly instead of weekly repayments, given the particularly acute time pressures experienced by borrowers in metros (many of who have long commutes). Swadhaar even gives them the option to pay a little extra to have their repayments collected at the doorstep. Also, doing away with center meeting makes a virtue out of necessity, since sufficient space for a gathering (let alone for a branch office) is prohibitively expensive, if available at all, in many urban localities.

It will be interesting to see how these innovations work out. Though, it should be noted though that not all urban MFIs are departing from the tried and tested. Arohan feels its present system is well suited to its clients,[32] while recognizing changes to it may be required for different segments, when they are covered (monthly repayments, for instance, for the salaried for personal loans).

5.4.3 Individual loans

The next logical step, of course, is to do away with JLGs altogether and introduce individual loans, which are already the norm in Latin America. The advantage of individual loans is that they can be more easily tailored to the loan size, gestation period, and other cash flow requirements of the specific activity chosen by each borrower. Individual loans are usually made to borrowers who have established a track record through group borrowing and who require larger loans. Their higher risk is usually addressed by security in some form and higher interest on account of the risk premium. Many MFIs have in fact already been making individual loans for housing purposes to senior group members, although, since funds for these usually come from the housing financing institutions, their interest rates are lower and tenor longer. What are more recent are loans made to small entrepreneurs and traders referred to by names such microenterprise loans, etc.[33] For most MFIs individual loans are still a small part of their portfolio, except for SEWA Bank, the MFI with the longest experience in India (and perhaps anywhere) of individual loans, as described in Box 5.6.

The next logical step, of course, is to do away with JLGs altogether and introduce individual loans, which are already the norm in Latin America. The advantage of individual loans is that they can be more easily tailored to the loan size, gestation period, and other cash flow requirements of the specific activity chosen by each borrower

5.4.4 SHGs or JLGs?

As a delivery vehicle, SHGs (instead of JLGs) would also be affected by the mobility and time-scarcity related constraints of urban life, perhaps even more so, since SHGs have more members than JLGs, which should make it even harder to find a time for meetings suitable for all members, and increase the likelihood of at least one member moving out of the locality. On the other hand, in theory at least, SHGs are better suited to handle urban heterogeneity since they are expressly designed to accommodate different loan amounts, and like chit funds can accommodate non-borrowing or net saver members who prefer to sit back and earn interest on loans taken by others. Moreover, given adequate accounting skills they should be able to accommodate heterogeneity in respect of variation in desired savings, both between members and over time. Despite this, their use is very much the exception, although Indian Bank's Microsate branch, SPMS, and Roshan Vikas (Box 3.5) rely on them exclusively, the last two as SHG federations.

On the other hand, in theory at least, SHGs are better suited to handle urban heterogeneity since they are expressly designed to accommodate different loan amounts, and like chit funds can accomodate non-borrowing or net saver members who prefer to sit back and earn interest on loans taken by others

Janalakshmi in Bangalore also relied on them exclusively in its previous avatar as Sanghamitra's Urban Microfinance Programme, but is reported to be moving away from them. Ujjivan also used them, outsourcing the task of forming them to existing NGOs, but like Janalakshmi has moved away from SHGs organized by others, to forming JLGs itself. In Ujjivan's case, the reasons had to do with lack of control over the quality of the groups formed, with some members frequently cornering all the funds, and instances of illegal commissions being charged from the groups by middlemen masquerading as NGOs. It also felt that the margin between what it charged the SHG and the rates paid by the ultimate borrower was unjustified. Finally, hoping to graduate borrowers in the medium term to larger individual loans, it felt JLGs gave it a much closer understanding of their credit and savings behaviour.[34]

Aajivika in Delhi actually initiated operations through NGOs who had an existing presence in slum clusters in activities such as health, literacy, and advocacy, but dropped this approach since it found that partners relegated microfinance very low on their list of priorities, and the groups formed were often short lived. It chose then to initiate direct operations in a huge new resettlement colony, but found the level of trust insufficient to mobilize 15 member SHGs. It settled finally on smaller groups of five clustered in centers of 8 along classic Grameen lines.

However, none of the problems encountered are inherent in the SHG channel, and warrant further investigation. The experience is mixed, and as noted above there are several examples of successful use of SHGs. For MFIs striving to attain rapid growth, however, JLGs give it more control over loan size and frequency, and this may be one of the decisive considerations in favor of the latter in most cases.[35]

5.5 Some other challenges

5.5.1 Human resources

While the MFI human resources challenge — not just training, but attracting and retaining staff — has been engaging the attention of the MFI community generally in the last few years, its severity in the urban areas has taken the new urban MFIs by surprise

While the MFI human resources challenge — not just training, but attracting and retaining staff — has been engaging the attention of the MFI community generally in the last few years, its severity in the urban areas has taken the new urban MFIs by surprise. Nearly all of them are finding it difficult to recruit and retain staff in conditions of a tightening job market, especially in cities like Bangalore where Ujjivan reports attrition rates of 20 to 30 percent a year. The skills field workers acquire are turning out to be in high demand in other parts of the financial sector, and also in marketing. Also, as Veena Mankar points out, many young entrants to the labour force find the multi-tasking nature of MFI field work too demanding, and prefer a more uni-dimensional job (and one offering, preferably, a little more "glamour" or office comfort). Finally, the relatively flat nature of the MFI pyramid does not help when it comes to promotion prospects. Clearly, better pay and incentives will have to be part of the solution, but will raise costs. Another solution being tried out is recruiting staff in the rural areas and providing them with accommodation.[36]

5.5.2 Borrower and external relations: "Money with respect"

Another aspect of urban operations MFIs are learning about is the much greater awareness of urban borrowers on financial and other matters, stemming partly from higher literacy, but also from the much closer presence of the formal sector.[37] As one CEO points out "one significant difference with rural operations is that you can't treat your customers as fools — you can't talk down to them." As another MFI leader put it "we impress on our staff that what we are offering is not just money, but money with respect." Borrower sophistication may be particularly high in West Bengal because of greater political awareness.[38] West Bengal MFIs have been particularly conscious of the need to maintain good customer and external relations. They keep local ward-level politicians informed of their activities and plans, and invite them to preside over functions. VWS has followed a conscious policy of developing borrower rapport and community goodwill through its diversity of microfinance plus activities, as well as schemes such as scholarships for children of borrowers who top in their classes, grants to local youth clubs, etc.[39]

As one CEO points out "one significant difference with rural operations is that you can't treat your customers as fools — you can't talk down to them"

5.5.3 Technology

The cost of space has already been mentioned, and is enhancing the interest in technological solutions such as branchless banking. For instance, Ujjivan is taking advantage of broadband connectivity in urban areas by centralizing all data entry at the head office and having the branches merely scan daily loan transaction data sheets and transmit them by email. (Alternatively, since the branches are located in the same urban area, the sheets can be hand-carried.) SEWA and Swadhaar are using biometric smart cards to make it easier for their members to operate savings accounts through ATMs, since they tend to forget their PINs. VWS has been given a grant by SIDBI to introduce 5000 smart cards and hand-held machines in each of the two branches.[40]

5.5.4 Competition

After what has been said earlier about the huge unsatisfied demand for credit in the urban areas, it may seem surprising that excessive competition between MFIs even figures as an issue is discussions of urban microfinance. However, there is clearly a perception among MFI leaders in several locations that competition could get out of hand and needs to be handled carefully. Allegations relate to poaching of customers, even whole groups, as well as staff, with some MFIs having acquired reputations for being particularly aggressive and even predatory. It is possible that some MFIs try to pre-empt others by planting the flag, so to speak, in new locations, by forming groups where the arrival of a rival is perceived to be imminent. It is possible also that there is a sort of herd mentality among MFIs as they follow others to new areas that have been shown to be operable by the first mover. It is surprising again that of all places, Kolkata, and the districts surrounding it, a huge urban and semi-urban conurbation with a population of about 30 million living within a radius of 50 km from Kolkata and accounting for about 40 percent of the population of West Bengal, should figure as a locus of concern about excessive competition.[41] Similar concerns are expressed in Bangalore and Hyderabad.[42]

...there is clearly a perception among MFI leaders in several locations that competition could get out of hand and needs to be handled carefully

Until technological advances make unique identifiers and credit bureaus economical, geographical separation would seem to offer one solution, but has not led to any explicit understandings anywhere, on account of fears of "cartelization" restricting competition and leading to anti-consumer behavior. However, even sharing of lists of borrowers is not practiced.

5.6 Conclusion

These are early days yet for urban microfinance. In the major metros, it seems to be growing relatively fast in Bangalore, Hyderabad, and Kolkata, but more slowly in Mumbai and Delhi, for reasons not entirely clear. Loan demand in Kolkata is particularly strong and staff easier to recruit because of higher unemployment among youth. Costs could also be lower. It will be interesting to see how the early experiences and issues discussed in this chapter develop.

Endnotes

1   The task of writing this chapter was made considerably easier by two reports presented at last years' Microfinance India conference: CARE, MSDF and ICICI Bank (2006), "A Promise to Pay the Bearer: An Exploration of the Potential for Urban Microfinance in India" and a companion volume of case studies, CMF (2006) "Reaching the Other 100 Million Poor in India." I am also indebted to a recent special issue of Microfinance Insights brought out quarterly by Intellecap, on "Reaching out to the Urban Poor" in March 2007, for a number of interesting articles and some of them written by the promoters themselves.

2   Examples are Janalakshmi and Ujjivan in Bangalore, Swadhaar in Mumbai, Mimo Finance in Dehradun, and Aajivika in Delhi.

3   Such as Arohan in Kolkata and Sonata in Allahabad.

4   The phrase is from CARE et al. (2006), as are also the phrases "Rural Converts" and "Pioneers" used below. All the "new generation" MFIs mentioned so far have been started by professionals, although not all by former bankers. One of them has worked for the UN, and another is a serving civil servant. It is too early to say whether this could become a trend in the rural areas too, but a former NRI has started a rural MFI in northern Karnataka recently with a strong emphasis on livelihood promotion.

5   Such as Spandana, SHARE, SKS, Bandhan, VWS, BASIX, Grameen Koota, Maheseman, and SWAWS, the last of which is almost exclusively urban, with operations in Hyderabad's Old City.

6   Examples are Satin Creditcare in Delhi, MAS Financial Services in Ahmedabad, and Yes Bank in Mumbai.

7   ACCESS is the successor organization to the DFID-assisted CARE-CASHE project, which incubated about 30 rural SHPIs in three states including West Bengal, using grants to build capacity and subsidize operational costs. In collaboration with SIDBI, ACCESS intends to incubate eight nascent MFIs in the Kolkata municipal area, assisting them to develop systems and capacity through mentoring services provided by an Urban Microfinance Resource Centre. It intends to achieve a collective outreach of 40,000 borrowers and a portfolio of Rs. 12 crores by the end of Year 1 (June 2008) going up to 1,32,000 and Rs. 120 crores by the end of Year 5. Loan funds will be provided by SIDBI, coupled with grants of up to 25 percent of the loan amounts for capacity building and overheads. The project aims to attain break-even for the MFIs by the end of the third year. ACCESS has similar projects in the MP and Rajasthan, but which are rural. Kolkata was chosen because it is the city in India with the highest population density, containing about 60 percent of the state's urban population, and because of the availability of suitable candidate nascent MFIs, and a history of operation in WB from CASHE days. It will be interesting to see how the incubation approach works out in comparison with the others described here.

8   Thus, Janalakshmi and Ujjivan both plan to grow to half a million clients within a few years. Now, Ujjivan has 4 branches each in Delhi and 7 branches in Kolkata apart from the 15 branches in Banglaore, and by March 2008 expects to grow to 100,000 clients within just over 2 years.

9   Data is lacking on the respective shares of their rural, peri-urban, and urban operations, although in some cases the last two are relatively important, going up to half, reportedly, in the case of

Spandana, which has been making daily collection loans in several urban areas for some time now. BASIX started expressly urban operations through a small pilot project in Hyderabad in 2004.

10 Yes Bank hopes to reach about 2000 borrowers, mostly the self-employed in need of working capital loans, by March 2008, and is targeting about 150,000 in 5 years out of all its branches, with an average loan size of Rs. 35,000. It does require security by hypothecating specific household goods like TV sets, which act as "reputational" collateral. The bank hopes to add new products soon, such as loans for the salaried, fixed asset loans, and home improvement loans. It has been urging the RBI to treat a microfinance-only branch (which it is willing to open in Dharavi) as fulfilling the requirement to open one rural branch for every three urban branches. It would also like to receive a license to open a microfinance-only NBFC.

11 The lower cost of SHG loans (as compared to individual loans) makes it possible for them to be extended at rates below the PLR.

12 The name Microsate comes from a plan to open mobile satellite branches, which was later dropped, although the name was retained. The branch is the subject of one of the case studies in CMF (2006).

13 Referring to the value placed by the Alliance in Mumbai (SPARC, NSDF, and Mahila Milan) on savings, for the moral discipline and commitment to the collective that it inculcates, Ruthven (2001) points out that the "mixed and complex agendas of urban development organizations can impose transactions costs on clients in their attempt to access financial services; it can even contribute to the unreliability of a service if more political agendas start to dominate".

14 Several of the statistics in this section are taken from various articles in Intellecap (2007).

15 Unlike urban poverty, rural poverty is declining both in relative and absolute terms. However, the number of rural poor is still three times higher than that of the urban poor.

16 See, for instance, Ghate (1992) and Rutherford and Arora (1997).

17 Or what has been called "reciprocal credit" in Ghate (1992).

18 For many migrants, of course, this may turn out to be a good thing. Not all of them join the pool of the unemployed, although one theory holds this pool will always exist, and its size will depend on the probability of getting a job.

19 This is clearly the case in the older, more settled, slums of which there may be a higher proportion in cities growing less rapidly.

20 Many of them have left without repaying. Similar drives appear to be fairly common in other metros too, as well as resettlement occasioned by the widening of roads and making space for higher income residential neighbourhoods, as in Delhi where Mukherjee describes the snapping of ties between job-work suppliers and workers resettled far away (coincidentally, in Holambikalan, the large new resettlement colony, where Aajivika also operates – see below). We are reminded, interestingly, from his study that mobility results also from re-shifting to the original or other neighbourhoods closer to work (Mukherjee 2004).

21 Inter-state migration according to the 2001 census increased by 30 percent over the decade of the 1990s. The largest in-migration states were Maharashtra (7.9 million), Delhi (5.6 million), and West Bengal (5.5 million) (Mukherjee 2007). Half a million people are said to migrate into Mumbai every year, most of them swelling Mumbai's slum population, which already accounts for 60 percent of

the total population of about 15 million. An estimate of the annual increment to Delhi's slums is 300,000 a year, or 3 percent of the city's population.

22 *She reminds us also that not all of them are poor. An estimate of mobility in the Mumbai occupational segments referred to below is that the average period for which an individual stays in the same house is 28 months.*

23 *The urban poverty line for a household of five is currently Rs. 2270 (Chapter 6). According to Ujjivan (2006), the share of Rs. 3000 to Rs. 7000 segment was only two-thirds of the 47 percent of the city's population below this income class. Arohan appears to reach lower down the Kolkata income distribution, with 38 percent of its loans being directed to the 31 percent of borrowers in the two monthly per capita expenditure classes below the Rs. 700 to Rs. 900 class in which its average borrower falls (Arohan 2007).*

24 *This recognition is of course not new. It has long been arrived at with respect to rural microfinance, and there is no reason why urban practitioners should feel defensive about it. Microfinance is ill-suited to solve the problem of chronic income deficits. However, it is also the case that there are many potential borrowers whose income deficits could be removed by credit, combined usually with other inputs. The challenge is to identify such persons and arrange for the provision of the other inputs by some other agency if necessary. There is also the question of the level of income at which such deficits turn from being usually temporary to becoming permanent. Defining the target group too conservatively finesses all these challenges. The method of exclusion used by one urban MFI is to set the monthly group savings requirement (referred to as a security deposit, which NBFCs are allowed to collect) high enough to be affordable only to the target group.*

25 *Having a fixed abode is a much less stringent requirement than owning or renting a house. Indeed as the customer satisfaction survey conducted for Arohan (2007) says, "in the slum areas there is rarely any rent being paid and the people dwelling there are staying since long and hence the accommodation pattern is taken as ownership." Those renting constitute 30 percent of the sample. In contrast among Ujjivan's members, as many as 40 percent own their accommodation, about 50 percent rent it, and 10 percent "lease" it (as defined below). Overall, only 61 percent of the urban population own their dwelling units as against 93 percent in the rural areas, according to NSS (2001) data.*

26 *They point out that while JLG members may be willing to pitch in for fellows when they are experiencing temporary cash flow problems, they tend to put their foot down after, say, three missed monthly installments. It is often forgotten that the quality of JLGs themselves varies. Arohan (2007) found that, of JLG members, only 44 percent could identify all other JLG members by name and purpose of loan taken. Seventeen percent could not identify some other JLG members by name, and 33 percent could not identify the purpose of the loans taken by some JLG members. Six percent could not identify any member by name or loan purpose. The situation varied by branch.*

27 *Aajivika tried this, but found that SHG members were unwilling to trust it with their savings unless deposited in their name in a bank.*

28 *In Arohan's case, the share of the self-employed is 55 percent. SEWA's very name indicates it is primarily for self-employed women.*

29 *Rag pickers and hawkers were found to have the lowest daily income (Rs. 60 and Rs. 80 respectively).*

30 Interestingly, migrant construction workers were not included, perhaps because in Mumbai construction workers are not as visible, as they do not live in temporary colonies next to the building site like those in smaller or more spacious cities, but tend to disperse themselves among the neighbouring population.

31 Interestingly, both MFI's educational loans are repayable in 10 monthly installments. VWS' carry a lower rate than other loans.

32 As the customer satisfaction survey says, "it is noted with pleasure that on the whole the customers are satisfied with loan tenure, its rate of interest, the EWI amount, other costs involved, repayment modalities and necessary formalities." The rate of interest is presently 30 percent, but is planned to be reduced to 24 percent. However, 90 percent of customers wanted larger loans and 20 percent fortnightly or monthly instead of weekly repayments. Minimum loan size is presently Rs. 5000. VWS has chosen the middle path and opted for fortnightly meetings and repayments, which gives field workers more time for group formation work.

33 Thus, in late 2006, SWAWS started making individual loans of between Rs. 20,000 to Rs. 50,000 at 15 percent flat, mostly for income-generation activities. Loans are disbursed as demand drafts and security is taken in the form of post-dated cheques and sureties by guarantors. They still account only for about 5 to 6 percent of the portfolio, but are finding a ready market in new centres such as Coimbatore to which SWAWS is expanding. VWS has a similar product, which is appraised by the branch manger instead of field staff. Spandana and the other large MFIs have been making individual loans for some time. It would be instructive to compare the profitability of individual loans with group loans for a group of MFIs. Their unit administration costs should be lower given larger average loan size.

34 It did attempt a closer than arms-length association with SHGs by requiring its own field workers to participate in training, and ensuring that proper group records were maintained. Apart from hoping to ensure that credit-histories of group members were built up, this was also in keeping with the Grameen tradition of monitoring the use of loans in accordance with its stated purpose. By making personal loans, Ujjivan and other MFIs have released borrowers from the pretense that the loan is being used for a "productive" purpose, but it does like to ensure that the loan is being used for the stated purpose, whatever that be.

35 See Box 5.5, on Swayanshree, an SHG federation in Cuttack, which has recently started organizing JLGs in addition to its SHGs.

36 Thus, Ujjivan has partitioned space off in branch offices for this purpose.

37 Reportedly, there are on an average two cooperative banks in every slum in Mumbai, and the number of credit societies operating in Mumbai is 100, including 10 in Dharavi.

38 It will be interesting to see whether the greater sophistication of urban borrowers leads to greater transparency on matters such as the effective interest rate.

39 Thus, VWS has an OPD centre in each branch with a doctor and generic drugs available at a 60 percent discount. Fees per visit are Rs. 35 for borrowers and Rs. 40 for members of the public. The scheme pays for itself at a break-even level of 50 patients a day. VWS also has a very popular compulsory health insurance scheme with an annual premium of Rs. 300 for a family of up to 4 members that includes maternity, caesarian, and fractures without the need for hospitalization. The scholarships of Rs. 100 go to students who come first, second, or third in classes 7 to 10. VWS legal form as a S25 company makes it easier to use surpluses for microfinance and charitable activities.

40   The cards will be able to handle all of the several VWS products. Card holders who pay a one-time charge
     of Rs. 50 will be entitled to borrow emergency loans or up to Rs. 2000 repayable within 8 weeks.

41   Especially in the North 24-Parganas just north of the Kolkata municipal area. Incumbent WB MFIs such
     as Bandhan, Village Welfare Society, and Arohan, and at least four SIDBI borrowers about to convert to
     NBFC status, have been joined recently by out-of-state MFIs SKS and Ujjivan. In addition, as mentioned
     above, ACCESS Development Services is in the process of incubating 8 MFIs in the inner Kolkata muni-
     cipality area. Bandhan with an outreach of 4.3 lakhs in January 2007 is by far the largest. Of its 300
     odd branches, 30 are urban of which 13 are in Kolkata proper. VWS had an outreach of 63,000 in March
     2007 with half its portfolio urban. Other MFIs with a presence in the greater Kolkata metropolitan area
     (including Kolkata municipality), are, in approximate order of size, Sahara Utsarg, Kalighat SDF,
     Rakapur SN, Ullon SSW, and HDC. Arohan has started operations in the inner Kolkata municipal area
     but has plans to expand outwards. The consumer satisfaction survey done for Arohan found that 15
     to 20 percent of its borrowers have borrowings from other individuals and institutions, formal and infor-
     mal, including 7 percent from other MFIs. Arohan has a policy of lending to persons who have up to one
     loan from another MFI, but no more. However, as Shubhankar Sengupta, the CEO points out, customers
     are not always candid about other loans. In the case of VWS the extent of overlapping was found to be
     about 40 percent in one branch. Aiming to build up a presence so strong that it will dissuade compe-
     titors from entering, VWS has opted for an "intensive" strategy in a limited number of blocks (which
     could increase to 25 from the present 18, in four districts) by covering at least half the target group
     of poor households in each block (or about 10,000 borrowers in each block). On competition in West
     Bengal, see also the article by Chandra Shekhar Ghosh, the CEO of Bandhan (Ghosh 2007). Since
     Ghosh's article was written, WB MFIs have formed an association to coordinate their activities. Also,
     the DMs have been asked by the government to hold a coordination meeting every month.

42   Janalakshmi and Ujjivan, both plan to grow to a size of about half a million in a few years, as we have
     seen, growing outwards from Bangalore city. Spandana and SKS have also commenced operations in the
     area. Spandana, SWAWS, Basix, and Roshan Vikas all operate in Hyderabad. It is interesting that
     SWAWS gives as the reason for dropping Grameen Bank's well-known 2:2:1 system, the need to become
     more accommodating with growing competition from Spandana.

References

Arohan, 2007, "A Survey and Critical Study on the Customer Satisfaction of the Customers of Arohan," Report done by Friday Solutions, Kolkata, mimeo

CARE, MSDF and ICICI Bank, 2006, "A Promise to Pay the Bearer: An Exploration of the Potential for Urban Microfinance in India," Report presented at Microfinance India Conference, October 29 and 30, New Delhi

Centre for Micro Finance (CMF), 2006, "Reaching the Other 100 Million Poor in India," Report presented at Microfinance India Conference, October 29 and 30, New Delhi

DHAN Foundation, 2005, "Impacting Urban Poverty Through Microfinance: The SPMS Experience," DHAN Foundation, Madurai

Ghate, Prabhu, 1992, "Informal Finance: Some Findings from Asia," OUP for ADB, Hong Kong

Ghosh, Chandra Shekhar, 2007, "Challenges of Scaling Up," *Intellecap*

Intellecap, 2007, "Reaching out to the Poor," Special issue of Microfinance Insights, Vol. 2, March, Mumbai

Mankar, Veena, and Lara Gidwani, 2007, "Metro Microfinance: Opportunities and Challenges in Mumbai," *Intellecap*

Mehta, Aditi, 2001, "Innovating Financial Services Delivery for the Urban Poor," *Intellecap*

Mukherjee, Piyasree, 2007, "Access to Finance: The Barrier to Mobility," *Intellecap*

Mukherjee, RK, 2004, "Study of the Demand for Micro Financial Services and Livelihood Promotion Services in Delhi," Conducted for Indian Grameen Services, New Delhi, Mimeo

Pasheva, Vanya and Manasee Desai, 2006, "Sewa Bank's Lifecycle Approach: 30 years of Urban Microfinance Inspired by Poor Urban Women," CMF 2006

Patole, M, O Ruthven, 2001, "Metro Moneylenders: Microcredit Providers for Delhi's Poor," *Small Enterprise Development* 13, 2

Rutherford, Stuart, and Sukhwinder Arora, 1997, "City Savers, How the Poor, DFID, and its Partners are Promoting Financial Services in Urban India," **DFID India Urban Poverty Office, Delhi**

Ruthven, O, 2001, "Money Mosaics: Financial Choice and Strategy in a West Delhi Squatter Settlement," Paper No. 32, Working Paper Series, Finance and Development Research

Programme, University of Manchester, also published in *Journal of International Development* 14, 249–271

Ujjivan, 2006. "A Study of Economically Active Poor Women in Bangalore – 2005," Report done for Ujjivan by Delphi Research Services, Bangalore

CHAPTER 6

Social Performance in Indian Microfinance

Frances Sinha[1]

For most Microfinance Institutions (MFIs) and those that work with MFIs (banks, investors, donors) microfinance is a social enterprise. As an enterprise, the organization is a business that aims to cover its costs and be financially sustainable. As a social enterprise, the business is a means to achieve social goals. Different organizations – or models of microfinance – may articulate some variation in their social goals or mission. Nevertheless, there is agreement that social goals in microfinance generally include serving poor people, serving people otherwise excluded from formal financial services, providing appropriate financial services, contributing to employment, contributing to positive change for clients and their households, contributing to poverty reduction, and being socially responsible.

Financial sustainability is important. An MFI that can cover its costs – has good financial performance – can grow to serve more clients in more areas. The growth in microfinance in India – and elsewhere in the world – is most probably due in large part to mechanisms that are financially sustainable, or on track to being financially sustainable. We have the systems to track financial sustainability, with definitions and indicators for reporting on financial performance. These are now almost routinely included in the annual reports of MFIs; over 35 MFIs in India report on them to the Microfinance Information Exchange (MIX)[2]; and these are the indicators applied in credit ratings.

On the social side, the reporting is less widespread. We have relied on impact assessments to provide the main evidence, with the focus on exploring the contribution of microfinance to various aspects of change. Impact studies are of varying complexity and quality – and their analysis is sometimes weak and not readily understood. Though, overall, the evidence tends to be positive, but nuanced.

In this chapter we present the new perspective on social performance that is wider than impact, but at the same time practical. Through defining different dimensions of social performance, we are able to look at ways in which MFIs can themselves manage their social performance, and identify the indicators that are relevant to social reporting

In this chapter, we present the new perspective on social performance that is wider than impact, but at the same time practical. Through defining different dimensions of social performance, we are able to look at ways in which MFIs can themselves manage their social performance, and identify the indicators that are relevant to social reporting. These indicators are currently being tested by M-CRIL in its pioneering initiative to develop social rating as a complementary activity to credit rating – a new form of social performance assessment.

So far, M-CRIL has undertaken seven social ratings in India supported by Friends of Women's World Banking and the Ford Foundation, and also nine poverty audits supported by SIDBI.

Some of the findings from these social assessments are summarized as part of this chapter. But first, what do we mean by social performance?

6.1 Unpacking the concept of social performance

A number of international initiatives have come together as part of the Social Performance Task Force[3] to reach consensus on the following definition of social performance. Social performance in microfinance is defined as "the translation of mission into practice in line with accepted social goals": These social goals relate to:

- reaching poor or excluded clients,
- improving the quality and appropriateness of financial services,
- contributing to employment and enterprise growth,
- improving the economic and social conditions of clients and their households,
- ensuring social responsibility to clients, to staff and to the communities in which they work.

Under this definition, impact, which refers to changes in the conditions of clients or the community that can be attributed to the microfinance programme, is just one aspect of social performance. Social performance is not only the end result, but the entire process of achieving that result. As such the focus shifts from trying to prove an end result to looking at the steps to get there, and managing and reporting on those steps that are likely to lead to positive social outcomes. Box 6.1 shows the different steps involved.

Social performance is not only the end result, but the entire process of achieving that result. As such the focus shifts from trying to prove an end result to looking at the steps to get there

---

Box 6.1   Dimensions of social performance

INTENT AND DESIGN

What is the mission of the institution?

Does it have clear social objectives based on its mission?

Do its objectives include formulation of principles of social responsibility?

INTERNAL SYSTEMS & OPERATIONS

Are systems designed and in place to achieve those objectives?

Does the institution have information to track performance towards those objectives?

OUTPUTS

Who does the institution serve? Is it reaching intended clients?

Is it serving poor people?

Are the financial services catering to their needs and capacities?

OUTCOMES

Have clients and their households experienced social and economic improvements?

> OR
>
> **IMPACT**
>
> Can these improvements be attributed to institutional activities?

[C-GAP, 2007, and Sinha, Frances, 2006]

- Social performance starts with analysis of the declared social objectives of institutions (intent and design):

  - Does the institution have a social mission and, whatever the social missions may be, are social goals clearly defined and articulated to conform to the social mission?

- Social performance includes assessment of internal systems and operations:

  - Are systems and operations aligned to mission and achievement of social goals?
  - Is progress towards these goals being tracked?

- Social performance includes social responsibility:

  - Does the institution have a policy on social responsibility – to clients, staff, community, and the environment?
  - Are there systems in place to ensure compliance?

- Social performance is about outputs:

  - Is the institution reaching large numbers of poor? excluded or marginal people?
  - Do products cater to the needs and capacities of intended clients?

- Social performance is also about outcomes – are clients improving their social and economic conditions, for themselves and for their families?

- And finally social performance is indeed about impact; exploring causality between programme participation and changes in the conditions of clients and their households.

6.2 Towards social performance management by MFIs

Most MFIs have a social mission. Putting that mission into practice – doing so in a systematic way – is what Social Performance Management (SPM) is about. Social benefits may result from microfinance interventions. But the basic principle of SPM is that social benefits are more likely to happen if an MFI deliberately manages the process towards achieving them. As part of routine financial performance management, an institution defines its organizational and financial targets, and puts systems in place to build efficiency and portfolio quality with regular monitoring, tracking and reporting on key indicators and ratios. A similar process can contribute to social performance management, a process which involves clarifying social goals and objectives, defining social responsibility principles, aligning strategies and systems to achieve those goals, strengthening the information system to monitor and assess progress and compliance, and using this information to improve performance.

...the basic principle of SPM is that social benefits are more likely to happen if an MFI deliberately manages the process towards achieving them

The process of starting SPM involves a set of core performance questions:

- Are you clear about: what type of areas you aim to work in? Who are your target clients? How do you define your target clients?
- Do you know whether you are reaching your target clients?
- Do you monitor and understand whether your services are appropriate to your target clients?
- Do you monitor how long clients stay with your programme?
- Do you monitor and understand why some clients leave or become inactive?
- Do you use this information to improve your services?
- Do you have clear policies and systems for social responsibility — especially to clients? And also social responsibility to staff, local communities, and the environment?
- Can you improve the systems and processes through which you answer these questions?

These questions look ambitious. They raise additional questions of definition, and tools — and low to address them cost-effectively. For example, many MFIs mention the "poor" as their target group. How then to define "poor," and measure poverty levels? Similarly, any clients may be leaving, but how to track the drop-out rate?

These questions look ambitious. They raise additional questions of definition, and tools — and how to address them cost-effectively. For example, many MFIs mention the "poor" as their target group. How then to define "poor," and measure poverty levels? Similarly, many clients may be leaving, but how to track the drop-out rate? What are the key elements of social responsibility relevant to MFIs?

These are areas that are now receiving technical attention. It took 10 years (yes 10!) to reach a level of consensus on financial indicators, definitions, and reporting systems. We are in the start-up phase for social reporting. And there is a lot of interesting work going on. Some of it is happening here in India, and part of this new area of social assessment is M-CRIL's pioneering of a methodology for social rating.

6.3 A new form of social assessment — social rating

The development of a social rating methodology has the potential to contribute to four important goals in microfinance:

- assist MFIs to identify both whether they are achieving their social mission and the institutional factors that may be facilitating or hindering achieving this target;
- assist potential investors and donors in their review of MFIs as part of their monitoring and due diligence processes;
- increase the transparency of the microfinance field;
- if adopted widely, establish social performance as equally important as financial sustainability in microfinance.

A social rating aims to be a relatively quick, low-cost assessment, similar to credit rating. As in credit rating, the social rating uses information available with the MFI to the extent possible, drawing on available documentation and data, and discussions with staff at all levels. It covers both the process (intent, policies, design, systems), and part of the results (outreach and appropriate services) along the dimensions of social performance as outlined in Figure 6.1. A social rating is not an impact assessment. That is a more complex exercise.

Figure 6.1 Assessing social performance

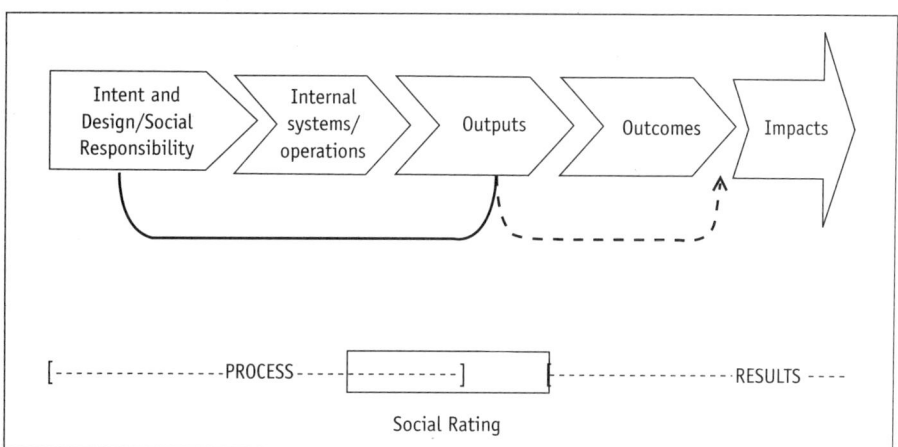

But if there is information on impact – or outcomes, and the information is robust, then the social rating can report on the impact findings.

How do we obtain information on the outputs, to understand: who the clients are? Do they match the MFI's target group? Are the financial services appropriate? Most MFIs do not have this information (some may, if they are implementing social performance management). So as to obtain direct client-level information about outreach to target groups and feedback on services provided, M-CRIL includes as part of the social rating exercise a small field survey, covering a sample of recent clients (to capture outreach profile on entry) and FGDs with older clients (for market feedback on MFI services). The field-work is undertaken in 3 to 5 clusters selected as representative of the MFI's current operations. The social rating sample covers a minimum of 127 clients from an average of four clusters. Hundred and twenty-seven is the minimum statistical level which gives a confidence level of 95 percent and precision of +/−10 percent.[4] A larger sample size might be preferred, and can be done, but would take more time and cost more!

A social rating aims to cover all the dimensions up to outcomes/impact. In covering the steps of the process that lead to impact, the social rating can be seen as a good predictor of impact, an assessment of whether the MFI is on track to achieve its social goals. Or, in rating terminology, it is an assessment of the risk of non-achievement – or mission drift.

6.4 Findings – social ratings and poverty audits

Key findings from the seven social ratings undertaken so far in India, with support from FWWB and the Ford Foundation, are summarized here, supplemented by additional information from a number of poverty audits undertaken with support from SIDBI. The social rating exercise, including the field work requires a team working up to 8 to 10 days with the MFI and in the field. The poverty audit was a quicker exercise, carried out over 3 to 5 days, with less detailed review of MFI systems, and client profiling based on FGDs with a smaller sample (therefore less robust than those from the social ratings). The presentation broadly follows the dimensions of social performance (as outlined in Figure 6.1), covering process (intent and design, systems) and results (outputs – outreach and appropriate services).

A social rating aims to cover all the dimensions up to outcomes/impact. In covering the steps of the process that lead to impact, the social rating can be seen as a good predictor of impact, an assessment of whether the MFI is on track to achieve its social goals. Or, in rating terminology, it is an assessment of the risk of non-achievement – or mission drift

6.4.1 Twelve MFIs

We have social performance data from 12 MFIs, 8 from the south, 4 from the north. These MFIs are quite representative of MFIs in the country: 5 follow the Grameen model, 3 the SHG model, 3 are cooperatives (MACS) and one follows the individual model. The data is mainly from 2006.

The 12 MFIs together represent over 1 million microfinance clients.

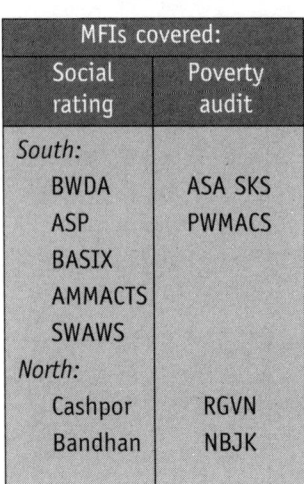

MFIs covered:	
Social rating	Poverty audit
South:	
BWDA	ASA SKS
ASP	PWMACS
BASIX	
AMMACTS	
SWAWS	
North:	
Cashpor	RGVN
Bandhan	NBJK

6.5 Institutional processes as part of social performance

6.5.1 Intent and Design

The mission statements of the 12 MFIs include reference to:

- serving the poor and vulnerable (10 MFIs),
- enhancing community capacities (4),
- women's empowerment (4),
- improved livelihoods (2),
- poverty reduction (2),
- quality services (2).

Accordingly, the mission is no more than a rhetorical statement or wish; it is not translated into social objectives that are the first step to putting mission into practice, objectives that are SMART (specific, measurable, adequate, relevant, time-bound) and strategic (what leads to what)

While the overall orientation is usually clear, the meaning of key terms is not so clear and is not usually defined by the MFIs. For example, who is "poor"? in what way will community capacities be enhanced? what counts as women's "empowerment"? what counts as poverty reduction? Accordingly, the mission is no more than a rhetorical statement or wish; it is not translated into social objectives that are the first step to putting mission into practice, objectives that are SMART (specific, measurable, adequate, relevant, time-bound), and strategic (what leads to what).

Out of 12 MFIs, three had clear definition of key terms (poor, vulnerable social groups, improved livelihoods). One of the three had gone further to develop SMART social objectives.

Governance appeared fairly well balanced in terms of financial and social experience and orientation, but reporting remains primarily financial – both within the organization, and externally, in, for example, annual reports.

6.5.2 Services and access

The range of services include general/enterprise loans starting at Rs. 2000 to Rs. 5000, some larger (individual) loans (Rs. 15,000 to Rs. 30,000) including in the MACS and SHG model MFIs. Along with credit, loan insurance and savings (or security deposits) are compulsory in 8 of the 12 MFIs. A few MFIs offer additional loans: an education loan of Rs 1000 to Rs. 10,000, emergency loan Rs. 500 to Rs. 1000, and offer insurance products (with linkages to formal sector insurance companies mainly for life and health). A few also offer non-financial services, directly, or through linkages to other providers – services such as agricultural/business

development support, health and education as part of community development, gender training, a school. Access to such services is quite low, usually under 10 percent.

Additional MFI services

Services	Number of MFIs providing	Percentage of clients accessing (prev yr)
Education loan	1	3
Emergency loan	1	<0.1
Life/medical other insurance	7	<20
Non-financial services	5	6–30

6.5.3 Internal systems

The conceptual framework for social performance includes an analysis of operational systems
to see whether they support the mission — in particular, targeting strategy, staff training and
incentives, and systems for MIS, monitoring, and reporting.

In terms of targeting, the main approach is area targeting. MFIs may select less developed
states and less developed regions within states, and slum or low-income areas in cities.
One MFI also strategically targets poor clients and monitors poverty profile at entry.
Another targets SC/ST and backward castes. Some MFIs are beginning to cater to different
market segments (with Joint Liability Groups, often men, alongside SHGs, and at different
income levels), though without specifically planning for what proportion of their clients
(or portfolio) should be from different segments.

In terms of targeting, the main approach is area targeting. MFIs may select less developed states and less developed regions within states, and slum or low income areas in cities. One MFI also strategically targets poor clients and monitors poverty profile at entry

In relation to human resources — orientation and incentives — the mission and values are usually part of staff induction. But in practice, the main emphasis is on financial management
and growth, as reflected in incentive systems that emphasis productivity (client numbers)
and on-time repayment. Though one MFI includes an incentive linked to coverage of poorer
clients.

In terms of monitoring and MIS, there is substantial scope for MFIs to strengthen their routine data collection and analyzing portfolio information from a social perspective. Many have
interesting information fields relevant to client profiling in their loan appraisal formats but
this is not being completed systematically or used for tracking outreach or market segments
(except by one MFI). Portfolio information can be analyzed not only to track growth and
arrears, but to track client retention over time, how many stay for how many loan cycles,
what is the drop-out rate, what differences are there for rural and urban clients, or for women
and men clients (if an MFI has both). A few MFIs have started applying or have commissioned
market research surveys, though most rely on informal feedback from staff.

6.6 Results — Outreach

6.6.1 Areas

For information on outreach, we first look at areas of operation, including rural/urban distribution and analyzing the district (branch) distribution of clients with reference to development ranking of districts in the country. Based on data from the 2001 Census, the 593 districts in the country are divided into development quintiles based on literacy rates, as a proxy for development level. Overall, in the sample, MFI outreach is more than proportionate (with 24 percent in the bottom district quintile, 56 percent in the lowest two district quintiles). Around five to six MFIs with no clients in the lower district quintiles are located in the southern states. The majority of MFIs have mainly rural clients. Rural/urban classification is usually based on administrative definitions.

MFI outreach – rural and less developed districts

Percentage of clients	0	<20%	21–55%	>55%	Average (%)
In bottom district quintile	6	2	3	1	24
In two lowest district quintiles	5		3	4	56
Rural	1		1	10	77

Beyond this broad (rural/urban) classification, it would be interesting to capture the extent of outreach in semi-urban/semi-rural areas. This would cover market town areas as a separate category (from rural) – with different implications for livelihoods, appropriate products, and MFI costs of operations.

6.6.2 Reaching the unreached (financial inclusion)

To capture exclusion, we analyse whether clients are from vulnerable communities (such as SC/ST) or from households without alternative access to formal or semi-formal finance. From the rating sample, we find that most MFIs have a proportion of SC/ST above the national average, reflecting substantial outreach to these communities

Second, we seek information to understand whether the MFI is serving the poor and excluded. To obtain this information, we undertake a small field survey of recent clients (noted above), that is, clients who have recently joined the MFI (within one year) so as to capture their profile on entry (before the likelihood of change). The sample size averaged 152/social rating and 48/poverty audit. The total sample for 12 MFIs is 1306.

To capture exclusion, we analyze whether clients are from vulnerable communities (such as SC/ST) or from households without alternative access to formal or semi-formal finance. From the rating sample, we find that most MFIs have a proportion of SC/ST above the national average, reflecting substantial outreach to these communities. Interestingly, though, we find that not all client households have been excluded from formal financial services. On an average, 26 percent have a bank or post office savings account; 12 percent have had a bank loan in the previous 3 years. This compares with the 36 percent national figure. And 6 percent of client households have members in another MFI, or an SHG (with this figure higher for southern MFIs).

Reaching the unreached

Percentage of recent client households	Range (%)	Average (%)	All India population[a] (%)
SC/ST	15–57	33	25
With savings in bank or post office	14–39	26	36
With bank loan in previous 3 years	2–21	12	
With client in other MFI or SHG	2–13	6	

[a] Census of India (2001)

A key question is poverty outreach. As we have seen, all the MFIs have a mission to serve the poor. How many clients are poor when they join? And how do we define poverty? A useful benchmark is the poverty line, the $1/day at Purchasing Power Parity (PPP) which, currently at Rs. 17.5/day or Rs. 524/person/month is just above the Indian poverty line (Rs. 395/person/month rural, Rs. 454 urban).[5] The social rating questionnaire includes two pages to estimate client household income in detail, from which the per capita per day figure can be calculated. Alternatively, and more easily, a poverty score card has now been developed for India (Schreiner 2007).[6] We have used both methods, to find poverty levels mostly at and less than the estimated poverty rate in the country.

Outreach to those below $1/day varies substantially around the average, which at 30 percent is slightly below the all India poverty incidence. Most of the MFIs rated are below the average. One MFI with a strong strategic focus on poverty outreach has 68 percent of its clients below the poverty line when they joined the programme.

Outreach to those below $1/day varies substantially around the average, which at 30 percent is slightly below the All India poverty incidence. Most of the MFIs rated are below the average. One MFI with a strong strategic focus on poverty outreach has 68 percent of its clients below the poverty line when they joined the programme. These figures are pause for thought. Is this the depth of outreach intended for microfinance?

6.6.3 Serving the poor

Percentage of recent client households	Range (%)	Average (%)	All India population[a] (%)
< $1/day at PPP	13–68	30	39

[a] NSSO (2005).

These figures are pause for thought. Is this the depth of outreach intended for microfinance? By MFIs whose stated mission is to serve the poor and contribute to poverty reduction? Are there elements in their operations which need strategic review, so as to align with a deeper poverty focus?

6.6.4 Microfinance and women

The majority of MFI clients are women, with eight MFIs working only with women clients. The balance in staff is skewed to men, due partly to issues of field mobility, especially in the northern states. Two MFIs have less than 10 percent staff who are women, including one in the south.

Women as clients and staff of MFIs

	<50	51–99%	100%	Average
% women clients	1	3	8	86%
% women staff	10	2		32%

Gender related indicators, beyond the number of women, relate to women's schooling at least up to primary (which at 35 percent on average can affect awareness and understanding of MFI information and services), whether the household is woman headed (which is an indicator of poverty especially if there are no adult male earners in the family), and women clients' involvement in managing an enterprise for which they have taken a loan. On average, just over one in the five women clients manage by themselves the enterprise for which they take credit, another 40 percent manage jointly with a husband or son, and a similar percentage pass the loan to a male relative. This has implications for women's empowerment. In one MFI, working with urban women, women's independent enterprise activity was the highest (over 70 percent).

Gender related indicators

Percentage of recent women clients	Range (%)	Average (%)
Have completed primary school or above	14–63	35
Are women heads of households with no adult male	3–10	4
Manage credit supported enterprise		
Yes – by herself	12–72	22
Yes – jointly with husband/son	25–44	40
No – husband/son manages (loan pass)	3–45	38

6.6.5 Microfinance and employment (indirect outreach)

Additional profile information from the rating survey relates to employment or "indirect" outreach. The majority of enterprises supported by microfinance are usually family based microenterprises, providing self-employment to family members. If hired labour is employed in an enterprise, microcredit can be seen to be supporting employment for others who are not direct MFI clients – and may be of a lower income category. This is likely for larger microenterprises or "small enterprises." In five MFIs for which we have this information, an average 8 percent of enterprises with credit have employed non-family labour, with an average employed of 2.4.

Employment in credit supported enterprises

	Range [5 MFIs]	Average
Percentage of supported enterprises with hired (non-family) employees	3–11%	8%
Average number of hired employees in such enterprises	1.6–3.7	2.4

6.7 Results – appropriate services

The first set of questions, under appropriate services, relates to client awareness of the financial products and terms of the MFI. This is a key element of social responsibility to clients, reflecting effective communication and transparency. These questions are covered as part of the rating survey, with reference to each MFI's specific services, and the responses are quantified. The findings are that clients are mostly aware of the notional interest on loans and interest receivable on savings deposits (though in a couple of MFIs awareness is 60 percent or less). Few clients (around half) on average are aware of the details of costs (interest on declining basis, break-up of loan fees), and loan insurance (what is covered).

The findings are that clients are mostly aware of the notional interest on loans and interest receivable on savings deposits (though in a couple of MFIs awareness is 60 percent or less). Few clients around half) on average are aware of the details of costs (interest on declining basis, break-up of loan fees), and loan insurance (what is covered)

Client awareness of financial services

Percentage of who know	Range (%)	Average (%)
National interest on credit and repayment installments	60–98	78
Interest on savings deposits	55–91	77
More details of costs (EIR, declining interest, break-up of loan fees)	31–90	52
Details of loan insurance	30–89	49

Client feedback is obtained through Focus Group Discussions with older clients. This provides both positive feedback, and some suggestions to the MFI.

Examples of client feedback on MFI services (from FGDs)

Clients like:

- timely credit, without collateral,
- savings – where available – no other option for saving small amounts,
- discipline of weekly repayments (mainly non-farm enterprises, in market centres),
- convenient repayment in installments,
- grace period (1 MFI): 46 payments over one year,
- lower interest rate than moneylenders.

Clients would like:

- loan products for other credit needs (education),
- larger loans, compare cost of dairy animal Rs. 7000 to Rs. 15,000); also demand from better-off clients (around 10 percent of clients interviewed), urban clients,
- monthly loan installments – rural,
- loan insurance to cover husband's death too (in case of women clients),
- avoid high up-front security deposit.

A strong indicator of client satisfaction or appropriateness of services is the rate of exit, particularly drop-out

A strong indicator of client satisfaction or appropriateness of services is the rate of exit, particularly drop-out. Of course, some clients who leave may be "fly-outs" who no longer need microfinance, or may be able to graduate to a formal service. But many who leave (as studies have shown) do so because the microfinance services do not match their requirements, for reasons of dissatisfaction, problems with repayment, other financial difficulties. The annual drop-out rate overall can be estimated from the loan portfolio, based on the number of clients at the end of the previous year, the number of new clients who joined during the year and the total number of clients at the end of the year.[7]

The data shows higher rates of exit compared to figures from 2002–03 of around 4 to 6 percent (M-CRIL data). Where MFIs are growing very fast, the large number of new clients in the year may mask the rate of drop-out (just as high disbursement of portfolio can mask the portfolio at risk).

Client exit

	Range (%)	Average (%)
Drop-out rate	5–17	11

Additional analysis would ideally include drop-out rate by time with the MFI (or by loan cycle) and by other client characteristics (poverty, social group). In future, we aim too to track client retention in terms of those who stay with the MFI for a certain period of time, say at least 3 years, or 5 years – which may be the minimum time within which to achieve change, or sustainable impact. Less than this is probably not long enough for substantial change, at least in terms of poverty reduction (provided, that is, it is not the poorer clients who have dropped out of the programme).

6.8 Future directions

The social rating tool has been under development. Its full form has now evolved in line with the understanding of what social performance is, and what are the key indicators of achieving social performance

The social rating tool has been under development. Its full form has now evolved in line with the understanding of what social performance is, and what are the key indicators of achieving social performance. It, therefore, now includes, for example, more details of social responsibility: whether MFIs are putting into practice key elements of the *Code of Conduct* towards clients, recently framed by Sa-Dhan.

The selected findings presented here are an example of social performance assessment, related to indicators that it is hoped MFIs will increasingly be able and willing to report on. And refer to as part of an internal system for social performance management.

They are indicators that are covered as part of a social rating. This does not go as far as to try to assess impact. But the social rating presents a range of information that is relevant to achieving mission and contributing social value. Therefore, It is a good predictor of impact, and an exercise which is faster and cheaper than impact assessment.

Endnotes

1   I would like to thank my colleagues in EDA and M-CRIL, past and present, who have worked on the social ratings and poverty audits that provide the material for this chapter. Particularly, Monika Agarwal, LB Prakash, Amit Brar, Komal P Rana, Nishant Tirath, and Sudipto Saha.

2   The MIX Market is the global microfinance information marketplace, providing financial data and profiles on microfinance institutions and the microfinance sector on the Internet, at http://www.themix.org.

3   For more information, please visit http://www.microfinancegateway.org/resource_centers/socialperformance/

4   See EDA Technical note: Estimating Sample Size, which explains the sampling formula. A larger sample of 340, or 510, would improve precision to +/- 5 percent.

5   Updated to 2006 based on relevant CPIs agricultural labourers and industrial manual labourers, from World Bank estimates of purchasing power parity for the international poverty line (SEEP, Donald 2006), and the Deaton adjusted national poverty line (Schreiner 2007).

6   The scorecard has 10 relatively simple questions which can be easily answered/observed about a household without much calculation or judgement. The indicators are: number of children under 17 years, whether house is pucca, whether own a TV, electric fans, almirah, sewing machine, pressure pan, land, primary energy source for cooking, number of acres of land, principal income source for the household. The answers to these questions are scored for their "poverty probability," with the scores derived from statistical regression of NSSO data. The scores can be linked to any poverty line. For India, they are linked to the international poverty lines – $1 and $2 per day. Thus, the poverty score card provides a simple but statistically robust method for measuring poverty levels.

7   M-CRIL applies the following formula:

    (Number of clients at beginning of year + New clients during the year – Number of clients at end of year)/ (Number of clients at beginning of year + New clients during the year)

    A "drop-out" or client who exits is defined as: "any client who has had not transaction with the MFI for the previous six months." See M-CRIL Technical Note: Estimating Exit Rate.

References

CGAP, 2007, "Beyond Good Intentions: Measuring the Social Performance of Microfinance Institutions," Focus Note Number 41, Washington DC

Census of India, 2001, "Population Tables," Government of India

Donald, Sillers, 2006, "National and International Poverty Lines: An Overview," United States Agency for International Development, http://povertytools.org?Project_Documents/Poverty_lines

EDA, 2006, "EDA Technical Note: Estimating Sample Size," http://www.edarural.com/publications

M-CRIL, 2006, "M-CRIL Technical Note: Estimating Exit Rate," http://m-cril.com/publications

NSSO, 2005, "National Sample Survey Organisation, Household Consumer Expenditure in India: NSS 59th Round, January–December 2003," Report No. 490, Ministry of Statistics and Programme Implementation, Government of India

Schreiner, Mark, 2007, "Is one poverty score card enough for India?" Washington DC, see http://www.microfinance.com/English/Papers/

Sinha, Frances, 2006, "Social Rating and Social Performance Reporting in Microfinance: Towards a Common Framework," SEEP Occasional Paper, Washington DC

CHAPTER 7

Micro Insurance

Sai Gunaranjan[1]

7.1 The importance of micro insurance for the poor as a tool to protect livelihoods

Financial inclusion of the poor by providing them with access to savings, credit, and insurance forms an integral part of the package of livelihood promotion services that the poor require. While a diverse set of both formal and informal institutions have evolved to cater to the savings and credit needs of the poor, there is still a huge gap with respect to insurance services available for the poor. It is also well understood that the vulnerability to various risks is highest for the poor. In the absence of proper risk hedging mechanisms like insurance, the poor stand to loose their wages, borrow, liquidate their assets, migrate and face several other hardships, which in turn only traps them into a deeper and vicious cycle of poverty. With the increasing prevalence of nuclear families, the informal support system of the joint family too is unavailable for most people today. The penetration of the formal insurance sector is very low today. Estimates put that less than 15 percent of the country's population is insured. The challenge for providing a whole of range of insurance products to cover the risks related to both lives and livelihood generating assets of the poor is huge. However, the current situation is also seen as an opportunity by many players in the insurance industry, to expand and deepen the insurance market in India. MFIs have made major strides to improve the access to credit and savings for the poor. It is imperative for MFIs to seize the moment by actively providing micro insurance services for the poor and thereby contribute to achieving comprehensive financial inclusion of the poor.

In the absence of proper risk hedging mechanisms like insurance, the poor stand to loose their wages, borrow, liquidate their assets, migrate and face several other hardships, which in turn only traps them into a deeper and vicious cycle of poverty

7.2 Issues related to the growth of micro insurance

The rapid growth of the microcredit movement in terms of scale has tempted many to expect a similar growth in micro insurance. To the extent that micro insurance has grown today, a large chunk of it comprises credit life insurance, which is automatically bundled with microcredit. However, providing insurance as a stand alone product for the poor has not been as easy. The reason for this contrast is not difficult to ascertain. Microcredit is largely a pull product (demand driven) whereas micro insurance, or any insurance for that matter, is a push product which requires significant marketing and sales effort to enrol customers. This transition from selling a pull product to a push product has not been easy for microcredit institutions. To enable this transition, one needs to look at a whole range of issues including capacity building of staff and incentive structures for the staff of microcredit institutions. However, the growth issues of micro insurance are not limited to the distributions channels such as MFIs alone;

they encompass other stake holders like insurance companies and their ability to provide suitable micro insurance products and service them.

Another issue which has to be addressed to promote micro insurance is the sustainability of such programs. The microcredit movement has grown with a strong focus on sustainability of the program to ensure scalability of the models. This has meant that institutions charged interest rates that covered both the cost of capital and cost of operations. In the overall analysis the interest rates charged by these institutions were viable for customers due to the customization of credit products and the hassle free lending procedures adopted. However, the focus on sustainability of insurance products has not received as much attention as required by MFIs. This situation is partly due to the fact that the actuarial science involved in pricing of insurance products may not be too well understood by MFIs. Therefore, there is a temptation on their part to bargain for rock bottom premium rates from insurance companies, without taking into consideration all the costs that may involved. This can seriously compromise the sustainability and continuity of such products. Currently, MFIs may not feel the pinch of such products as they do not underwrite the risk, and given the current market scenario where several new insurers are trying to get a foothold in the market, there is always another insurer who may be willing to underwrite for a brief period such unsustainable products. The advantage of meeting rural and social sector obligations in a quick manner with such under priced products may more than offset the loss making microrisks that an insurer underwrites. The answer to this problem is the need for MFIs to work towards building internal capacities to understand and provide sustainable micro insurance products, as they have done in the area of microcredit.

...the focus on sustainability of insurance products has not received as much attention as required by MFIs. This situation is partly due to the fact that the actuarial science involved in pricing of insurance products may not be too well understood by MFIs

7.3 Challenges to be overcome to achieve sustainable and scalable micro insurance models

7.3.1 Creating actuarial data for micro insurance, rather than searching for actuarial data to get micro insurance started

Most poor people have not had access to insurance in the past as in the present. This translates into absence of data regarding frequencies of various risks faced by them. In the absence of this data, insurance companies are often constrained in their ability to offer products, as the availability of historical data is critical to the design of insurance products. This perpetuates the problem of making insurance products available to the poor. To break the deadlock, insurance companies should be willing to introduce products even in the absence of adequate actuarial data. The incentives for doing this would be:

(1) It would help to build data on various risks for this segment of the market, which is huge. This data, and with the experience in administering micro insurance policies, would serve as an asset for the insurance companies in expanding their penetration of the huge and untapped rural market.

(2) The marginal error in pricing micro insurance policies in the absence of historical data would not seriously affect the insurance companies as the financial value of risk in micro insurance policies is very marginal compared to the traditional high value insurance contracts underwritten by insurance companies. This marginal risk too can be mitigated by taking a conservative approach to

pricing of the micro insurance policies in the inception years and then reviewing the price, based on actual claims experience in subsequent years.

(3) Global reinsurers are also beginning to recognize the potential of micro insurance, in order to expand the overall insurance market size. Munich Re and Swiss Re are examples of Global reinsurers who have been actively studying and promoting micro insurance in the Indian insurance market. The willingness and the interest of these reinsurers provide an opportunity to local insurance companies to enter the micro insurance market, by ceding a portion of micro insurance risks to global reinsurers. The reinsurers would be in a better position to absorb the risks from micro insurance programs where the market experience is still in a very nascent stage.

7.3.2 Rationalizing underwriting procedures for micro insurance to make it accessible to target clients

A major roadblock for rolling out insurance products for the poor has been the gap between expectations of insurance companies about completing a certain kind of paperwork for issuing insurance contracts, and what the poor can actually provide. The poor and especially those in the rural areas are in a disadvantaged position in terms of their ability to access hospitals, schools, and various public utility service providers. The certificates issued by these institutions often serve as proofs for establishing identity and also age to be considered for an insurance contract. In such scenarios, as in the case of BASIX, the micro insurance service providers have worked with the insurance companies to accept alternative age proofs like declaration of age by community members like SHGs, or even declaration by the individual or the household itself as sufficient for the purpose of extending insurance (Box 7.1). This has helped in extending insurance to individuals who would not have otherwise been insured due to non-availability of formal certificates of age and residence.

A major roadblock for rolling out insurance products for the poor has been the gap between expectations of insurance companies about completing a certain kind of paperwork for issuing insurance contracts, and what the poor can actually provide

---

Box 7.1 Providing sustainable and competitive insurance products to rural customers

BASIX, a livelihood promotion institution set up in 1996, provides both financial and technical assistance services to about half a million households spread over eight states in India. In October 2002, it began its initiative to provide life insurance cover to customers who took microcredit. BASIX took a group policy from AVIVA which covered its borrower for 1.5 times of the loan amount taken by him or her during the loan tenor. In the absence of any past experience of mortality for the customer profile served by BASIX, AVIVA priced the product conservatively at Rs. 8.61 per thousand sum insured. By October of 2004, the experience of covering more than 50,000 person years was completed. The positive performance of the product by this stage allowed the insurance company to lower the premium rate to Rs. 6.89 per thousand sum insured. A year later in 2005, over 100,000 person years were covered cumulatively. The claims experience gained till then allowed the insurance company to reduce the premium rate to Rs. 3.98 per thousand sum insured. Based on the actual performance of the product, BASIX and AVIVA could reduce the premium rate by more than 50 percent in a 3-year period. This further allowed BASIX to extend cover to the spouses of the borrowers, as the premium was much more affordable now. This experience proves that a sustainable approach to pricing of micro insurance, combined with proper administration of the products, allows the partners to add value to the small premiums paid by its customers.

In the area of health insurance, traditionally, insurance companies have required that a hospital should have at least 10 beds to allow policy holders to qualify for re-imbursement of expenses. However, most hospitals in rural areas do not have this kind of infrastructure. Therefore, to allow customers to take treatment at rural hospitals, the policy conditions have been simplified in health insurance policies so that customers can get admitted and treated at any registered hospital, even if it does not have the mandatory 10-bed infrastructure. This kind of flexibility in re-looking at traditional procedures in administering insurance policies holds the key to unlocking the availability and access of micro insurance to the poor.

7.4 Creating a conducive environment for the growth of micro insurance

Several stages of innovation have yet to be undergone before micro insurance reaches the position where microcredit is today, in terms of productization and operating systems. While microcredit is of interest today for many stakeholders ranging from private to public purpose institutions, it should be remembered that the sector has reached its current stage over a span of three decades. During this period, several grass-root organizations have grappled with a host of issues to make microcredit work. These included addressing financial capital and grant requirements for the sector, regulatory bottlenecks, and also product and operating system design and implementation. Each of these areas has gone through various phases of maturity and iterations to enable the microcredit movement to reach the stage where it is. This long journey has to be kept in mind, while work is being done to replicate the success of microcredit to micro insurance. While the journey of progress in micro insurance can be accelerated, the issues cited need to be addressed and cannot be bypassed or overlooked. A unique challenge that the micro insurance movement has to confront is the rather complex task involved in designing and distributing a diverse range of insurance products where knowledge and technical expertise is required from several fields like health care systems, animal husbandry, enterprise valuation, agriculture, etc. This calls for a more collaborative approach in actual delivery of micro insurance products, where expertise from insurers, distributors, and service providers (e.g. health care) needs to be synchronized to achieve a seamless delivery of micro insurance products. The complexity involved in micro insurance is quite evident from the relatively slow introduction and growth of micro insurance among practitioners of microcredit. There is certainly a strong case for greater investments into capacity building for potential micro insurance distributors and collaborative partnerships for scaling up of micro insurance.

The growth in a nascent sector like micro insurance will also be strongly influenced by the regulatory environment. A major impetus for the growth for micro insurance in India has come from the rural and social sector obligations stipulated under the IRDA Act. This has ensured that all insurance companies in India develop and distribute products for the rural and social sector. Taking this effort forward, IRDA introduced the micro insurance regulations in December 2005. These regulations aimed at making certain enabling provision to encourage both insurers and micro insurance distributors to actively promote micro insurance. The regulation enable SHGs, societies, and co-operatives to function as micro insurance agents and carry out a lot functions like premium collection, policy bond distribution, and claims administration. However, a large number of MFIs which are registered as S25 companies or as NBFCs, with outreach to millions of rural household, are not recognized as micro insurance agents by micro insurance regulation and are, therefore, constrained from using the enabling provisions made under these regulations to spread micro insurance on a large scale.

7.5 Livestock insurance: Insuring the wealth of rural India

After agriculture, it is livestock which is the most common source of income for rural households. Very often it provides a supplementary source of income for rural households, helping them to tide over loss of income from other sources. According to the 17th national livestock census conducted in 2003, there were 284 million cattle in India. There was no growth in the cattle population of the country between 1997 (when the 16th livestock census was conducted) and 2003. In the year 2002–03, according to the Department of Animal Husbandry & Dairying, Ministry of Agriculture, 18 million cattle were insured, which means that only 6 percent of the cattle population was insured. Traditionally, livestock insurance has always been seen as an unattractive portfolio for insurance companies due to its poor financial performance on account of the behavioural risks associated with both customers and service providers. One of the requisites for offering livestock insurance has been the need for getting a certificate from a veterinary doctor. Many remote places still do not have the services of a veterinary doctor and to get this only adds to the cost of obtaining livestock insurance. To overcome this difficulty, which seriously compromises the ability to offer livestock insurance in rural areas, BASIX worked with Royal Sundaram to enable the certification of livestock insured through its field staff who are adequately trained in assessing the economics of cattle rearing, and the insurable status of cattle. While this arrangement greatly simplifies the ease of insuring animals, great care has to be exercised by BASIX staff to ensure that proper controls are in place to ensure that no adverse selection of high risk animals happens. Also, in the event of a claim, if a death certificate cannot be given by a doctor, an inspection and report from a field facilitator approved by the insurance company is considered for settlement of claim. There are other key issues that had to be addressed to make cattle insurance more attractive to rural customers as discussed in the following sections.

7.5.1 Assessment of market value at the time of claim

Traditionally cattle insurance policies are indemnity based contracts, that is, the claim amount paid is based on the market value of the animal at the time of death of animal. If the value of the animal is greater than the sum insured only then is the sum insured paid. It is known that the market value of milching cattle follows an almost cyclical path based on the reproductive stages that they go through. Thus, if the death of the cattle takes place when the market value is at the low end of the cycle, then the farmer suffers considerable loss of future value. Besides, it is also difficult for the farmer to come to terms with the fact that while he has paid a premium for a certain sum insured, he gets paid an amount less than that. In order to overcome these situations, BASIX worked with Royal Sundaram to convert the policy to a full benefit policy, that is, one where the claim paid is equal to the sum insured. To ensure that the principle of indemnity is not compromised, the cattle were insured for about only 80 percent of the animal value. This also ensured that there was an element of self insurance by the farmer, which would translate into better care of the animal.

...a large number of MFIs which are registered as S25 companies or as NBFCs, with outreach to millions of rural household, are not recognized as micro insurance agents by micro insurance regulation and are, therefore, constrained from using the enabling provisions made under these regulations to spread micro insurance on a large scale

...if the death of the cattle takes place when the market value is at the low end of the cycle, then the farmer suffers considerable loss of future value. Besides, it is also difficult for the farmer to come to terms with the fact that while he has paid a premium for a certain sum insured, he gets paid an amount less than that

7.5.2 Reducing adverse selection

Avoiding adverse selection is a major challenge in livestock insurance. A field staff who is not too technically trained in veterinary science cannot easily asses the exact health status of cattle from mere visual observation. To overcome this challenge, most insurance policies have a window period of 10 to 15 days from the date of tagging after which the risk cover period commences. To further minimize adverse selection, customers are also sometimes incentivized to insure all the cattle in the household by providing a premium discount for insurance of multiple animals.

Since most of the lending in microfinance is not necessarily targeted at a single economic activity, most MFIs have not entered the space of insuring the livestock of their clients. Among those MFIs which do lend to specific activities like purchase of livestock, combinations of factors like (i) high premium rates (ranging from 3 to 8 percent of the insured value), (ii) inordinate paper work, (iii) a poor history of claims settlements, and (iv) issues related to adverse selection deter them from making livestock insurance compulsory for their clients. Only in specific locations where the above issues can be addressed, do MFIs encourage their customers to take livestock insurance on a voluntary basis. BASIX has cumulatively insured over 40,000 livestock so far. In the recent 2 years, BASIX has also begun providing preventive vet care services on a fee basis under its Business Development Services (BDS) program. It currently has close to 50,000 customers who are availing of these services. BASIX expects that the BDS services will result in reducing the risk and thereby, reducing mortality of livestock owned by its customers. This would eventually translate into reduction of premium of premium rates for livestock insurance, making it more attractive to enrol larger number of customers for livestock insurance.

7.6 Life insurance

Life insurance has perhaps had the longest innings in the domain of rural insurance, where it is popularly associated with LIC. One of the consequences of this legacy is that insurance in the rural areas is closely associated with savings, under which on maturity of the contract, the customer gets back his premium with some return on it. However, a high percentage of lapsation of such policies has translated into erosion of the savings of the poor to the tune of a few crores of rupees. Due to the seasonality and unpredictability of their incomes, the poor cannot often pay timely renewal premiums, resulting in policy lapsation. In spite of this past experience, the focus on selling savings policies is perpetuated as the insurance agent stands to earn a hefty commission on the first year's premium on such policies. However, what the poor need most is risk protection, which is offered through pure-risk term policies. The lower premium installments of such policies also make the pure-risk term polices more affordable for the poor.

As the margins in pure-risk products (term insurance) are thin compared to savings products for the insurance companies, innovative approaches need to be taken to reduce the transaction costs involved in providing term insurance

As the margins in pure-risk products (term insurance) are thin compared to savings products for the insurance companies, innovative approaches need to be taken to reduce the transaction costs involved in providing term insurance. One way to address this is to take the cue from how microcredit has addressed the problem of transaction costs through the group approach. Today all BASIX borrowers and also their spouses are covered under a group policy called Credit Plus, a product from AVIVA. This group product covers each of the insured individuals to 1.5 times of the loan amount taken. This ensures that in an unfortunate event of the death of the insured person, not only is the loan amount written off, but the dependent also gets some additional financial support to cover immediate financial needs.

Another unique feature of the Credit Plus policy is that it provides borrowers with the convenience of paying the insurance premium in small monthly instalments to the insurance company along with their loan repayments. By the end of September 2007, BASIX had covered 0.5 million individuals under this policy. Cumulatively, it has settled life insurance claims to about 2000 families amounting to Rs. 3 crores.

Under the IRDA act, all insurance companies are mandated to achieve a certain number of policies in the rural and social sector. This combined with the new micro insurance regulations are giving a new impetus to provide affordable term policies for the poor. Today, with 16 life insurance companies operating, a reasonable number of term insurance products are available in the market.

7.7 Health insurance

For many poor who do not have any significant assets, their body is their only asset. They earn their livelihood, which often borders on subsistence, by engaging in both farm and non-farm labour. Health risks seriously affect such households, as they not only lack the financial resources to pay for health care, but also stand to loose their only source of income from labour. However, the perils of ill health do not restrict its impact to the above category of people. It also has a serious impact on not-so-poor people, as health care costs are spiralling, and are unaffordable even by middle class income standards. This problem is further compounded by reduced public spending on health care, leaving most people to meet health care costs out of pocket. Given the enormity of the challenge involved in providing health care financing options, it is not surprising that the microhealth insurance sector has seen numerous initiatives, making it one of the most active and innovative fields in the domain of micro insurance. There are a variety of models which are emerging in this sector, some which are underwritten by insurance companies, some self-managed within the community or an institution without a tie with an insurance company and some of which are hybrid of both formal and in-house insurance arrangements. A compilation of the various microhealth insurance programs carried out by ILO under its STEP program indicate that close to 9 million people are insured in about 90 microhealth insurance programs in India. Of these, the two biggest schemes are (i) Yashashwini which is managed by a trust with contributions from the state government and users from cooperatives in Karnataka, currently covering over 2 million individuals. This makes it one of the largest micro insurance programs in the world and interestingly the risks are not underwritten by an insurer. (ii) The Sampoorna Suraksha health insurance scheme introduced by SKDRDP trust is based at Dharmasthala in Karnataka. It covers today over 7 lakh individuals, and the risk is currently underwritten by ICICI Lombard. The uniqueness of both these models is that the health insurance program is independent of any microcredit program. It is a clear indicator that the penetration of micro insurance on a large scale does not have to be entirely dependent on the availability of the microcredit vehicle. While this may be the case, microfinance institutions certainly possess the necessary outreach and experience in financial services to give a major fillip to providing access to micro insurance for the poor. An increasing number of MFIs are introducing microhealth insurance to

Given the enormity of the challenge involved in providing health care financing options, it is not surprising that the microhealth insurance sector has seen numerous initiatives, making it one of the most active and innovative fields in the domain of micro insurance

their customers along with life insurance cover. SEWA from Gujarat stands as an example for providing a whole suite of financial services for its customers. Its customers today have access to savings, credit, and a whole suite of insurance products. Its composite insurance product offers risk cover for life, health and household assets and SEWA currently covers close to 2 lakh individuals under its health insurance policy.

While there are several promising models of microhealth insurance emerging, the problems of adverse selection and moral hazard continue to challenge all players in their attempt to deliver affordable, hassle free and sustainable health insurance products. While adverse selection can be controlled by covering well-defined groups, moral hazard (e.g., inflated billings) continue to challenge insurance providers. This problem is further perpetuated by poorly defined and poorly implemented protocols for health care management in India. There exist an ever growing number of health care service providers in the market, mainly in the private sector, and implementing standards of quality and health care procedures across so many providers remain a challenge. While current health insurance providers continue to innovate around these problems, the growth of health insurance will depend a lot on the proactive role played by public institutions to establish standards and quality in health care systems in India.

7.8 Enterprise insurance

A large percentage of rural customers are engaged in various forms of non-farm enterprises. These enterprises are often housed in kacha premises and face a high level of risk from elements like fire, floods, storms, etc. and from external impact damage. It is important to safeguard them against these risks. In recent years some of the private insurance companies have begun to offer insurance cover for such kacha enterprises where enterprise value may be as small as Rs. 10,000 to Rs. 20,000. The key to scale up outreach on microenterprise insurance would be to have simplified products for valuation of such enterprises and simplified claims procedures to survey and settle their claims.

7.9 Managing agricultural risks

The crop insurance schemes have also not been very popular with farmers as the claim assessment process is not very transparent and claim payments are often delayed. Alternative models to manage crop risks are now being explored to find a more sustainable approach to managing agricultural risks. Index based weather insurance is now emerging as a promising alternative

India has a large exposure to weather risks, where the majority of the population is dependent on rainfed agriculture. In the past two decades, large scale attempts have been made to cover the risks of farmers through state sponsored crop insurance schemes, aimed at covering multiple risks faced by the crops. These schemes have, however, imposed significant fiscal pressure on the states even though they cover only about 10 percent of Indian farmers. This situation has arisen due to the adverse claims experience, where the claim payouts have been more than four times of the premium collected. Besides a 50 premium subsidy offered by the government, all the excess claim payouts have been borne from state finances. The crop insurance schemes have also not been very popular with farmers as the claim assessment process is not very transparent and claim payments are often delayed. Alternative models to manage crop risks are now being explored to find a more sustainable approach to managing agricultural risks. Index based weather insurance is now emerging as a promising alternative.

A simple weather index insurance product would work in the following manner. In the event of a shortfall of rain from a predetermined level (index) during a particular period of the crop season, the farmer would be compensated based on a predetermined formula, which takes into account the probable loss incurred due to the extent of shortfall in rain. This allows for an objective way to measure claims payable to the insured farmer. As the claim payout formula is predetermined, it automatically leads to timely settlement of claims to farmers, allowing them to reinvest in their next crop or to meet their immediate consumption needs. With the availability of historical weather data, the pricing of the insurance product can be done on an actuarial basis, leading to a more financially sustainable product. The availability of international reinsurance for weather insurance helps to transfer the local weather risk to the global weather risk market and thus, provides for a the pooling of risks.

BASIX works with a large number of households whose livelihoods depend on agriculture, without any assured source of irrigation. Between 2000 and 2002, BASIX undertook several research projects to provide cover for crop risks. These efforts culminated in a collaboration with the Commodity Risk Management Group of the World Bank and ICICI Lombard, to launch the first index based weather insurance in 2003 in Mababubnagar district of India covering 230 farmers in the first pilot program. In subsequent years, the index based weather insurance market in India has scaled up, covering more than 300,000 farmers. Today, there are more companies offering weather insurance in India, including the government-owned Agriculture Insurance Company. However, for taking weather insurance to a larger scale, there are challenges to be overcome. One of them is to increase the density of weather stations in a big way, so that rainfall measured in a particular weather station is better correlated to the actual rainfall in a particular farm (Box 7.2).

...for taking weather insurance to a larger scale, there are challenges to be overcome. One of them is to increase the density of weather stations in a big way, so that rainfall measured in a particular weather station is better correlated to the actual rainfall in a particular farm

Box 7.2   SEWA and rainfall insurance

The Self-Employed Womens' Association (SEWA) developed, in collaboration with ICICI Lombard, an insurance product to insure against risks arising out of deficit and excess rainfall. While the insurance product offered by ICICI Lombard has gone through several cycles elsewhere in India, the product requires customization to local agro-climatic settings. One challenge is the understanding of the precise relationship between rainfall and rural income, particularly given the paucity of data on rural income. A well-designed product should pay the poor precisely when they need income the most. One goal of SEWA was to make the product accessible to even its poorest members. As a result, the minimum unit size for purchase was quite low, available to anyone whose income varies with the weather.

This project aims to (i) evaluate the potential of rainfall insurance to improve the livelihood and sustainability of rural poor in Gujarat, India, (ii) understand how behavioral biases and risk aversion influence decision making at the household level, and (iii) evaluate the effectiveness of different marketing and communication strategies in encouraging take up of the product.

For the purposes of rolling out the insurance product, 100 villages have been identified that are within 30 km of an IMD-recognized weather station in 3 districts – Ahmedabad, Anand, and Patan. Since, SEWA will initially be able to offer weather insurance to only a limited number of villages, 33 villages were selected at random, where insurance is offered. In the second year, it expanded to a group of 50 villages.

The baseline and the midline surveys have been completed in a little over 1500 households. Based on the data and experiences from the first year, the insurance product and the marketing strategy are being redesigned to serve the needs of the clients more effectively.

While weather insurance can protect farmers from significant deviations in weather performance, there is still a need and huge scope for providing risk minimization and productivity enhancement services needed by farmers. These advisory services are needed to complement the index insurance product. In the absence of these services, weather insurance would carry too much of the weight of farmer's expectations and prove to be an incomplete solution or promise to the farmers.

7.10 Making micro insurance more affordable and accessible

The biggest constraint involved in the distribution of micro insurance is the disproportionate cost of distribution and servicing, in comparison to the value of the premium and the sum insured of these policies. One of the key learnings from the field of microfinance has been that the poor can save and pay in frequent and small instalments. Most insurance policies require premiums to be paid in annual instalments. This makes the premium instalments quite unaffordable for the poor. The key to enhancing outreach of insurance for the poor would be to make provision for collecting premium in more frequent and smaller instalments. However, this benefit can be outweighed by the increase in transaction costs for collecting such small premiums. A solution to this could be to bundle the premium collections with other forms of financial transactions like savings and credit repayments.

The key to enhancing outreach of insurance for the poor would be to make provision for collecting premium in more frequent and smaller instalments. However, this benefit can be outweighed by the increase in transaction costs for collecting such small premium s. A solution to this could be to bundle the premium collections with other forms of financial transactions like savings and credit repayments

Another key to the success of micro insurance is the simplicity in documentation. One of the earliest products introduced by AVIVA for the rural sector goes by the name of "Jan Suraksha." This is a pure term life insurance product with a sum insured limit of Rs. 50,000. The proposal form for this policy contained 4 pages. In collaboration with its micro insurance partners, AVIVA developed and recently introduced a new life term micro insurance product by the name "Gramin Suraksha" with similar policy limits. However, the proposal form for this policy has been shortened to a single page. This ensures that minimal and relevant data is captured from the customer and the scope for errors in documentation are minimized. It also reduces the transaction costs involved in selling micro insurance policies.

The level of risks covered under micro insurance policies is often of a small value, in the range of Rs. 5000 to Rs. 50,000, as compared to regular insurance policies where the risk cover is often in excess of Rs. one lakh. Given the small value of insurance benefits that come with micro insurance products, it is important to ensure that the products have minimal exclusions and fine print that is usually associated with insurance policies. This is essential to ensure that the poor perceive the insurance products to be fair and to encourage greater enrolment of customers under such products. Some of the microhealth insurance products currently being offered in the country cover both pre-existing diseases and maternity related treatments under such policies and some have demonstrated that they can be offered on a financially sustainable basis.

7.11 The role of public institutions in developing micro insurance

The government and its institutions wear several hats in the insurance industry. They together perform several roles: that of a regulator, a development agency, an insurer, a re-insurer, and an insurer for the uninsured — in the form of various welfare and relief programs run by the government. Some of these functions are also performed by several private and non-profit institutions. It is often a tough balancing act for the various public institutions to perform, so that they function effectively in each of these roles, and also ensure that no one function works at cross purpose with any other function. A case in point is that of the several insurance schemes announced by both the central and state governments which aim to cover rural clients or special categories of social sector clients, with a premium subsidy provided by the government. Sometimes these schemes can crowd out the development of market based insurance products for the poor, making the poor perpetual dependent on such schemes. In other cases, such schemes do not reach the targeted population. An example of a recent state government sponsored scheme is the Mukhyomantri Jibon Jyoti Bima Achoni[2] launched by the Assam state government in July 2005, covering all the 30 million population in the state, where each individual is covered for hospitalization expenses up to Rs. 25,000 per annum. The state government paid a premium of Rs. 250 million to ICICI Lombard General Insurance Company for this cover. Within one year of this policy, that is, up to July 2006, about 4205 people (out of 30 million!) are reported to have benefited from this policy with about Rs. 90 million paid in claims.

Such low utilization of the benefits can be attributed to the low awareness of the policy among the insured population. The question that arises is the right manner in which the public subsidy should be targeted. There is certainly a case for subsidizing the poorest of the poor for their premiums. But the above example also indicates that unless investments are made to educate the poor on the benefits of insurance, such subsidies do not really help the majority of the targeted population. A part of the subsidy should be apportioned to programs for improving awareness and education about the benefits of micro insurance for the targeted population. The latter holds the key to laying a strong foundation to scale up and develop a healthy micro insurance market in India.

A part of the subsidy should be apportioned to programs for improving awareness and education about the benefits of micro insurance for the targeted population. The latter holds the key to laying a strong foundation to scale up and develop a healthy micro insurance market in India

Endnotes

1   *Manager, Insurance Business, BASIX.*

2   *See Central Bureau of Health Intelligence (CBHI), Ministry of Health and Family Welfare, Government of India; http://www.cbhi-hsprod.nic.in/retopt2.asp?SD=21&SI=9&ROT=1*

CHAPTER 8

Microfinance and Technology
Prasanth V Regy and Vijay Mahajan[1]

8.1 Technology: The key to efficient microfinance

8.1.1 Technology for microfinance: Why?

As one of the authors, Vijay Mahajan, predicted a decade ago, "the day we can marry the power of the microprocessor with the power of microfinance, we will have developed a terrific solution to provide microfinance transactions to poor people in a low-cost, user-friendly way." The proper use of information and communication technologies can be very beneficial to MFIs. A well-designed and well-thought-out Management Information System (MIS) is essential to achieve scale, improve efficiency, and reduce cost. By reducing manual work, it decreases the possibility of error and fraud. Such a system can serve as the backbone of the MFI's processes. It can provide decision-making support to the management by facilitating the analysis of data. It can also help the management to monitor the activities of the MFI on a day-to-day basis. Further, such applications can help in managing complex products, allowing the MFI to offer tailor-made products to its customers with marginal extra effort. They are also very useful for HR purposes, including recording employee information and calculating salaries and commissions.

As one of the authors predicted in 1998, "the day we can marry the power of the microprocessor with the power of microfinance, we will have developed a terrific solution to provide microfinance transactions to poor people in a low-cost, user-friendly way"

MIS is not the only application of IT in microfinance. Another technology fast gaining importance is that of various Point-of-Sale (POS) devices, which can make transactions faster and safer. This chapter is an attempt to examine the use of various technology products and channels in the delivery of microfinance in India.

Within *microcredit*, the key activities involved are registration, appraisal, disbursement, repayment, and monitoring.

Registering a customer involves recording details about her name, age, and other personal and household details. In addition, data about the livelihoods, education, and assets of the household are also usually captured. This data can help in the assessment of the social and economic impact of the activities of the MFI. Depending on the delivery model, we may also need to record details about the group, centre, JLG, guarantor, etc.

During appraisal, information about the cash-flow of the activity, and of the household, needs to be captured. Repayment is an activity that will happen over and over again, so it should be quick and fraud-proof. The MIS should generate the demand statement and it should also help in monitoring the portfolio by generating statements of PAR, NPA, etc.

The regulatory requirements for being able to provide *microsavings* services are much more stringent than those for microcredit. In India, only banks and certain NBFCs are allowed to accept savings. An effective assets and liability management application will be useful in risk monitoring. In contrast to microcredit, where most products involve regular transactions, microsavings products would have to be flexible enough to accommodate irregular savings.

The information requirements for *micro insurance* are slightly different from that of microcredit. MFIs selling micro insurance are retailers for insurance companies. This requires collaboration between the MFI and the insurance company, and the MFI's MIS would need to be able to output data in the format required by the insurance company. The amount of data to be entered is also very high, since insurance is often offered for the whole family. Further, the data accuracy needs to be higher as compared to microcredit.

8.1.2 The current usage of IT by MFIs

A survey on the use of technology in DCCBs and MFIs in India was conducted recently by Saral Services (2007). The results are quite interesting.

Ninety-four percent of the MFIs used software applications for internal accounting. Sixty-four percent reported that they used loan-tracking software, and only 30 percent used payroll software. Fourteen percent used PDA applications to capture field transactions. In the 64 percent of the cases, the head office of the MFI has a LAN. All the MFIs had internet access in their HO and branches. It is also notable that the cellphone network was accessible from almost all the MFI locations.

When asked about the factors that inhibited the adoption of technology, the most commonly cited constraint was budgetary. Lack of adequate expertise, training, and support were contributing factors. Another issue was the lack of awareness about technology providers. While irregular power supply is also a problem, it is one that could be rectified by using a UPS, which is again expensive

When asked about the factors that inhibited the adoption of technology, the most commonly cited constraint was budgetary. Lack of adequate expertise, training, and support were contributing factors. Another issue was the lack of awareness about technology providers. While irregular power supply is also a problem, it is one that could be rectified by using a UPS, which is again expensive.

8.2 MIS solutions – a survey

The microfinance software vertical has seen a lot of activity in the last year. Along with well-established MFIs offering software that they themselves use, a few new application developers have entered the arena. What follows is a review of some MIS applications, classified according to the various microfinance models. This is not a comprehensive list, but it will help to give us an overview of this sector.

8.2.1 Software for SHGs

Since SHG–Bank linkage is the predominant microfinance model in India, several applications have been developed for it. Most of these applications are meant to help the promoting MFI or NGO to track all the financial transactions that happen at the SHG meetings:

- McFinancier of Sharada Computer Services, Gurgaon: This is a software system solely targeted at SHGs. It can handle group-wise books, and provides all the required administration, tracking, and accounting functionalities. It is used by PRADAN, Sarvodaya Nano Finance Ltd., etc.

- SafalFin of Safal Solutions Ltd, Hyderabad: SafalFin is an integrated solution for NGOs, which helps to track internal credit, deposit, and insurance transactions of the members of SHGs promoted by the NGO/MFI. It keeps track of the day-to-day loan activities of these MFIs in addition to managing their member, staff, SHG, accounts, and other details.

- MTech developed a product named "SHG–MIS", which is meant to help the SHGs track their operations, and also to help the promoting organization track the SHG performance. After every SHG meeting, the transaction sheets are sent to a centralized location, where it is entered into the MIS and the next demand sheet is printed and returned to the SHG. This product was jointly developed with Andhra Pradesh's Velugu, so that it could be used by all the Velugu groups.

- Mahila Sphurthi, developed by Co-options: This software is intended to be an integrated information system to streamline SHG activities. This product also attempts to bridge the digital divide, by bringing relevant information to the villager about agri-inputs, market intelligence, sanitation and health, etc.

- Ekgaon's Mahakalasm MIS: This MIS will allow the promoting NGO/MFI to track the performance of its SHGs. Ekgaon has also designed a unique and accessible system of paper forms for data entry in the field.

An interesting innovation in this field has been PRADAN's Computer Munshi (CM). Many SHGs remain dependent on the promoting NGO for book-keeping. Even when they can maintain the daybooks themselves, they are usually unable to produce the group financial statements. PRADAN conceived the idea of a community-based computer entrepreneur, the CM, who would provide accounting services to the SHGs for a reasonable payment. He could offer his services to about 200 SHGs, resulting in viable employment. Most CMs supplement this income with other activities, such as STD PCOs, internet, and photocopying facilities.

PRADAN conceived the idea of a community-based computer entrepreneur, the Computer Munshi (CM), who would provide accounting services to the SHGs for a reasonable payment. He could offer his services to about 200 SHGs, resulting in viable employment

8.2.2 Software for the Grameen model

The Grameen model of microcredit, which originated with the Grameen Bank of Bangladesh, has been used heavily in India with significant improvements. One of the most commonly used applications for monitoring Grameen-style microcredit, Portfolio Tracker, was developed by Grameen Communications (GC) of Bangladesh, an IT service provider and a member of the Grameen group of enterprises. Together with modules for performance monitoring and accounting, this application reduces paper work considerably and raises work efficiency. In India, it is used by CASHPOR, SKS, and several other Grameen replicators.

8.2.3 Software implementing multiple methodologies

Various lending models have been tried out in the field of microcredit. Lending may be to individuals or to small groups (SHGs, Grameen groups, and JLGs), and at the other end of the spectrum, to Federations and MACTS. There are a variety of methods to calculate interest and schedule payments. The organizations that offer multiple models and several kinds of products need software that can handle the complexity.

8.2.3.1 FAMIS PLUS

FAMIS is short for Financial Accounting and Management Information System. It was developed by BASIX's software partner, Sathguru Management Consultants, based on BASIX's specifications. It was designed to be a comprehensive solution for accounting and management information needs. While it is no longer used within BASIX, it continues to serve more than 36 other MFIs at 140 installations, to whom BASIX provides ongoing support.

FAMIS PLUS is a very mature application, satisfying the requirements of 36 MFIs throughout India. It runs on Windows, and requires minimal maintenance and support. It is very rich in features, being able to support credit, savings, and insurance. It has extremely rich reporting features, which have enabled its users to track metrics that could not be tracked earlier, leading to better recoveries. It is highly configurable software, easily adaptable to any terminology, interest calculation method, and lending/saving methodology.

FAMIS' main negative has to do with the database it uses – FoxPro. This database is not as robust as the other databases available, and is not perceived very favourably today.

8.2.3.2 Delphix

Delphix, designed to be an MIS for livelihood finance, was also developed by Sathguru, based on BASIX's specifications. It drew heavily from BASIX's previous experience of creating FAMIS. In particular, it is highly robust and customizable, and is based on the Oracle platform

Delphix, designed to be an MIS for livelihood finance, was also developed by Sathguru, based on BASIX's specifications. It drew heavily from BASIX's previous experience of creating FAMIS. In particular, it is highly robust and customisable, and is based on the Oracle platform.

BASIX uses Delphix for all its lending operations, serving more than 200,000 customers in more than 60 units. New features are being added to Delphix, including savings, life insurance, and agricultural and business development services. It is a highly capable system, based on a rugged and proven platform. Box 8.1 describes the evolution of MIS applications in BASIX.

Box 8.1   The evolution of MIS in BASIX

FAMIS was BASIX's first effort at a comprehensive solution to our accounting and management information needs, and it served us from 1997 to 2005. It was first developed on a Visual Basic/FoxPro/MS-DOS platform. After the release of the first version in 1997, several more versions were released, each adding to functionality and robustness.

At that time, there was no other software on the market which had the functionality needed by MFIs. Most MFIs used manually prepared charts to determine repayments

At that time, there was no other software on the market which had the functionality needed by MFIs. Most MFIs used manually prepared charts to determine repayments. In the year 2000, FAMIS was supplied to its first external user, ASSEFA. This version was named ASSEFAMIS, and it was installed in ASSEFA offices in Maharashtra, Rajasthan, Madhya Pradesh, and Bihar. This involved not just providing the software, but also setting up the requisite infrastructure, including buying generators and UPS, as well as training the operators who would use it.

RGVN, who had centres in Orissa, Assam, and Bihar, was next. They lent to groups as well as to other NGOs, and these two activities were very different in the software functionality that they demanded. RGVN had a wider portfolio of products, including savings and grants, and required many new reports as well. Our analysts spent a lot of time on the field understanding their processes and requirements, and then we converted them into software specifications that we passed on to the developer. This was our first experience in customizing our software for external users. RGVN installed FAMIS in 16 locations.

This was followed by a very large number of other MFIs. It may be noted that BASIX charged these users only for training and customization. In each case, our analysts invested a lot of time in understanding the requirements and tailoring FAMIS accordingly. As may be imagined, every MFI had different lending methodologies and interest calculation methods. Other requirements like savings and grants were also integrated into FAMIS. The complexity quickly increased, till there were 10 different versions of FAMIS for 10 MFIs! This large number of versions obviously created several problems for us, and so we decided to combine these different versions into one. This unified version was called FAMIS PLUS. This is the only version that is used today.

The main problem with FAMIS was the database that it used. While it works very well for small MFIs, it could not keep up with the growth of BASIX. In the year 2000, inspired by the information system employed by DID Canada, plans were laid for the creation of a new software, Delphix. It drew heavily from our experience of creating FAMIS. It was based on the Oracle platform, which, we expected, would be able to handle large amount of data.

The design of the new system was done in the year 2000, and the development largely took place in 2001. The development was done by the same company who developed FAMIS. In 2002, we pilot tested it in three units, entering data in Delphix in parallel to FAMIS. However, there were several problems including migrating data from FAMIS to Delphix. In addition, Delphix was immature at that time. So, there were several issues in the way of moving to Delphix completely.

The pilot testing continued in the year 2003 and 2004, with seven more units taking part in the pilot. In 2004, all our software development efforts were focused at building features for handling insurance in FAMIS, so Delphix development was stopped during that time. All this while, the parallel entry into Delphix continued in the 10 pilot units.

In 2004 September, the first round of systems auditing was done by our auditor, who identified several issues with Delphix. These issues were fixed, and then another round of audit done. After this round, in which only minor issues were reported, we inducted Delphix into all our units.

8.2.3.3 Micro Financier

Java Softech's Micro Financer is a flexible solution capable of supporting a variety of models, including SHGs, Federations, Grameen, and individual loans. It also has a full-featured savings module. It enables the capture of several kinds of socio-economic data, and it can generate a variety of reports. It comes integrated with a financial accounting module.

Its clients in India include SERP, CARE, Gram Utthan, and several MACS and federations.

8.2.3.4 BankSoft

BankSoft is an integrated suite of applications for banking, created by Processware Systems, Bangalore. It enables branch automation, head office consolidation, and inter-branch reconciliation. A user-friendly software package, BankSoft provides integrity, flexibility, and security to the user.

BankSoft has been installed at more than 300 locations in Karnataka, Andhra Pradesh, and Goa. It supports multiple delivery channels such as Internet, PDAs, Touch Screen Kiosks, Mobile phones, and ATMs. It enables the bank to generate all the statutory reports required by RBI. It was chosen by BASIX for use in the Krishna Bhima Samruddhi Local Area Bank

(KBSLAB). Responding to the requirements of KBSLAB, Processware added several features to BankSoft, making it a suitable product for microbanking.

8.2.3.5 MIFOS

The MIFOS Initiative was established by Grameen Foundation's Technology Center to address the microfinance industry's information management challenge. The initiative aims to deliver an open source information management system for the global microfinance industry via a collaborative development and support community. The open source framework allows microfinance institutions to select local developers to assist with the customization, implementation, and maintenance of their software. MIFOS is still under development and is not currently recommended for use in a production environment.

8.2.4 Hosted solutions

As internet connectivity improves, a different kind of application software is now possible – one that is hosted by the solution provider on its own servers, rather than being installed locally. The data is entered and accessed over the internet, through a browser. Installing and upgrading software locally is replaced by a subscription-based model, in which data is stored remotely. FINO and Salesforce.com are among the prominent players in this space.

Software development and its maintenance are not the core competencies of an MFI. Rather than spending money and resources on purchasing (or, worse, developing), installing, configuring, maintaining, and upgrading application software and hardware, it may be more economical to just use a ready-made application hosted elsewhere and accessible through the browser

This model has many advantages. Software development and its maintenance are not the core competencies of an MFI. Rather than spending money and resources on purchasing (or, worse, developing), installing, configuring, maintaining, and upgrading application software and hardware, it may be more economical to just use a ready-made application hosted elsewhere and accessible through the browser. This will also lead to lower manpower requirements. The solution provider will take care of ensuring data protection and data redundancy, which are requirements that are typically neglected by MFIs. Thus, such applications can deliver benefits at reduced costs and risks.

There are disadvantages to this model as well, the first being that it requires internet connectivity. The internet is not available or is highly unreliable in large parts of our country. If only very limited functionality is required, it may still be possible to use a hosted solution with once a day connectivity. But for more complex usage, the information will be required to be cached locally and synchronized with the hosted server whenever possible. This may require local installation of caching software, which neutralizes some of the advantages of such hosted solutions. Another problem is that of regular subscription payments. This payment is typically based on the number of groups or customers handled by the application.

There are also data-ownership issues: MFIs may not wish to part with their customer data to solution providers, if they fear that the data may be shared with others. In addition, the fact that the data is stored by the solution provider may tie down the MFI, if it later wishes to migrate to a different solution.

8.2.4.1 FINO platform

Financial Information Network and Operations (FINO) Ltd. was set up by ICICI, which still owns 20 percent of it. It provides a technology platform to MFIs to manage their data electronically. It has been designed to support all the common lending methodologies.

This solution is based on a central Core Banking Solution (CBS), which will be the repository of all the customer accounts. FINO is able to provide multiple levels of reports for MFIs that choose to be hosted on their platform. It also claims that it can even support MFIs who wish to host their accounts themselves – the MFI can upload the data to it, and use the reporting and analyzing abilities of the platform. FINO also offers the ability to handle smart cards. FINO is described further in Box 8.2

Box 8.2   A hosted solution: FINO

Indian startup Financial Information, Network, and Operations Ltd. (FINO) has recently become the first company in the world to offer a complete end-to-end technology solution to MFIs. While back-end data management software designed for microfinance operations has been available on the market for years, FINO is the first to link a back-end software system with a front-end based on biometric smart cards for customers, and field devices for credit officers, to offer a complete, integrated solution.

While back-end data management software designed for microfinance operations has been available on the market for years, FINO is the first to link a back-end software system with a front-end based on biometric smart cards for customers, and field devices for credit officers, to offer a complete, integrated solution

The basics of the FINO product are simple. FINO is targeted at Business Correspondents, governments, MFIs and in fact, at any organization that intends to reach the unbanked sector. Customers of the organization are given biometric enabled smart cards which store the customers' fingerprints, account details, a unique identification number, and photo. Transactions are recorded using a field device equipped with a smart card reader, fingerprint reader, and small printer and then automatically uploaded from the field device to the back-end FINO software via a phone line. At the back-end, all data is stored and maintained by FINO itself and accessed by the organization via web browsers. In addition to the full solution described above, FINO also allows organizations to purchase just the front- or back-end portions of the system. (So far, several MFIs have opted to adopt the back-end only.)

A key application of FINO would be to enable the Business Correspondent (BC) model. The BC model can work only if there is quick and accurate flow of information between the BC and the bank (Section 8.6.2). The bank needs to be able to monitor and control the services offered by the BC to the end customer. FINO provides offline-mode capability and detailed report-generation systems, thus, making it feasible and safe to adopt the BC model.

Another obvious application of the FINO product is to streamline the existing operations of MFIs. By replacing rote paperwork with automatic data transfer, FINO allows MFIs to reduce labour costs, lessen the chance of fraud, create reports more quickly, and gain better overall insight into the performance of their portfolio. In addition to cutting costs, FINO also benefits MFIs and their customers by allowing MFIs to offer new products such as remittances and flexible savings accounts to their customers. Without the enhanced security, data management capacity, and connection to the existing financial system which FINO allows, these products would be nearly impossible for an MFI to offer.

The FINO product holds potential for increasing financial inclusion in India and elsewhere in other ways as well. In addition to MFIs, banks may also use the FINO platform to directly engage in microfinance activities. Similarly, governments may use the FINO platform to deliver wages and other benefits to the public more efficiently and with less leakage. Finally, FINO may benefit the microfinance sector as a whole by serving as a platform for the development of a credit bureau for the sector. Because FINO collects the fingerprints of all customers it gives smart cards to, and stores this information in a central location, FINO could easily be used to track and share the credit histories of customers as they move from MFI to MFI. FINO has already begun working on a credit model to predict customer credit profile. A credit bureau would allow MFIs to cut down on the cost of screening clients, reduce overall defaults, and allow customers to more easily move from MFI to MFI, or to graduate from microfinance lending to bank lending. It can also enable the MFI to offer individual loan products instead of group-based products.

Whether these potential benefits are realized depends greatly on how much FINO is able to bring down the costs of the system for the MFI as well as the amount of support commercial banks give FINO. Up until now, many MFIs have been reluctant to adopt the FINO system due to the high initial investment and yearly fees. For more MFIs to be convinced that adopting FINO is a smart move, these costs will have to be brought down. FINO could see easier acceptance in the Business Correspondent sector, since the initial investments would be borne/subsidized by banks.

Despite a slow start, FINO is gaining steam. The company has signed up about 15 MFIs for its solution and a few of them have already gone live. It has carried out about 3 lakh enrolments, and has issued 1.5 lakh cards. The AP government is already using the FINO platform to deliver government benefits to recipients as a pilot, and it intends to replicate it in the entire state. In addition, Corporation Bank, ICICI, Indian Bank, and Union Bank of India have all made major investments in the company. Having these banks on board will do much to help ensure the success of the company. But FINO will need to sign up far more MFIs and gain the support of several more players, including governments. For FINO to be truly successful, it will also have to reduce costs by delivering multiple services through the same cards.

8.2.4.2 Salesforce.com

Salesforce.com is the leading provider of hosted enterprise applications internationally. In fact, a large part of the credit for creating the hosted enterprise solutions space goes to them, due to their pioneering work in web-based customer relationship management applications. They are in the process of developing a web-based tool for MFIs. Being at an early stage, they are looking for MFI partners who are willing to test their application.

8.3 Transaction Support Technologies

In microfinance, transaction costs have traditionally been high. Innovations like the Grameen model, SHG, and JLG, made large-scale microfinance possible by bringing down this cost significantly. In this section, we examine how technology can be used to further bring down transaction costs:

- they should be easy to use, even by people unfamiliar with technology,

- they should be able to handle even small ticket transactions in an economically feasible manner,

- they should take minimal time and effort,

- they should protect the interest of customers,

- they should have the checks and balances necessary to avoid frauds.

In practice, the transactions are usually captured manually in the field by an agent of the MFI, who gives the customer a receipt. This data is then fed into MIS loaded on a PC in the MFI branch office. The problem with this approach is the amount of time and effort this requires, and the possibility of error and fraud. The information entered into the MIS is the same as the information written down in the receipt – if this duplication of effort is avoided, then it can lead not only to a savings in effort, but also to greater accuracy.

8.3.1 Hand-held devices

One way to avoid this error- and fraud-prone duplication is to use portable POS devices that can electronically capture transactions. BASIX has experimented with several hand-held devices, including Simputers, for this purpose, before settling on devices manufactured by Edgar Interactive, Bangalore. When the field agent enters the transaction, the device records it and prints out a receipt for the client. When the agent comes back to the field office, he connects his hand-held device to the server, and the data is synchronized. Such devices are already being used in bus ticketing, electricity billing, etc.

One way to avoid this error- and fraud-prone duplication is to use portable POS devices that can electronically capture transactions

8.3.2 Rural ATMs

IIT Chennai, the Tenet group, and ICICI Bank have designed a secure, low cost, and low maintenance ATM called the Gramateller. The idea behind this is to increase financial institutions' outreach and penetration in rural areas.

The Gramateller can use existing connectivity in rural areas to enable a bank to extend its services to the poor in an efficient and cost effective manner. It can use smart cards or fingerprints for authentication. It also has a battery backup to deal with power outages.

8.3.3 Mobile phone based solutions

Cellular networks have recently become ubiquitous in India. It is estimated that there are more than 180 million cellphone subscribers in India, and their numbers are fast increasing. The cellphone combines processing power, storage, and wireless communication. Cellphones are falling in price, while their memory and processor power have been increasing. Increasingly, cameras and Near Field Communication (NFC) chips are built into them, as cellphone manufacturers try to make them more and more useful in an effort to supplant the PC as the primary personal computing device. Extrapolating these trends, it can be safely said that cellphones will play an important role in transaction capturing in microfinance.

Increasingly, cameras and Near Field Communication (NFC) chips are built into them, as cellphone manufacturers try to make them more and more useful in an effort to supplant the PC as the primary personal computing device. Extrapolating these trends, it can be safely said that cellphones will play an important role in transaction capturing in microfinance

8.3.3.1 A Little World

This company has come up with an initiative that envisages the mass deployment of multi-application smart cards through a network of service delivery points, with the POS device being a cellphone. It has the following components:

- agent/employee with an NFC-enabled mobile phone,

- customer with a NFC-enabled smart card,

- MFI/Bank,

- centralized card management system.

NFC is a short range (a few cm) wireless communication technology that works through magnetic induction. In A Little World's (ALW) model, the smart cards issued to customers have NFC-enabled chips on them, allowing them to transfer small amounts of data wirelessly and almost instantaneously.

The model is relatively low cost. A smart card is estimated to cost around Rs. 100 and the equipment with the agent (comprising a mobile phone, a finger print reader, and a printer, all NFC-enabled) around Rs. 20,000. The initial investment costs of the cards and the equipment are high, so this system is best for MFIs that intend to become BC, where the bank can bear the setup cost. Compared to the cost of establishing and operating a physical bank branch in the rural area, this system would be extremely cost effective. The operating costs of the model are expected to be minimal and can be easily absorbed by banks.

ALW has already deployed this technology in collaboration with banks in Pithoragarh in Uttarakhand, Aizawl in Mizoram, and Medak in AP. This technology is now being deployed with IGS acting as the BC of Axis Bank in Delhi and in Muzaffarpur, Bihar, as described in Box 8.2.

8.3.3.2 Acceltree

The solution provided by Acceltree is a mobile phone based technology that provides a low cost mechanism to computerize microfinance processes. Here, again, the mobile phone (or a wireless PDA) itself operates as an on-/offline terminal. This device connects to a low cost central server.

Acceltree provides an easy to configure framework that enables quick deployment after customizing the application software to suit local business and government rules. The application can be made available in local languages with little effort.

8.3.3.3 Ekgaon

Ekgaon has developed a mobile information services framework called CAM. This framework comprises a cellphone application, paper forms with bar-codes that embed processing instructions, and a server. This system offers the ability to have a hybrid system, combining paper-based processes with automated systems, using bar-codes and image recognition through cellphone cameras. The system also offers a voice-based menu, which will be helpful for illiterate users. It can deal with situations where the cellular network is not available. Further, the system is easily localizable. This system can be used by SHGs as well as by BC.

8.4 Caveats

This section details some of the key aspects MFI managers should keep in mind as they implement a technology solution.

8.4.1 Proper design and integration

Using multiple software to handle related services results in dissipation of development energy and managerial attention. If the different services are used by the same customers, it might be useful to build in the functionalities required for the different services into one program

Often, when new features or services are being developed by an MFI, it may choose to prototype it using a new application. But, once the service becomes standard and mainstream, it is felt that it is too much bother to change the application, and so the MFI continues to use the prototype application for production purposes.

Using multiple software to handle related services results in dissipation of development energy and managerial attention. If the different services are used by the same customers, it might be useful to build in the functionalities required for the different services into one program, or alternatively, to ensure that the different applications for the multiple services can talk to each other. This is important in enabling us to have a unified view of the customer base.

The operations staff has to be inducted into the application development project right from the conceptualization stage to ensure that the solution meets the requirements of the end users. They play a vital role in the success of the project, and their feedback should always be taken into account. This will help to ensure that the application is easy to use for those who actually use it.

8.4.2 Pilot testing

It is vital to test the software/hardware thoroughly in a few locations in the field before deploying it company-wide. This will help the field staff to get used to the new way of doing things, and also will catch issues before they become serious. In particular, it should be recognized that software design is essentially iterative, and that the early versions will need to be refined over a period of time before they can be used in a production environment.

8.4.3 Project management and documentation

Good project management is essential to the success of any project. The project should be monitored by all the concerned parties, and the MFI should work closely with the IT partner to resolve issues immediately. If a new product or process is being introduced, the development of the software required should start well in advance. Otherwise, the unavailability of the software may delay the new product.

In the IT industry, the employee turnover is generally very high. Hence, the application development/deployment project should be process driven and not person driven. Documentation can play a key role in ensuring this. If the required documentation is in place, the maintenance of the application will become easy later. Proper documentation also helps us to evaluate whether we got what we asked for.

8.4.4 Security

It is generally seen that the security aspects of using technological solutions are often overlooked. This is perhaps due to the assumption that most users, particularly field agents, do not have the skills required to manipulate the software/hardware. It should be noted that while technology can help prevent frauds, it can also enable a skilled hacker to perpetrate frauds on a large scale. This can be avoided by a proper security architecture, including appropriate access permissions, logging, regular backups, and encryption.

It should be noted that while technology can help prevent frauds, it can also enable a skilled hacker to perpetrate frauds on a large scale. This can be avoided by a proper security architecture

8.5 A guide to the perplexed

So, as the CEO or CTO of an MFI, how should you decide what solution to go for?

The kind of MIS required will change according the size of the MFI. Even a small MFI would need at least basic tools like a spreadsheet application or Access. As the size of the MFI increases, the demands from the MIS increase as well, requiring more features, robust databases, and easy to use user interfaces (Intellecap 2006). An MFI with a country-wide presence may require a solution with a three-tier architecture, in which the data, business logic, and presentation are split into distinct layers. This can web-enable the MIS and also provide the extensibility required to be able to work with other applications and partners.

Thus, MFIs may need to migrate from one solution to another as they grow. Migration is usually a long and messy process, and it is best if planning is done in advance so as to avoid it or, at least, to minimize the disruption caused by it.

A rough typology of the MIS features required by MFIs of various sizes is given below. These numbers are indicative: an MFI with a very simple model might be able to serve millions of customers with a very simple MIS, and another with more flexible and complex products may need a more advanced solution from an early stage. Since the actual feature requirements will vary according to factors such as the operational model of the MFI, and the number of products it offers, these figures are order-of-magnitude estimates.

MFI Size (number of customers)	MIS Features
<100	Manual, paper-based system may be sufficient
<10,000	Excel/Access based solution
<100,000	Robust Database with good consolidation and reporting features
>100,000	Web-based and extensible, can work with other applications, enables high-level analysis

Whether to purchase a ready-made product or to develop a new application altogether is another key question. The answer to this question depends on several factors: the microfinance model followed by your organization, the size of your organization, the criticality of the software to you, the quality of the external developer, and the comparative costs of development. Obviously, this will vary from organization to organization, and even within an organization, from service to service.

In general, for small organizations or organizations using standard microfinance lending models, it is better to source the software externally, and have the vendor customize it to one's specific requirements. For large organizations, or where the requirements are specialized, it may be possible or necessary to develop a custom application

In general, for small organizations or organizations using standard microfinance lending models, it is better to source the software externally, and have the vendor customize it to one's specific requirements. For large organizations, or where the requirements are specialized, it may be possible or necessary to develop a custom application. In this case, one should carefully factor in the implications of developing in-house versus outsourcing the software development to an application developer. Given the problems inherent in employing software engineers in-house, including their management, their high salaries and their high attrition, outsourcing to a technology partner may be the more attractive solution.

The selection of the technology partner plays a vital role in determining the success of the project. The options that the partner can offer you are limited by his knowledge and experience. Hence, we should carefully research his technological capabilities to ensure that he is knowledgeable enough to be able to choose the best technology. We should also satisfy ourselves that his project management capabilities are good enough that he will be able to deliver the most cost-effective and robust solution, and support it over a long period.

The decision to go for a particular MIS or to develop a new one should be guided by a clear idea of the costs and the benefits of that solution. The upfront price of the package may only a very small part of the entire cost (Ivatury and Pasricha 2005). The larger chunk will be made up of the costs of personnel, training, support, and maintenance. One should also account for the costs of the underlying operating system, database, hardware, and security costs.

As mentioned above, the particular technologies that are chosen will depend on the capabilities of the technology partner. However, there are some aspects that the MFI should pay close attention to:

- Robustness and suitability: We should ensure that the technology is well suited to the use it will be put to, and the scenarios it will be used in. Buying extremely expensive and unduly high-end hardware or software can be as bad as buying underpowered components.

- Cost: In general, open standards, whether in hardware or in software, are attractive because it leads to low prices. Also, in addition to the development or purchase costs, one should pay attention to the maintenance costs and any licensing or subscription costs of the operating system and database.

- Life: We should ensure that the software and hardware technologies we use do not become outdated too soon. A technology solution should be able to serve your needs at least 3 to 4 years into the future. Both hardware and software should be maintainable locally.

The technology platform is another issue. Most solutions seen so far run on Microsoft Windows. This is primarily due to pervasiveness of that platform, and the large number of developers familiar with it. There are a few solutions that run on free platforms like Linux. The advantages of such a platform are that the costs are much lower, systems are generally more secure (free of viruses, trojans, worms, etc.), hardware requirements may be lighter, and one is free to upgrade at one's convenience. A similar situation obtains for databases. While large organizations may require expensive and high-end databases such as Oracle, SQL Server or DB2, it is usually seen that most of the functionality exists in free/open source databases like MySQL and Postgres. Grameen Foundation's MIFOS, and Ekgaon's various products are based on open-source technologies. The vendors of most of the high-end databases now offer "express" or "lite" versions of their products, which can be deployed in applications for free. Some of the high-end features are disabled, but that is generally not a problem for MFIs.

The Microfinance Gateway and the MIX Market offer some online information about various technologies, products, and vendors.

8.6 The way ahead

8.6.1 New technologies

The field of microfinance is becoming mainstream, and along with it, so is the technology for this field. Several interesting players are just stepping in. With the advent of new players like FINO, Grameen's MIFOS, Atyati's Ganaseva and Salesforce.com, and of new technologies like the use of mobile phones, smart cards, and NFC, MFIs can look forward to having more and better technology options at their disposal in the coming years.

The field of microfinance is becoming mainstream, and along with it, so is the technology for this field

Some of the technologies mentioned above, particularly smart cards and cellphone based readers, may be especially suited to banks providing savings services. Their costs are also currently high enough that they can be afforded by banks only. This raises the question, would banks take over microfinance, rendering MFIs superfluous?

On the other hand, MFIs have several strengths of their own. They specialize in assessing and originating microloans, in educating the customer, and in dealing with delinquencies. Even if banks were to enter this field in a more direct manner, they would need to build up these competencies. They might instead, prefer to continue to "outsource" these functions to MFIs.

8.6.2 Regulatory environment

One of the recent initiatives of the RBI has been the Business Facilitator and BC models (RBI 2006). The BC model is meant for the conduct of banking business. Only NGOs/MFIs set up under Societies/Trusts acts, Societies registered under Mutually Aided Cooperative Societies Acts or the Cooperative Societies Acts of States, S25 companies, and post offices may act as BC.[2] The RBI has made it clear that the Bank is responsible to the customer for the acts of the BC. Further, considering that the objective is to extend banking services to the unbanked, the RBI has also allowed banks to rely upon certificates of identification issued by the BC for the purpose of satisfying KYC norms.

BCs can perform a wide range of activities, including: assisting in the enrolment of new customers, disbursal of small value credit, collection of small value deposits, recovery of principal and collection of interest, receipt and delivery of payment instruments including remittances, and the sale of third-party financial products. Thus, the BC model enables a pooling of competencies between the bank, which can create financial products, but which may not be able to deliver these products to all segments of the population, and the BC, which does not have the ability to offer financial products, but which does have existing infrastructure that can be used as a delivery channel to reach the financially excluded.

The RBI has explicitly exhorted banks "to adopt technology-based solutions for managing the risk, besides increasing the outreach in a cost effective manner."

The RBI has explicitly exhorted banks "to adopt technology-based solutions for managing the risk, besides increasing the outreach in a cost effective manner." Using an IT solution is in any case, almost a regulatory requirement, since transactions need to be reflected in the bank's books by the end of the day or the next working day. Within the guidelines issued by RBI, banks and BCs have a fair amount of latitude in determining the payment systems to be used.

For example, IGS, a BASIX group company, has become a BC of Axis Bank. This project is being operationalized first in Delhi and Muzaffarpur, Bihar, and it is particularly directed at migrants from Muzaffarpur working in Delhi who want to remit money back home to their families. To reduce the operational risk, customers are given smart cards which store their fingerprints. Transactions are authorized and settled electronically, with the communications happening through the mobile phone. Customer information is collected by IGS and passed on to the bank. The bank opens a no-frills SB account for the customer. The information captured for every customer, including his photograph and his fingerprints, is stored in the smart card issued to him. He can withdraw and deposit money using this smart card at the terminal of the IGS agent. Transactions are authenticated biometrically, using the stored fingerprints. A printed receipt is provided to the customer for every transaction. The project is described in more detail in Box 8.3.

Box 8.3   TAFI: Putting mobile phone technology to work as a BC for remittances

BASIX, in collaboration with Axis Bank and A Little World (ALW), has launched an initiative in Delhi and Muzaffarpur, Bihar, called Technology Assisted Financial Inclusion (TAFI). This started as a result of BASIX's efforts to provide financial access to migrant workers. Studies have found that rural people in Bihar have become highly mobile due to poor local employment prospects. The destination is often determined by social networks: people tend to go to places where others from their village and caste have previously gone. Delhi is one of the major destinations. Migrants remit a large part of their income, and these remittances greatly improve the standard of living of their families. Many remittance mechanisms are used, including money orders, private agents, and hand-carrying. Deshingkar et al. (2006) quote Rs. 450 crore as the amount of money sent through money orders to Bihar in 2005–06. Most of this would be due to migrants. The amounts they hand-carry or send through private agents are each likely to comparable to this amount.

Migrants find it very difficult to open bank accounts, and to save or borrow money from formal sources. Money orders were also not preferred due to the cost (both official and unofficial), unreliability, and frequent delays. This forces them to rely on less-favoured unsafe/illegal methods to send money back home, at a high cost. This issue could be easily solved if the remitter and the payee each had access to a savings bank account. Also, such an account could provide a proof of income and of credit-worthiness, allowing them to borrow from the formal financial system. Hence, BASIX saw savings accounts as key to achieving financial inclusion. We approached Axis Bank and ALW to be our partners. The plan was for IGS (a BASIX group S25 company) to become Axis Bank's Business Correspondent (BC), at Delhi and at Muzaffarpur, using the technology provided by ALW. By using common delivery mechanisms to provide the BC services and our other services, we hoped to keep the costs low.

We surveyed households in several areas in Muzaffarpur, and found that most households had sent male family members to work outside the state, particularly to Kolkata and Delhi. In Delhi, migrants from Muzaffarpur were concentrated in the slum area of Mandavali. From our survey in Muzaffarpur, we were able to get the names and addresses of a large number of migrants in Delhi. On an average, they send around Rs. 1000 to Rs. 1500 per month back home. They commonly use money orders, private agents, and sometimes, even bank drafts. We decided to offer our services to the migrants in Mandavali and other slum dwellers. In Bihar, we decided to open our Specified Point of Transaction (SPOTs) in Muzaffarpur town and in a few villages in the district.

We initially explored opening a joint account for the migrant in Delhi and his wife/relatives in Bihar. But we soon learnt that they would prefer to avoid joint accounts – the migrants didn't want their families in Bihar to have access to all their money! So, we planned to open separate no-frills savings accounts for the migrants and their families. Remittance would be just an account-to-account transfer. We needed a safe, secure, and robust method for identifying and authenticating customers, so we chose fingerprint-based authentication. After data is collected and verified for each customer by IGS, Axis Bank vets it and opens a no-frills savings account for him. A smart card which stores his fingerprints, photo, and other details is issued to him.

But we soon learnt that they would prefer to avoid joint accounts – the migrants didn't want their families in Bihar to have access to all their money! So, we planned to open separate no-frills savings accounts for the migrants and their families

Operating the account has been made as easy as possible. Each IGS agent has a kit: a mobile phone, a fingerprint reader, and a printer. All these communicate with each other through the NFC chips built into them. To withdraw cash, the customer authenticates himself at the fingerprint reader. When successfully authenticated, the reader authorizes a single transaction on the card. Now, the agent presses his phone to the card. The phone reads the information in the card, and displays a menu on its screen. The agent then chooses the appropriate menu item and enters the amount the customer wishes to withdraw. The mobile phone checks the customer's balance, and if there is enough money in the account, it informs the server about the transaction, and gives the agent the go-ahead. The agent then pays the customer his money. To print a receipt, the printer is brought in contact with the cellphone. The transaction is committed only after the receipt is printed, ensuring safety. At the end of the day, an IGS agent will visit the nearest Axis Bank branch to square the accounts.

For remittances, a customer (say, in Delhi) can register other customers (his wife in Bihar) with us, as his payees. Then, he can transfer money from his account to theirs, and IGS shall inform the recipient. The remittance fee is proposed to be just 0.5 percent of the amount. In the initial stages of the project, the recipient shall have to come to the nearest SPOT to withdraw the money. Later, our agents will travel through the villages, providing doorstep service to the customers. The recipient will be paid within a day.

This technology is new to customers. To encourage them to use this mode of transaction, we incentivise our agents by paying them a commission per transaction. However, this needs to be carefully monitored, as it can be misused. The agents will be based at units situated close to the customers. The project is still in its very early stages — at the time of writing, only a month had passed since its inauguration. Within this short time, 1000 customers (both migrants and non-migrant slum-dwellers) had already enrolled. We hope to achieve break-even in about 2 years.

It is interesting to note that nations such as Brazil, South Africa, and the Philippines are ahead of India in using such technological and structural arrangements to promote financial inclusion (Lyman et al. 2006). In Brazil, a variety of retail agents are allowed to offer financial services on behalf of banks, including post offices, lottery kiosks, and supermarkets. These "banking correspondents" have ensured that every single municipality in Brazil — 5800 of them — have access to formal financial services. Similarly, in the Philippines, Globe Telecom offers an e-money product tied to the mobile phone SIM card of the subscriber. While this is meant to be used as a payments and remittance mechanism, many poor people also use it as a savings account. In South Africa, mobile phone operators have tied up with banks to offer cellphone based bank accounts.

Today in India, technology makes it possible to have a one-man bank branch, at any place one wishes. One individual, armed with a mobile phone, can do most of the cash-in, cash-out functions of a bank teller

Today in India, technology makes it possible to have a one-man bank branch, at any place one wishes. One individual, armed with a mobile phone, can do most of the cash-in, cash-out functions of a bank teller. While the BC model enables us to tap into this possibility, further changes in regulations will be required to make the BC model feasible on a large scale (Tankha 2006).

8.6.3 Technology fund

We already know that business process innovations backed by technology can make financial services accessible to the poor. However, much work needs to be done to investigate the ways to upscale these innovations to achieve complete financial inclusion. In his budget speech, the Finance Minister has promised to create a Financial Inclusion Technology Fund, with the objective: "to meet the costs of research and development, pilot testing and scaling up of appropriate and cost-effective technologies for enhancing financial inclusion." This fund, if properly utilized, will be of great help in promoting innovative ways of taking banking to the unbanked. It can target projects that use technology to address financial exclusion by reducing the transaction and monitoring costs, increasing the reach and scale of operations, and preventing fraud. Some of the promising technologies it could support could be:

> technologies which use the increasing ubiquity of mobile phone networks and the internet for financial inclusion;

- methods to standardize and automate the calculation of customer credit risk to the extent possible;

- cheap, reliable, and rugged ATMs;

- development of cheaper identification/authentication mechanisms;

- inexpensive smart cards and other secure ways of reducing – ideally eliminating – cash.

Endnotes

1   Prasanth V Regy is Manager, Strategic Initiatives, BASIX and Vijay Mahajan is an electrical engineer and Chairman, BASIX.

2   In the original circular (issued in January 2006), registered NBFCs not accepting public deposits were also allowed to become BCs, but in a subsequent circular, RBI advised banks to avoid the use of NBFCs as BCs (with the exception of those NBFCs licenced under S25).

References

Saral Services, 2007, "Information and Communication Technology Survey of DCCBs and MFIs in India," Saral Services, Sheffield Hallam University, Oxford University, ODI

Intellecap, 2006, "The Way Forward: Technology in Indian Microfinance," Report for CARE India, Mumbai

Ivatury, Gautam, and Nicole Pasricha, 2005. "Funding Microfinance Technology," CGAP, Washington DC

Deshingkar, Priya, Sushil Kumar, Harendra Kumar Chobey, and Dhananjay Kumar, 2006. "The Role of Migration and Remittances in Promoting Livelihoods in Bihar," Overseas Development Institute, London

RBI, 2006, "Financial Inclusion by Extension of Banking Services," Mumbai

Lyman, Timothy R., Gautam Ivatury, Stefan Staschen, 2006, "Use of Agents in Branchless Banking for the Poor," CGAP 2006

Tankha, Ajay, 2006, "Challenges and potential for Indian banks to implement the Business Facilitator and Business Correspondent Models," NABARD and GTZ

CHAPTER 9

Regulation: The Microfinance Bill: An Opportunity Being Lost?

Finalization of the draft of microfinance bill promised by the finance minister in his budget speech of February 2005 has not only turned out to be a lengthy affair, as is common with microfinance bills around the world, but the bill has undergone considerable modification from the original version of the bill proposed by Sa-Dhan, the network of MFIs in India, after extensive consultations within its membership. The fundamental changes in concept undergone by the bill in its various versions are described at greater length in Box 9.1.[1] The bill was introduced in parliament as the Micro Financial Sector (Development and Regulation) Bill, 2007, on 20 March 2007, and was referred by the Lok Sabha to the Standing Committee of Finance, which was still considering it at the time this chapter went to the printers (in the first quarter of 2008). The chapter first describes the main objectives of the bill as it presently stands. Then, it discusses the major issues arising out of it. It does so because whatever the fate of the bill, the issues it raises will remain relevant to the sector for a long time.[2] Finally, it draws attention to two regulatory steps the RBI could take immediately that would have a much greater short-term impact on the sector than the bill itself, even if it gets passed in its present form.

Box 9.1   The microfinance bill: A case study in dilution

The draft bill initially prepared by Sa-Dhan envisaged that the regulator would be an independent professional body appointed by the central government. It also proposed the creation of a two-tier structure for the sector, with two categories of microfinance service providers. Micro Finance Organizations (MFOs) would be allowed to mobilize savings only from members and be subjected to simple reporting requirements. Once they had a loan portfolio of more than Rs. 1 crore, however, they would have to convert themselves into companies as "Micro Finance Institutions," but with a lower entry capital requirement than is required currently for NBFCs (Rs. 25 lakhs instead of Rs. 1 crore). This special window would have made it much easier for NGO–MFIs to transform to company status, which is more suited to microfinance operations as discussed earlier. MFIs, on the other hand, would be allowed to mobilize savings from the public subject to several conditions.

However, after extensive inter-agency consultations led by the Ministry of Finance, the bill actually submitted to government in August 2006 for inter-ministerial discussion and Cabinet consideration took the form of an amendment to the NABARD Act, which nominated NABARD as the regulator, giving the Council only an advisory role. In this modified version not only was the two-tier structure abandoned, NBFCs were dropped from the bill

---

altogether. In the third and final version that was presented to parliament, it became apparent that four further changes had taken place.[50] The bill was no longer an amendment bill to an existing act (the NABARD) act, but a bill relating to a new act, and was renamed the Micro Finance Sector (Development and Regulation) Bill, 2007. The composition of the Council, which had already become merely advisory, was changed from being primarily non-official and professional, to predominantly official. Not-for-profit S25 companies were dropped from the definition of MFOs, who were to consist now only of societies, trusts, and cooperatives. Finally, the proposal to create an ombudsman went from being mandatory to merely enabling. Table 9.1 summarizes the major differences between the three versions, and Table 9.2 differences between MFOs and the new "MFIs" (the proposal to create which has now been dropped).

Table 9.1 Successive versions of the microfinance bill

	Original bill proposed by Sa-Dhan in consultation with members and key government agencies	Modified bill circulated by Ministry of Finance for inter-agency discussion	Current version approved by Cabinet and introduced in parliament
Name	Micro Finance Development Council Act, 2005	National Bank for Agriculture and Rural Development (Amendment) Bill, 2006	The Micro Financial Sector (Development and Regulation) Act, 2007 (Bill No. 41 of 2007)
Scope	All existing categories of MFIs, including a new category of "MFI" registered as a company with an entry capital of Rs. 25 lakhs (see Table 9.2)	New category of "MFI" dropped, but MFOs defined to include all non-profits, including S25 companies	Only NGO–MFIs registered as societies, trust, and cooperatives (i.e. excluding NBFCs an S25 companies)
Structure envisaged for sector	Two-tier, with MFOs and "MFIs" (apart from NBFCs)	One tier, MFOs only (apart from NBFCs, who along with banks are included in data gathering requirements)	One tier, MFOs only (apart from NBFCs and S25 companies, but no provisions applicable to them)
Savings authorization	"Thrift" for MFOs, public savings for special category "MFIs"	Only "thrift" for MFOs	Only "thrift" for MFOs
Regulator	Microfinance Development Council	NABARD	NABARD
Micro Finance Development Council	Independent body of experienced professionals with executive responsibilities	Advisory body, but with majority of members representing the sector	Advisory, with majority consisting of officials representing specified agencies exofficio
Ombudsman	Not specifically provided, but MFDC to establish mechanism for redressal of grievances	MFDC required to set up ombudsman	MFDC "may" set up ombudsman

Table 9.2 "MFOs" and "MFIs"

	Original bill proposed by Sa-Dhan in consultation with members and key government agencies		Modified bill circulated by Ministry of Finance for inter-agency discussion	
	MFO	"MFI" (as defined in bill with capital of Rs. 25 lakhs)	MFO	MFI (in generic sense)
Size-trigger for registration as "MFI"	Credit outstanding not to exceed Rs. 1 crore or 10 times NOF, whichever is less	Above the limits for an MFO must incorporate an "MFI" company if MFO is a society or trust (if cooperative, must comply with norms for "MFIs")	Since "MFIs" dropped, none. Bill includes all non-profit forms of registration including S25 companies	NBFCs
Capital	Must maintain a capital adequacy ratio of 10 percent	NOF of not less than Rs. 25 lakhs, of which at least 10 percent promoter's contribution (with provision for exemption for cooperatives) and CA ratio of 15 percent	NOF of at least Rs. 5 lakhs and a capital adequacy ratio of 15 percent	As per existing NBFC regulations
Type of savings	Only thrift from members	Deposits from the public	Only thrift from members	As per existing NBFC regulations
Limit on savings/ eligibility conditions	Not more than Rs. 25 lakhs in aggregate, and Rs. 5000 or such other amount specified by Council per individual	No limit, but certificate of registration as "MFI" to be granted only to MFO with aggregate thrift of not more than 4 times NOF, or more than aggregate loans outstanding, whichever is less	No limit, but must have had surplus income in at least the year before applying for registration, and compliance with rating norms	As per existing NBFC regulations
Restrictions on thrift	Not be repayable in less than three months	No restrictions	No restrictions	As per existing NBFC regulations
Reserve fund	Must transfer not less than 10 percent of surplus to RF	Must transfer not less than 15 percent of surplus to RF	Must transfer not less than 15 percent of surplus to RF	As per existing NBFC regulations

9.1 The proposed microfinance bill

The latest version of the bill being considered by the parliamentary standing committee on finance applies only to three categories of not-for-profit MFIs: societies, trusts, and cooperatives These are collectively referred to in the bill as Micro Finance Organization (MFOs). It does not cover the bulk of the sector in terms of share of borrowers and loans outstanding, which is accounted for by MFIs registered as companies (for-profit NBFCs and not-for-profit S25 companies)

The latest version of the bill being considered by the parliamentary standing committee on finance[3] applies only to three categories of not-for-profit MFIs: societies, trusts, and cooperatives. These are collectively referred to in the bill as Micro Finance Organizations (MFOs). It does not cover the bulk of the sector in terms of share of borrowers and loans outstanding, which is accounted for by MFIs registered as companies (for-profit NBFCs and not-for-profit $25 companies).[4]

The bill contains both prudential and non-prudential provisions. The former seek to allow MFOs to offer what are referred to as "thrift" services, defined as savings collected through groups,[5] after obtaining a certificate of registration from the new regulator created by the bill, NABARD. NABARD may grant approval to an MFO to collect thrift, if it has been in existence for at least 3 years, has net owned funds of at least Rs. 5 lakhs, and if NABARD is satisfied about the "general character" of the management of the MFO. Every MFO granted approval to offer thrift services shall create a reserve fund out of transfers to the fund of not less than 15 percent of its net profit or surplus every year, and will prepare financial statements by the end of the year, in such form as may be specified, to be audited by an approved auditor.

Cooperatives are, of course, already empowered to offer much more than "thrift" to their members as defined in the bill, since cooperative thrift or savings and credit societies offer their members individual savings accounts as well as fixed deposits. It is widely accepted that as mutual organizations prudential regulation of cooperatives can be much lighter than for entities accepting non-member (or public) deposits. Now they find themselves being treated on a par with societies and trusts. Sections of the cooperative movement feel understandably aggrieved that they were not consulted during formulation of the bill,[6] and feel threatened by the uncertainties introduced by the arrival of the new regulator. A section of the cooperative movement has opposed the bill vocally, as discussed below.

While one of the main objectives of the bill is to allow NGO–MFIs to accept savings in the limited form of group savings, the bill prescribes in addition the "duty" of the regulator to achieve the much broader non-prudential objective of promoting the "orderly growth of the microfinancial sector so as to ensure greater transparency, effective management, good governance...

While one of the main objectives of the bill is to allow NGO–MFIs to accept savings in the limited form of group savings, the bill prescribes in addition the "duty" of the regulator to achieve the much broader non-prudential objective of promoting the "*orderly growth of the microfinancial sector* so as to ensure greater transparency, effective management, good governance..." Among the measures suggested through which it may do so are: (i) setting benchmarks and performance standards, (ii) facilitating the development of credit ratings norms, (iii) specifying accounting and auditing standards, (iv) facilitating institutional development through training and capacity building, (v) supporting sector related research, (vi) documenting and disseminating information relating to fair practices, (vii) laying down a code of conduct, and (viii) promoting consumer education.

The last three of these activities will support a third objective of the bill which is to create *a consumer protection regime* by enabling the regulator to appoint "as many Micro Finance Ombudsmen as it may deem fit" with powers to redress grievances by issuing directions to MFOs. A strict reading of the definition of MFO would seem to preclude the benefits of the ombudspersons from applying to the clients of NBFCs and not-for-profit S25 companies.

A fourth objective of the bill is to create a *national database* "in the public domain" and disseminate it through a "national dissemination network." To this end, every MFO whether providing thrift services or not will be required to file at the commencement of the act and at intervals thereafter, duly audited returns. While on the one hand no minimum size for the purpose of filing returns is laid down for the societies, trusts and cooperatives falling within the purview of the bill, that is, those offering "microfinance services,"[7] the bill on the other hand provides no authority to seek returns from NBFCs. This is the case also for the first three of the "orderly growth" activities listed above. With the exception of the training and research activities, the orderly growth activities will apply only to MFOs. It is hard to see how, therefore, the bill will succeed in promoting orderly growth for the sector as a whole, including equipping it with a much needed database.

Fifth, the bill provides for the setting up of *a Micro Finance Development Council to advise the regulator* on the "formulation of policies, schemes, and other measures required in the interest of orderly growth and development" of the sector. The Council shall consist of an experienced "person of eminence" as chairman, 7 official members,[8] and 6 non-official experts with experience in rural banking and microfinance.

Sixth, it provides for the continuation of the existing *Micro Finance Development and Equity Fund* to receive grants from the government and donors, to make loans to MFOs, to invest in their equity or quasi-equity, to make grants to them for capacity building, and to pay for the various functions of the regulator enumerated above.

Finally, although this would be an effect rather than an explicit objective of the bill, it could be argued that by recognizing the legitimacy of their microfinance activities, the bill will *enhance the legal status of NGO–MFIs, and will in effect protect them* from arbitrary state government action. However, it provides no protection against state moneylenders acts, or even for that matter the central government's own Usurious Loans Act 1918, which is still on the statute books. S21A of the Banking Regulation Act expressly exempts the rate of interest charged by banks from state moneylender acts, as well as from any other law related to indebtedness in force in any state. There is no such provision in the present bill. In fact, quite the opposite. S36 says its provisions "shall be in addition to, and not in derogation of, the provisions of any other law for the time being in force."

9.2 Major issues

9.2.1 The bill excludes the bulk of the sector

One of the major omissions in the bill is that it excludes MFIs registered as NBFCs and S25 companies, which account for nearly all the large MFIs and the larger part of total microcredit in the country. Their number is steadily increasing as they are joined by more and more NGO–MFIs transforming themselves into companies in order to be able to attract equity investments with which to leverage borrowed funds, and at the same time escape the vicissitudes of state government policy towards NGO–MFIs (NBFCs are regulated by the RBI).[9] However, by including only societies, trusts, and cooperatives, the bills is proposing to cut out at one stroke 60 percent of the sector in terms of portfolio outstanding on March 2007, and 55 percent of the total number of borrowers.[10] It is doing so on the mistaken grounds that NBFCs are already regulated by the RBI. They are – RBI regulations recognize 10 categories of NBFCs including loan, leasing, investment, and hire-purchase companies, and even a "residual" category of NBFCs like Sahara and Prudential. But microfinance is not one of the recognized categories. Nor have any of more than two dozen NBFCs conducting microcredit (defined in the bill as loans smaller than Rs. 50,000 for most purposes, and smaller than Rs. 1.5 lakhs for housing) managed to satisfy the stringent requirements that have been laid down by NBFC regulations to become eligible to mobilize savings.

The irony is that not only can NBFC—MFIs not accept public deposits, but by virtue of being excluded from the bill they will not be able to accept the savings of their own borrower—members who will continue to have to rely on less convenient, riskier[11] lower yielding, and often socially less productive savings instruments (such as ornaments). There is understandable reluctance to allow MFIs to mobilize public deposits, without putting in place the necessary safeguards, for sound prudential reasons. But the vast majority of MFI members are net borrowers of the MFI at any one time.

They borrow to finance their larger investment requirements, but simultaneously save small amounts regularly to finance their liquidity requirements, provide for emergencies, build up a cushion to tide over the lean season when agricultural wage employment is scarce, and aggregate savings into amounts large enough to make useful investments, repair the hut, send a daughter to high school, or a son to the big city to look for work.

The argument adduced for keeping NBFCs outside the purview of the bill (the need to avoid duality of regulation) is equally applicable to district, state, and urban cooperative banks which are governed by the Banking Regulation Act in respect of banking activities, while conforming to the cooperative law in other respects. Like them, NBFCs would be governed by the microfinance bill in respect of thrift activities, without any dilution of their capital, reserve, or liquidity requirements as NBFCs, until they qualify under NBFC regulations to mobilize not just thrift from members, but hopefully, also, public savings. It is true that dual regulation of cooperative banks has not been a resounding success. However, as Sinha (2007b) points out, UCBs are financed primarily by deposits, whereas MFIs, even after being allowed to accept thrift, will always depend primarily on borrowings from the banks and the financial institutions, and therefore, will be subjected to due diligence exercised by their lenders.[12]

However, as Sinha points out, UCBs are financed primarily by deposits, whereas MFIs, even after being allowed to accept thrift, will always depend primarily on borrowings from the banks and the financial institutions, and therefore, will be subjected to due diligence exercised by their lenders

In confusing the form of incorporation with the substantial nature of the institution, or form with function, the act will also deprive more than half of borrowers (the proportion is set to grow) from the protection of the ombudsman, and the sector as a whole from the benefits of universal performance standards in respect of microfinance activities and a much needed database.

9.2.2 It allows NGO—MFIs to mobilize thrift, which is a small step forward

India's attitude to savings mobilization by non-banks has been more restrictive than elsewhere, an attitude strengthened by periodic scams which affect the savings of the urban middle classes and which therefore receive widespread publicity in the press. Most of the countries of South Asia, which share the same legal heritage, now expressly allow savings in their microfinance legislation. Bangladesh, where conditions are closest to India, and where the MFI model originated, has recently passed the Micro Credit Regulatory Authority (MCRA) Act 2006, which allows the MCRA to permit MFIs to offer savings withdrawable on demand. In Sri Lanka also NGO—MFIs are allowed to mobilize deposits once they have received the regulators permission.[13] The provisions in the bill enabling savings, albeit in a limited form, are probably the single most important contribution of the bill. However, ironically it is this aspect of the bill that has been the most widely misunderstood by critics. These misunderstandings are dealt with separately in Box 9.2.

Box 9.2   Misunderstandings about savings

The provisions in the bill enabling savings, albeit in a limited form, are probably the single most important contribution of the bill. However, ironically it is this aspect of the bill that has been the most widely misunderstood and attacked by critics, who have alleged that NGO–MFIs must not be allowed to mobilize "*public*" savings. However, this is not what is proposed. The savings in question are the savings of borrower–members, the vast majority of whom are net borrowers of the MFI at any one time. To argue, as some people do, that borrowers are not "*members*" of the MFI in the same sense that members of mutual institutions are, depends on whether one defines membership in a strictly technical sense or according to the substantive nature of the bond it creates.

Under the Grameen Bank methodology, borrowers have to meet eligibility conditions, receive week-long training, and pass a test before qualifying to receive their first loan. Thereafter, they are in contact with the MFI at least once a week, when the MFI field worker comes to collect loan repayments, which is much more frequent than in mutual organizations. The peer pressure to repay loans exercised through joint liability groups is often much stronger than in the larger and far looser primary groups of mutual organizations. MFIs recognize and reward long-standing "members" when graduating them to larger, housing, or other individual, loans. The loyalty of members to their MFI is usually every bit as strong as in a mutual institution, in which, as has been pointed out, the boundaries of membership can be porous, depending on the nature of the "common bond" of the mutual institution. If the common bond is area-based, or geographical, membership can be given to anyone in the area who wants to make a deposit. In any case, in practice, as the 2005 Union Task Force on the Revival of Cooperative Credit Institutions points out, membership with full voting rights is usually given only to borrowers, with depositors being categorized as nominal members without voting rights, which is why borrowers rather than net savers tend to dominate cooperative boards, although this is not the case with the new mutually aided cooperative society acts passed in nine states, and is an issue that the ongoing cooperative reform is trying to set right.

Thus, if an MFI "*flies by night*" (the second misunderstanding), then it will stand to lose much more than it gains, since most members will owe the MFI much more than it owes them. Also, an MFI cannot "fly by night," because it is first and foremost a credit institution. Unlike an unlicensed finance company, it needs dozens, if not, hundreds of field workers, who work out of branch offices as it expands. These huge establishments and infrastructure requirements cannot disappear overnight. The MFI can of course collapse from incompetence or fraud, but if it does so (and no recognized MFI out of the approximately 1000 societies, trusts, etc. estimated to be conducting microfinance in India, is reported to have done so yet), it will again be borrowers who will be the net gainers in a strict financial sense, provided the norms recommended earlier are followed. The regulator is in any case required to assess the "general character" of an MFI before approving it for thrift.

Last, and this is the third misunderstanding, the mere act of mobilizing savings, or financial intermediation, does not constitute "banking" as has been widely alleged in the debate on the bill. If it did, NBFCs approved to collect deposits would not remain non-banks, and every cooperative credit society would be a bank. An essential element of banking, in the wider sense understood by economists, is money and credit creation through the money and credit multipliers of fractional reserve banking, which connects banks to the wider financial system in a systemic way. This is not the case with small stand-alone financial institutions such as cooperatives and MFIs. Even more important, they do not participate in the payments system by issuing cheques.

There is also a widespread misconception that the poor are too poor to save, and that they need credit, not savings facilities and services. On the contrary, savings is probably a more widely felt need than credit, and takes place through a variety of savings mechanisms and institutions in the informal sector, such as itinerant deposit collectors,[14] small community chit funds, informal credit unions (such as the bishis of Maharashta), investments in livestock or ornaments (which can later be liquefied through the pawnbroker and moneylender), or by lending to a friend in need so that the lender can borrow reciprocally when required.[15] The phenomenal growth of the SHG movement in which rural women meet with unfailing regularity once a month to save small sums ranging from Rs. 10 to Rs. 50, and the fact that poor urban slum dwellers, far from earning interest on their savings, are willing to pay to have their deposits collected at the doorstep and stored safely until they amount to a useful sum, and countless other examples, attest to the importance of the almost universal need to save. Like the rest of us, the poor are looking for savings services which are convenient, safe, liquid, and can preferably be used to leverage loans.

By allowing at least MFOs to meet this need, the draft microfinance bill takes a long overdue, albeit small step forward.[16] Quite apart from the benefits to MFO members, there will be benefits to the MFOs themselves — their cost of funds will come down, and their members' sense of ownership in their MFO will increase, since a part of the loans they will be getting will be their own money coming back to them, giving them a further incentive to maintain high repayment

Because Indian MFIs have had to rely exclusively on funds borrowed from the banks, their financial expense ratios (cost of funds as a proportion of total costs) are the highest in the world

rates. Because Indian MFIs have had to rely exclusively on funds borrowed from the banks, their financial expense ratios (cost of funds as a proportion of total costs) are the highest in the world (see Chapter 4 of last year's report). In Bangladesh, on the other hand, interest rates are slightly lower than in India, because as much as a third of the funds base comes from member savings. Many Bangladeshi MFIs also pay a slightly higher rate to savers than the banks, because of the cost efficiencies that ensue from economies of scope in being able to use existing field staff, who have to meet borrowers once a week anyway to collect loan repayment installments and disburse fresh loans. Grameen Bank mobilizes in fact more savings than it disburses as credit (as does Bank Rakyat Indonesia, further examples of how savings are as valued by poor clients as credit).

How can it be ensured that the vast majority of MFIs members remain net borrowers at any one time? (i) First, by licensing MFIs to collect savings only after they have established a track record as lenders, (ii) Second, once licensed, by limiting acceptance of savings only to their borrowers and not the public, (iii) Third, by ensuring that not more than a small proportion of the borrowers of the MFI are net savers at any one time, or in other words have more savings deposited than loans outstanding,[17] (iv) Fourth, by laying down a ceiling on the total savings that can be mobilized as a proportion of the liquid assets of the MFI in the form of loans outstanding at any one time, the savings/loans outstanding ratio could be set, say, at 50 percent, which would ensure that the MFI would also have to borrow to fund its loans and thereby subject itself to the normal scrutiny that any lender such as bank or financial institution would exercise (Sinha 2007b). (v) A further prudential measure would be to prescribe a liquidity reserve, the size of which should depend on the liquidity of savings offered.[18] While the bill provides for the first two of these conditions, Section 10(1)(e) enables the regulator to lay down the remaining three or any other condition it deems appropriate.

9.2.3 ...however, it remains a rather small step: Compulsory versus voluntary savings

While the proposal to allow thrift is welcome and long overdue, it is important to note that it is only the first small step forward in introducing savings. Quite apart from the fact that it only applies to MFOs, thrift is defined in the bill as monies collected by a microfinance organization only from "a group, or by a group from its members through the group mechanism..." What this definition seems to have in mind is the kind of uniform, mandatory, monthly savings service offered by SHGs in India, and by the smaller joint liability groups used by MFIs in Bangladesh, the Philippines, and in more than 45 other countries which have MFIs based on the Grameen Bank model.

While many savers welcome the discipline of compulsory savings, they tend to belong to the better-off among the poor or to the "near-poor" above the poverty line. On the other hand many of the poorer members of SHGs (and most of the self-excluded non-members), who have highly uncertain and variable incomes, would prefer to save *small variable amounts, with variable frequency* (Rutherford 2005). Several surveys have found that the main reason for why only half the members of SHGs are below the poverty line is the inability of BPL persons to commit themselves to the required mandatory savings amounts and periodicities. Uniform mandatory savings are also the most frequent reason cited by drop-outs for leaving SHGs.[19]

A concomitant of mandatory savings products is their illiquidity. While illiquid savings protect the savings of the poor from daily demands, and are suited to accumulating lump-sums for *expected purposes* such as life-cycle events or school fees or adding a new room to the hut, they are unsuited to coping with *unexpected emergencies* including sickness and disease, or consumption smoothening in the lean season, or replacing a leaky roof in the middle of the monsoons (CGAP 2005a). While the SHG movement provides for unexpected demands to some extent, through small intra-group loans, and the MFI model does so through "emergency loans," these are an imperfect substitute for being able to access ones own savings quickly in an emergency.

Indeed, recognizing the *liquidity preference* of the poor for many although not all savings purposes, several MFIs in Bangladesh, and indeed worldwide, who have the requisite accounting systems, are moving to a system of voluntary savings in which the saver has some choice over the timing and amount of savings and withdrawals. Some Bangladesh MFIs have introduced "open access" savings (in which savers have access to their savings whenever they like), and have found that the inflow of total savings far from declining has in fact increased[20] (see Box 9.3 and Wright 2000).[21] It is not being suggested that most small Indian NGO–MFIs have developed the requisite systems yet to be able to able to offer such a savings product,[22] or that mandatory savings do not have their advantages for certain purposes.

Indeed, recognizing the liquidity preference of the poor for many although not all savings purposes, several MFIs in Bangladesh, and indeed worldwide, who have the requisite accounting systems, are moving to a system of voluntary savings in which the saver has some choice over the timing and amount of savings and withdrawals

Box 9.3   Grameen II and flexible, voluntary savings

Under Grameen II, each member opens *a personal savings account*, into which she may pay whatever she likes, subject to a weekly minimum that depends on the value of her loans from the bank, and withdraw whatever she likes whenever she likes, for any purpose, subject to being up-to-date in her loan repayments. Deposits are made at the weekly "centre" meeting, but withdrawals are made at branch offices (normally within a half-hour's rickshaw trip or so). When she takes a loan, 2.5 percent of its value is deposited to this account (but may be withdrawn). Deposits earn interest at 8.5 percent per annum; a higher rate than passbook savings in commercial banks...

Withdrawal symptoms: At first, many staff feared open withdrawals. They sincerely believed that members would quickly drain their accounts, leaving them with no reserves to fall back on, and Grameen with no implicit cash collateral for the loans. Then, during 2003 some managers began to allow withdrawals for "approved" uses, such as health emergences and marriage ceremonies, while denying them for making loan repayment installments. Finally, in 2004 the product began to be administered as designed: HQ issued passbooks with the message that "you may withdraw cash from your personal savings at any time" printed on every page. Staff learned that open withdrawal wasn't the disaster they had feared. Members, finding withdrawals easier, began to use their accounts for the (often short-term) storage of larger sums, in addition to their small regular weekly deposits. The chart shows the growing number of withdrawals in our sample branches.[51]

Balances: Average balances per member in personal savings accounts did not change much during this period (Note Q3 2002 to Q3 2004). In two of our branches, it grew but fell in the third, and ranged between 500 and 800 taka ($8–13). Membership grew rapidly, pushing down average balances as new accounts opened, so it is clear that members did not choose to exhaust their accounts as withdrawals became freely available.

Uses: Mrs NB, a member in sample branch S, is one of the Grameen clients whose financial behaviour we are tracking. In 2004, her personal savings account transactions amounted to $64 in 48 (mainly weekly) deposits and $60 in five withdrawals, leaving her with a year-end balance of just $9. She used the withdrawals for household consumption and health care, to lend to others, and to make repayment installments to Grameen and other MFIs. The personal savings account, for her, is becoming a convenient current account. Large flows of cash in and out of such accounts, resulting in small balances, is both common and rational among the poor, whose small and fragile incomes require them to resort to saving and borrowing to finance even small items of expenditure such as a visit to the doctor or the purchase of a new sari. This useful service did not exist in Grameen before Grameen II, but is now one of the bank's most popular products.

Extracted from Member Savings by Stuart Rutherford, MicroSave Briefing Notes on Grameen II #2

However, provision should be made for the day when a larger number of NGO–MFIs have developed the requisites systems and capacity to offer voluntary savings.[23] Since voluntary savings are more conveniently offered as individual savings (because voluntary savings amounts and frequency will always vary from individual to individual), it would seem essential to allow the regulator the option to approve individual, voluntary, savings products in appropriate cases after due diligence by the regulator on a case-by-case basis.

In order to do so, the words "or by other means" need to be inserted after the words "group mechanism" in the definition of thrift in clause 2(1) of the Bill. Also, the exclusion in the definition of thrift of current accounts and demand deposits needs to be removed. These would be enabling provisions in the case of most MFOs for now, but a very useful one when the time comes (given the difficulties of securing amendments to a legislative act in the future).

A third amendment required it to clearly exclude SHG federations from the definitions of groups. The phrase in the definition of "group" or "a group called by any other name" has created apprehensions to the contrary. The definition requires a group to provide microfinance services to individual members of the group, which many federations do (see Chapter 3).[24]

9.2.4 Should cooperatives be covered by the Act?

Cooperatives are defined in the bill to include all cooperatives except cooperative banks and cooperatives "engaged in agricultural operations."[25] India has had for a long time a large thrift cooperative movement which at one time was one of the strongest in the world.[26] There is no estimate at present of the number of thrift cooperatives, or even of those registered under the new MACS acts (see below). At one time, NABARD did publish data on cooperatives on the basis of information received from state registrars but has for some years stopped doing so.[27] The responsibility for regulation and supervision of PACS is being transferred to NABARD under the central government's Revival Package for the Rural Cooperative Thrift and Credit System.[28] With the present bill, a similar responsibility is being conferred on NABARD for thrift cooperatives.

The responsibility for regulation and supervision of PACS is being transferred to NABARD under the central government's Revival Package for the Rural Cooperative Thrift and Credit System. With the present bill a similar responsibility is being conferred on NABARD for thrift cooperatives

The issue with respect to bringing thrift cooperatives under the bill is that cooperatives, as mutual organizations are already allowed to accept savings from their members. Indeed the term thrift has been in use by thousands of cooperatives in India for several decades now[29] and has been further popularized by the Cooperative Development Foundation, a well-known civil society organization registered as an NGO in Andhra Pradesh, which spearheaded the movement for cooperative reform, and lobbied with the AP legislature to enact the Mutually Aided Cooperative Societies Act or APMACS Act in 1995. This was followed by the enactment of similar acts in eight other states and a central multi-state act to provide for a new type of "mutually aided" or "mutual benefit"[30] cooperative which would be much truer to cooperative principles than traditional cooperatives under existing state acts, and enjoy much more autonomy and freedom from government interference of the kind that has led to the deterioration of traditional cooperatives.[31]

CDF has set up 450 "mutually aided," women's and men's thrift cooperatives under the new act in Warangal, and two neighbouring districts of AP, which exercise a powerful demonstration effect on how savings and credit cooperatives should function. With meticulous accounts, good governance, compulsory monthly thrift ranging from Rs. 20 to Rs. 50, and membership of about 250 each, they have mobilized own funds or member savings in various forms to the tune of Rs. 46 crores (by March 2007), of which Rs. 40 crores has been lent back to members. CDF is strongly opposed to MACS being brought under the bill, since they are already empowered to mobilize thrift. It fought a long battle to rescue cooperatives from the ill advised attempt over the years to assist cooperatives with subsidies so as to convert them into vehicles for political patronage, and is understandably worried about coming under the oversight of an organization it fears may not understand the MACS ethos. It is strongly opposed to MACS being brought under the bill.

The bill does indeed empower the central government to exempt a particular class of microfinance organization from any or all the provisions of the Act, and it will have to do so for SHGs of which there were 2.86 million by March 2007, and which cannot possibly be expected to apply for registration to mobilize savings individually. However, CDF and the MACS community (including, reportedly, the AP government setting up SHG federations registered as MACS under IKP) are understandably reluctant to depend on government to exempt them as a class after the bill becomes law. As a vocal civil society organization CDF has experienced considerable opposition from the state government on a host of issues in the past, an instance of which was the AP government's action to foreclose the MACS option for dairy cooperatives, a matter which CDF took to the AP High Court and had overturned. A more recent instance is the ban the AP government has placed on further registration of thrift cooperatives as MACS. CDF is likely to lead the challenge to the bill on the grounds that as mutual organizations cooperatives are already allowed to mobilize thrift under the principle of mutuality, and on other grounds.

The alternatives, however, are not clear. There has been little effective supervision of thrift cooperatives by the state registrars of cooperative societies, even under the new acts. None of the states with MACS acts have appointed a separate set of registrars at the state of district level, who continue to exercise jurisdiction under both acts. Perhaps for reasons of lack of proper orientation under the MACS acts the registrars have shown little inclination to discharge the functions entrusted to them under the statute.[32]

Although prudential concerns are greatly softened by the member-owned nature of cooperatives, they are not entirely eliminated. While it is unique among the nine MACS acts in this respect, the AP MACS act allows societies to accept deposits even from non-members and many of them do

Although prudential concerns are greatly softened by the member-owned nature of cooperatives, they are not entirely eliminated. While it is unique among the nine MACS acts in this respect, the AP MACS act allows societies to accept deposits even from non-members and many of them do. Also, as the Union Task Force on Revival of Cooperative Credit Institutions points out, most cooperative members restrict membership with full voting rights to borrowers. Depositors are categorized as nominal members[33] without full voting rights, or are not given any membership status. Cooperative boards tend, therefore, to be dominated by borrowers. Thorat and Wright (2006) have suggested that restrictions on loans to board members and strengthening the presence of net savers on cooperative boards will lead to more effective pressure on cooperative management to ensure prudent governance and protect the interest of savers.

Effective supervision is important not only at the primary level, but also at the secondary level. SHG federations registered as MACS have become important players in the sector in AP, where the two tiers of SHG federations at the village and mandal level, as we have seen in Chapter 3, have either already been, or are slated to be, registered as MACS. Orissa, where federations have been formed in every panchayat of the state (but are not yet active) has also registered its federations under the Orissa Self-Help Cooperatives Act, the equivalent of the MACS in the state. Other states may well adopt the MACS form of registration for their federations. At present, according to one observer, the relationship of such federations with the MACS act ends as soon as they have been registered, and they simply exist in the books of the district registrar.[34]

The supervision of thousands of thrift cooperatives all over the country is going to be a huge task compared to the supervision of the much smaller number of societies and trusts providing microfinance services whose number is estimated at not more than a thousand. Rather than seeking to supplant the registrars all over the country, it might be more practicable (and certainly more in accordance of the spirit of cooperation) for the states to energize the state registrars and ensure they carry out their obligations under the old and new acts.

A third alternative is for MACS conducting microfinance to set up a system of self-regulation, a possible solution being studied by APMAS.[35] At the very least, a careful study of the situation on the ground would seem desirable before rushing into a supervisory solution that might not be practicable (apart from being possibly unconstitutional, unless the states sign on to it as some of them have to the broader cooperative reform programme[36]). Also, as discussed below, while NABARD does have a presence in the field, it is not clear whether it is willing to employ the resources necessary to supplement it if required by the added workload. The decision should hinge on which agency is likely to have greater commitment, resources, and expertise.[37]

As already noted, one of the purposes of the bill is to create a database in the public domain containing essential information such as the number and type of MFOs of different kinds, the number of borrowers (and now savers), the quantum of lending and savings (or in other words something as basic as the size of the sector), and a host of other variables the lack of which is an important gap in the knowledge base essential for sound policy making for the sector.[38]

However, despite the reporting requirements in the MACS acts, data on MACS is as deficient as it is on societies and trusts. It would seem advisable, therefore, to find a way of at least including cooperatives in respect of the reporting requirements of the bill, and perhaps also those relating to its consumer protection provisions, since not all cooperatives, whether traditional or MACS, have as good and responsive a governance as those organized by CDF.[39] At the very least, the actual position with respect to this and other issues needs to be examined at the field level and discussed much more widely and openly than they have been so far.

9.2.5 Who should the regulator be?

The bill initially prepared by Sa-Dhan envisaged that the regulator would be the Micro Finance Development Council itself, which would have body corporate status, and consist of a chairperson, not more than five whole-time members, and not more than four part-time members. All the members were to be persons of experience in microfinance and related disciplines, with not less than half representing the microfinance, NGO or the rural development sectors. Members would hold office for up to 5 years. The Council would be much more than an advisory body. Apart from all the powers of the regulator listed above, it would be the registering authority for MFOs and MFIs as well as for the empanelment of rating agencies and chartered accountants.

Although it would have been the appointing authority of the Council, the government felt unable to cede regulatory authority to an independent professional authority and opted for NABARD as the regulator in the version of the bill that was submitted to parliament. Considerable unease has been expressed in the sector at his choice, primarily on grounds of its conflict of interest with NABARD's role as the promoter and champion of one particular model of microfinance, the SHG–Bank linkage model. Other observers have identified the alleged source of conflict as coming from the opposite direction, from the fact that NABARD is an investor in, and lender to, MFIs through the MFDEF. However, this is an unlikely source of bias – the major criticism of the MFDEF is that it has been extremely slow so far in getting off the ground on account of excessive caution by NABARD on account of bureaucracy and lack of familiarity with the MFI model. Besides the MFDEF board has non-official sector representatives on it.

The bill initially prepared by Sa-Dhan envisaged that the regulator would be the Micro Finance Development Council itself, which would have body corporate status, and consist of a chairperson, not more than five whole-time members, and not more than four part-time members. All the members were to be persons of experience in microfinance and related disciplines, with not less than half representing the microfinance, NGO, or the rural development sectors

What is surprising, however, is that after NABARD had been named the regulator in the pending bill, it announced that it was planning to float a huge retail MFI of its own called NABARD Financial Services, or NABFINS, as an NBFC. The proposal was reportedly motivated by a desire to act as a role model to the sector.[40] As has been pointed out NABFINSs would be more of a role model if it were to be set up in one of the underserved parts of the country. Being a majority owner of an MFI would be a clear conflict of interest for NABARD.

Some observers have argued that the regulator ought to be the RBI.[41] The RBI, of course, already regulates MFI–NBFCs, along with thousands of other NBFCs. Even if it is able to create a separate category of NBFCs with requirements more suited to microfinance, as recommended below, their number is not likely to exceed more than a few dozen for at least some years, which is surely a manageable supervisory task. However, it would not seem feasible for the RBI to supervise MFOs, even without cooperatives.

Sa-Dhan in its submission to the Standing Committee is reported to sought to have attempted to partly retrieve the original concept of an independent authority by urging that 50 percent of the members of the Council's proposed 14 members be selected from the microfinance sector (instead of, as currently proposed, 7 from officialdom, 6 non-official experts and a chairman) and also that the Council's decisions should be binding on the implementing agencies under the act. It is unlikely that this good suggestion will be accepted.

9.2.6 What about supervision?

"*it is relatively easy and interesting to craft regulations, but harder and less attractive to do the concrete practical planning for effective supervision...the result may be regulation that is not enforced, which can be worse than no regulation at all*"

There has been virtually no discussion of what arrangements NABARD envisages to implement its regulatory responsibilities through supervision. As CGAP (2003) points out "it is relatively easy and interesting to craft regulations, but harder and less attractive to do the concrete practical planning for effective supervision... the result may be regulation that is not enforced, which can be worse than no regulation at all." We have already touched on the problems of regulating thousands of thrift cooperatives. To supervise societies and trusts, field supervisory personnel will have to be trained in microfinance methods and operations, and special skills such as portfolio testing. NABARD does have a field presence in the districts but it may have to supplement it, not just to carry out supervisory responsibilities but to assist the ombudspersons and participate in the data-gathering effort. The extra costs will have to be realistically estimated, and provided for.

9.2.7 Consumer protection

Although the bill does not explicitly use the term consumer protection, and the final version of the bill now merely enables the appointment of one or more ombudspersons rather than make it mandatory, and that too only for NGO–MFIs, it specifies several of the important features of a consumer protection regime by suggesting such measures as a code of conduct, disseminating information on fair practices, and promoting consumer education. The last three of these are also a fruitful area for collaboration between the regulator and the industry through self-regulation.

Among the positive effects of the Krishna district episode in March 2006 (Chapter 4 of last year's report) was the fact that many of its lessons for MFI practices were recognized and codified in Sa-Dhan's interim code of conduct (Box 4.1 of last year's report). The interim code emphasized among other things the need to (i) avoid over-financing of the same household by different MFIs, (ii) make interest rates more transparent, (iii) ensure that staff do not use abusive language or intimidation tactics while collecting repayments, (iv) ensure high standards of corporate governance by including on MFI boards eminent independent board members, and (v) stay in touch with government authorities, banks, and the media on a regular basis.

The interim code was replaced with a statement of "core values and a voluntary mutual code of conduct" released at Sa-Dhan's annual conference in January 2007. The first part of the statement, relating to core values reiterated that MFI services will be delivered in an "ethical, dignified, transparent, equitable, and cost effective" manner. Clients should be educated about the terms of loans offered to them, and a balance struck between respect for a client's dignity, an understanding of her vulnerability, and a "reasonable pursuit" of loan recovery.

The Code of Conduct itself is part II of the statement, parts of which are reproduced in Box 9.4. Part III of the statement provides for the setting up of an Ethics and Grievance Redressal Committee to look into cases of non-compliance by member MFIs, leading to expulsion from Sa-Dhan if warranted.

Box 9.4   Sa-Dhan's voluntary mutual code of conduct

"To ensure that all our activities and dealings with clients are in compliance with the above core values, we all agree to adopt the code of conduct as elaborated hereunder...:

2.1 We all agree to

(i)   Promote and strengthen the microfinance movement in the country by bringing the low-income clients to the mainstream financial sector.

(ii) Build progressive, sustainable, and client-centric microfinance institutions in the country to provide integrated financial services to our clients.

(iii) Promote cooperation and coordination among microfinance institutions and other agencies to achieve higher operating standards and avoid unethical competition in order to serve our clients better.

2.2 In order to achieve the aforesaid, we all agree to follow the following practices mentioned below:

2.2.1 Integrity

We agree to

(i)   Act honestly, fairly, and reasonably in conducting microfinance activities.

(ii) Conduct our microfinance activities by means of fair competition, not seeking competitive advantages through illegal or unethical microfinance practices. No officer, employee, agent or other person acting on our behalf shall take unfair advantage of anyone by manipulation, concealment, abuse of privileged information, misrepresentation of material facts, or any other unfair practice.

(iii) Prominently display the core values and code of conduct on the notice board of head office and all branches, and put systems in place to ensure compliance.

(iv) Ensure that our staff and any person acting for us or on our behalf are trained or oriented to put these values into practice.

2.2.2 Transparency

We agree to

(i)   Disclose to clients all the terms and conditions of our financial services offered in the language understood by the client.

(ii)   Disclose the source of funds, costs of funds and use of surpluses to provide truthful information to clients.

(iii) Provide information to clients on the rate of interest levied on the loan, calculation of interest (monthly/quarterly/half-yearly), terms of repayment, and any other information related to interest rates and other charges.

(iv)   Provide information to clients on the rate of interest offered on the thrift services provided by us.

(v)   Provide information to clients related to the premium and other fees being charged on insurance and pension services offered by us as intermediaries.

(vi)   Provide periodical statements of our accounts to the clients.

2.2.3 Fair practices

We are committed to follow fair practices built on dignity, respect, fair treatment, persuasion, and courtesy to clients. We agree to

(i)   Provide microfinance services to low-income clients irrespective of gender, race, caste, religion, or language.

(ii)   Ensure that the services are provided using the most efficient methods possible to enable access to financial services by low-income households at reasonable cost.

(iii) Recognize our responsibility to provide financial services to clients based upon their needs and repayment capacity.

(iv)   Promise that, in case of loans to individual clients below Rs. 25,000, the clients shall not be asked to hand over original land titles, house pattas, ration cards, etc. as collateral security for loans except when obtaining copies of these for fulfilling "know your customers" norms of the RBI. Only in case of loan to individual clients of Rs. 25,000 and above can land titles, house pattas, vehicle RC books, etc. be taken as collateral security.

(v)   Interact with the clients in an acceptable language and dignified manner and spare no efforts in fostering clients' confidence and long-term relationship.

(vi)   Maintain decency and decorum during the visit to the clients' place for collection of dues.

(vii) Avoid inappropriate occasions such as bereavement in the family or such other calamitous occasions for making calls/visits to collect dues."

Excerpted from the Statement of Core Values and a Voluntary Mutual Code of Conduct" released at Sa-Dhan's annual conference in January 2007

The existence of a code of conduct should make it unnecessary for the regulator to prepare its own, although it will have to adopt it formally (with modifications if need to be) so as to give it legal sanction, and bring within its purview NGO—MFIs that are not members of Sa-Dhan. As discussed in last year's report, many difficult questions remain in translating the general principles in the code of conduct into specifics, such as when exactly competition become unethical, or what constitutes over-lending, or above what level interest rates become "unreasonable." Individual grievances brought before the ombudsmen (if and when appointed) will also serve to put flesh and bones on these principles, just as the decisions of the courts continue to add to the general law.

A much broader role for self-regulation was envisaged as early as 1998, when a task force was set up by the RBI under the chairmanship of NABARD (Box 9.5). Although nothing came of the initiative, and there are no examples of comprehensive self-regulation being successful anywhere in the world, consumer protection is one area where self-regulation has a major role to play (CGAP 2005b). Now that the sector has experienced at first hand how bad practice by some members can undermine the reputation of sector as a whole, members of the committee will hopefully be more likely than before to overcome any natural reluctance they may feel about making adverse evaluative judgements about their peers, which has been the Achilles Heel of self-regulation in other areas. It is all the more important that they do so in view of the fact that the legal backing of the bill will be available, if at all, only for breaches of the code by NGO—MFI members. The precipitating factor behind the chain of events set into motion by the Krishna district episode on the other hand were allegations of misconduct by NBFC members. The advantage of the Sa-Dhan code is that it applies to all members.

Now that the sector has experienced at first hand how bad practice by some members can undermine the reputation of sector as a whole, members of the committee will hopefully be more likely than before to overcome any natural reluctance they may feel about making adverse evaluative judgements about their peers, which has been the Achilles Heel of self-regulation in other areas

Box 9.5   A bit of history: Self-regulation backed by legal sanctions

In 1998, a task force was set up by the RBI under the chairmanship of NABARD, which proposed that all MFIs (including credit-only MFIs) register themselves with an Self-Regulatory Organizations (SRO) (with recognition of the SROs to be conferred by the central bank). However, MFIs were defined to include only entities with a recognized legal identity, so that CBOs not registered as societies or trusts would continue to operate informally and remain outside the purview of reporting and prudential controls below a certain size. The registration with the SRO would be provisional for the first 3 years, during which time the MFI would either attain the standards specified by the SRO, or have its registration cancelled. Societies and trusts would have to transform themselves into cooperatives or companies once the sum of their deposits and loans exceeded a certain level, tentatively proposed at Rs. 25 lakhs. Prudential norms for all MFIs irrespective of size or form of organization were proposed as follows: (i) a reserve requirement of at least 10 percent of deposits, to be deposited in a bank, (ii) a provision equivalent to the entire principal outstanding and interest thereon for loans which were past due by 90 days at the end of the financial year, (iii) interest recognition on an accrual basis to stop at that time, and (iii) limits on loan sizes to any one individual, group, or other MFI.

It was further envisaged that for a large country like India there could be different SROs recognized by the central bank for different states, given the fact that there was as yet no single apex body of MFIs for the country as a whole. State level Recognized SROs (RSROs) would also be able to take advantage of local knowledge, and of proximity for purposes of on-site visits and inspections. An RSROs would have to establish mandatory standards for its MFI members, which would have to be approved by the central bank. The RSRO would require periodic returns from its members, and would submit periodic summary returns to the central bank. The RSRO would suspend the registration of an MFI which failed to submit returns or comply with prudential norms, and bar it from carrying on further business. The central bank would have the right to derecognize an RSRO if more than say one-fifth of its members were reported to be in non-compliance of standards.

Clearly, a great deal of further consensus building and preparatory work remained to be done and the RBI never took a view on the task force recommendations. Given the uneven spread of MFIs in India, it might have been possible to start with one or more regions which had a relatively high concentration of MFIs and a few that were role models, and then proceed incrementally, developing and revising performance standards and prudential norms on the basis of experience, identifying potential SRO members in other regions, and training them and MFIs generally.

Thus, the proposed regulatory framework recognized the advantages to MFIs of starting up as societies and trusts, given the relative ease of registration under these forms of organization, but required them to transform into cooperatives or non-profit companies or non-bank financial companies above a certain level of total business. This was also the approach taken in the initial bill prepared by Sa-Dhan with the difference that it gave NGO–MFIs the special-window option of registering as an "MFI" which would be a company with an entry capital of Rs. 25 operating in conformity with requirements custom-made to microfinance. Unfortunately this concept was dropped.

9.7 Two other regulatory issues are as important as the microfinance bill

There are two important areas of reform that would have a more immediate impact on financial inclusion, at least in respect of credit services, than the bill as presently drafted, essential though legislation is in the long run, if microfinance in India is to "enter the arena of licensed, prudentially supervised financial intermediation" (CGAP 2003) as it has in most other countries with microfinance acts. Both areas lie within the jurisdiction of the RBI. The first is less intractable politically, and depends very much on the attitude and stance of the RBI towards commercial microfinance through for-profit institutions such as NBFCs. The real questions with respect to the first area, therefore, is RBI's vision of the role of microfinance in India as discussed in Chapter 1.

If the RBI wanted to, it could easily create a new category of Microfinance NBFC more suited to microfinance than that the RBI's present NBFC guidelines. If the microfinance bill is not amended to include NBFCs, or enacted at all, the RBI could take the liberal view that thrift contributions do not constitute public deposits,[42] and allow these new MFI–NBFCs to mobilize member-savings. After all, this is the implicit view taken by the bill with respect to NGO–MFI member-savings, and would be in keeping with the RBI's own bold view taken in the mid-1990s that SHG member savings do not constitute public savings because SHGs partake of the nature of member-owned mutual institutions despite being purely informal. Without this interpretation by the RBI at the time, the SHG–Bank linkage programme would never have happened. As noted earlier, the regulatory task of supervising the relatively small number of new MFI–NBFCs will remain manageable.[43]

The second area is more sensitive politically, and relates to the interest cap on loans below Rs. 2 lakhs for commercial banks, which is fixed at the prime lending rate. This issue has been discussed in detail elsewhere, including last year's report, and will not be expanded upon here, but it is important to note that it relates to a restriction that is self-imposed by the RBI, although the RBI would no doubt want to consult the government before removing it. The main effect of the restriction is to deny credit to poor borrowers, and its removal is likely to see a significant expansion of micro and small loans, whose share in total lending and number of accounts has been steadily declining. It will be interesting to see whether the Committee on Financial Inclusion will have the political will to include it in its recommendations.[44]

Because the cap applies to the business correspondent model too, it has effectively killed that model on the lending side. As discussed in last year's report (Chapter 7A) the PLR does not allow enough headroom for the bank to compensate the correspondent for its loan initiation, monitoring, and collection services.

9.8 Conclusion[45]

The bill makes a small beginning in introducing savings to less than half the sector, but in far too limited a form. Savings are defined much too narrowly as "thrift" or small compulsory periodic savings. One does not have to agree with much of the microfinance literature which argues that these contributions are not savings at all, but are viewed by most borrowers as part of the cost of borrowing, which they passively accept as a condition of accessing loans rather than value for their own sake. This does not seem to be generally true in India, where savings have been the most successful part of the SHG programme (too successful it could be argued, because productive opportunities to use the savings haven't kept pace with their growth). But it is the case that the inflexibility of compulsory savings has kept the poorest out of the programme, as many surveys show.

So ambivalent is the bill about savings that it does not use the word "savings" even once. Even "thrift" is not included in the bill in the definition of "microfinance services." It has even been suggested that the primary motivation of the RBI, if not of the government, in promoting the bill, is to address the concern expressed by some that the whole SHG programme is illegal, because it allegedly violates the Banking Regulation Act. This concern is unfounded, since SHGs, although purely informal and unregistered, are mutual organizations. As noted above, it was this bold view taken by the then RBI governor that allowed the banks to lend to SHGs and give rise to the largest, and so far one of the most successful, microfinance programmes in the world. The approach at present seems timid in comparison.

So ambivalent is the bill about savings that it does not use the word "savings" once. Even "thrift" is not included in the bill in the definition of "microfinance services"

Second, by excluding companies, the bill not only denies a large part of the sector the direct benefits of the bill (mobilization of member savings, and possibly consumer protection if the regulator decides to provide it), it denies the sector as a whole the indirect sector-wide benefits. While some "orderly growth" activities could be taken care of by the RBI for NBFCs, such as setting performance and accounting standards, it is unlikely to be able to set up a consumer protection regime or build a database, even for the MFI–NBFCs under its purview,[46] for lack of supervisory resources.

The bill confers a modicum of legitimacy on the most vulnerable part of the sector, the NGO–MFIs, but is careful not to step on the toes of the states by failing to assert that the principle of cost-recovering interest rates takes precedence over caps on interest rates under state moneylender acts, although this principle has recently been implicitly recognized by the Technical Group to Review Legislations on Moneylending (RBI 2007).[47] The group has recommended that societies and trusts should be exempted from the purview of moneylender acts, and that state governments in setting interest rate caps, should "look at the range of interest rates being charged by microfinance entities."

The bill violates the spirit and intent of the new MACS acts in reducing the role of government in cooperation. It is true that the registrars under the new acts are not performing supervisory, data gathering, and consumer protection functions any better than the old ones, but will the new regulator be able to do a better job for thousands of thrift cooperatives all over the country? In any case cooperation is a state subject, and the states will have to sign on, unless the courts take the narrow view that accepting thrift even from one's own member—borrowers constitutes "banking," which is a central subject.

The bill does not provide the sector with a form of registration uniquely suited to microfinance. It leaves NGO—MFIs with no alternative between remaining NGOs and having to raise enough capital to become NBFCs.[48] Societies and trusts were not designed as vehicles for financial operations, and although NGO—MFIs are non-profits, they have a hard time convincing the local income tax authorities that their surpluses are intended for expansion and leverage of borrowed funds. Yet Rs. 2 crores is too much for many NGOs to raise, especially as an NGO is not allowed to contribute its accumulated surpluses to the equity of a new NBFC for tax reasons.[49] Rs. 25 lakhs as the entry capital requirement for the special-window "MFIs" envisaged seemed about right when the first version of the bill was formulated. However, it could be increased to Rs. 50 lakhs now. Special-window MFIs would constitute a valuable intermediate stage of incorporation between remaining an NGO and becoming a full-fledged NBFC.

Given these and other limitations of the bill, and the fact that amendments to an act once passed are not easy to make, many observers feel that it may be desirable for the sector to wait a little longer till further debate, advocacy, and field studies, where necessary, lead to a better understanding of microfinance among policymakers, and indeed among many sector players themselves

Finally, as we have seen the nature and composition of the Microfinance Development Council leave much to be desired. Given these and other limitations of the bill, and the fact that amendments to an act once passed are not easy to make, many observers feel that it may be desirable for the sector to wait a little longer till further debate, advocacy, and field studies, where necessary, lead to a better understanding of microfinance among policymakers, and indeed among many sector players themselves. They would argue that some of the benefits of the bill can be partly provided through self-regulation, such as those relating to consumer protection and the "orderly growth" activities, and that the costs of postponing enactment of the bill are lower than enacting it without major amendments. The main cost would be the loss of the limited go-ahead to "thrift" services, and of the modicum of legitimacy the bill should impart to public and state level bureaucratic perceptions of microfinance.

It is not an easy choice, but at least it needs to be widely debated by the sector before the parliamentary committee completes its work.

Endnotes

1   *For a detailed discussion of the "twists and turns" taken by the bill up to January 2007, see Sinha (2007a). Generally, this is a good source on recent regulatory concerns. Other sources for background on regulatory issues in Indian microfinance are Radcliffe and Tripathi (2006) and Eschborn (2004). Small parts of this chapter are taken from two articles by the author, Ghate (2007a, b).*

2   *Another reason for doing so is that the State of the Sector report is intended to serve as a sort of "moving" reference document for posterity, through a series of annual snapshots. It is recognized, though, that this chapter may well be out of date soon after it appears. Apart from being amended the bill could expire unless reintroduced.*

3   *Bill No. 41 of 2007.*

4   *The title of the bill has, therefore, become a misnomer – it does not apply to the bulk of the sector.*

5   *Thrift is defined as "any money collected (other than in the form of current account or demand deposit) by a microfinance organization from a group" and a "group" is defined to mean "any association of eligible clients formed either as self-help groups or joint liability groups or a group called by any other name for the purpose of providing thrift and microfinance services to individual members of such association".*

6   *The Ministry of Finance did not make copies of the bill available to sector participants other than to Sa-Dhan, and Sa-Dhan felt constrained not to share the bill with non-members (members are almost entirely MFIs and a few service providers, which leaves out a large number of sector participants affected by the bill such as cooperatives, banks, equity investors, rating agencies, consultants, researchers, microfinance policy analyst, etc.). A Ministry of Finance spokesman said at the annual Sa-Dhan conference in January 2007 that the bill had not been put onto the ministry's web-site in order to save time. During the whole process of discussion of the bill, several versions of the bill were floating around simultaneously, making for much confusion. It was only when the bill reached parliament that copies of it became available. The Standing Committee on Finance has initiated a process of widespread consultation on the bill by inviting a cross section of sector participants and interested observers to send in their views and appear before it, if required. Civil society organizations have been urging persons to send in their views to the committee.*

7   *These are defined as credit, insurance, pension, and any other services that may be specified by the regulator. This leaves open the possibility of adding money transfer services. It is surprising that savings services are not mentioned, not even as "thrift."*

8   *These are to be the two officers nominated by the ministries of finance and rural development, two representing NABARD and one each nominated by the RBI, SIDBI, and the National Housing Bank.*

9   *The Indian microfinance sector has seen a steady migration of NGO–MFIs in the last few years from the society and trust form of registration to the company form of incorporation, most of them becoming NBFCs, but many of them preferring to retain their not-for-profit status as S25 companies. The transformation is taking place worldwide, for several reasons. First, companies have to meet more stringent disclosure, transparency, and audit requirements, more suited to financial operations, than those laid*

down for registered societies and trusts, which were designed for charitable, welfare, or educational activities. Second, by providing for capital or equity in the form of shares, companies encourage a stronger sense of ownership on the part of promoters, leading usually to stronger governance and management. An NGO has no "owner" of the net owned funds built up out of grants and operational surpluses. This combination of advantages gives banks and financial institutions lending to MFIs the essential comfort without which the sector will never attract the funds to expand fast enough to make a rapid dent on poverty and challenge of financial inclusion. The steady stream of transformations has been assisted by the advent of private investors, both social and commercial, who are willing to provide transforming as well as start-up MFIs not just the Rs. 2 crores required as entry level capital, but the much greater investments required to give them the capital adequacy to support the more than Rs. 3000 crores of borrowing by MFIs that took place last year (see last year's report), and the projected rapid growth in the near future.

10 *These figures are derived from Sa-Dhan's Quick Report 2007 and represent the share of 17 NBFCs and 13 S25 companies out of a total 129 MFIs in the survey (Sa-Dhan 2007).*

11 *While a similar study does not exist for India, evidence exists for Uganda that of the formal, semi-formal (MFI), and informal sectors in Uganda, the last was the riskiest for savers (Wright and Mutesasira).*

12 *Nearly all large Indian MFIs have been rated not just once but several times in order to qualify for loans from SIDBI, which makes a satisfactory rating a condition for its lending, as do increasingly many of the banks.*

13 *According to World Bank 2007, "there is an increasing sense worldwide that NGOs mobilizing deposits from members need not be regulated like banks..."*

14 *See "City Savers" by Rutherford and Arora (1997). Savings safe-keepers are referred to as "money guards" in Africa. In India door step cumulative savings collectors have given rise to huge organizations like Peerless and Sahara.*

15 *See Ghate (1992) for a comprehensive review of different types of informal finance in India and five other Asian countries, Das-Gupta et al. (1989) on urban informal finance in India, Bouman (1998) on the bishis of Maharasthra, and Rutherford and Arora (1997) on urban informal savings mechanisms in India.*

16 *Restrictions proposed in the initial version of the bill on maximum savings per member and the aggregate savings liability outstanding of the MFI as a ratio of net owned funds and total assets, and a liquidity reserve requirement, have been dropped, presumably because they are hard to monitor. The liquidity reserve would have been desirable, since liquidity is a particularly highly valued attribute of savings among the poor, as discussed in Section 9.2.3.*

17 *For most MFIs, a small proportion of borrowers will be between loan cycles, and some others as they approach the end of the repayment cycle will temporarily have more savings to their credit than loans. A ceiling could be fixed for the proportion of net savers. Compliance could be monitored through periodic returns and occasional on-site checks where necessary. There are some MFIs in other countries, those offering "open access" savings (see below) such as BURO Tangail in Bangladesh, whose savings products are so popular that they have a fairly high proportion of net savers and indeed of pure savers at any one time. However, these will be special cases for the foreseeable future, especially in India, which is a late starter in offering savings services, and they can always be dealt with through special exemptions after due diligence on a case-by-case basis.*

18 Liquidity is an important attribute of savings for the reasons discussed below. The bill proposes that 15 percent of profits be transferred to a reserve fund, but this is not quite the same thing as a reserve fund created out of savings, since profits and surpluses may not accrue for several years initially. Transfers to the fund should come from savings, not profits.

19 These were some of the findings of EDA (2005), the first and most comprehensive impact evaluation so far of SIDBI's MFI partners (who conduct lending through SHGs as well as JLGs). The second evaluation of the SIDBI project, which was undertaken by the Agriculture Finance Corporation, has yet to be released by SIDBI although it was completed in August 2006.

20 Although, initially, there is a massive out-rush as clients "test" the system to see if they really will be permitted to withdraw their savings!

21 Nearly, all Bangladeshi MFIs offer a variety of savings opportunities to their borrowers apart from compulsory savings, as "special savings," contractual savings, time deposits, and daily savings.

22 These systems include (i) strong governance and management, (ii) high portfolio quality, (iii) liquidity management (asset and liability management) skills, (iv) good information systems, and (v) strong internal controls.

23 Some of them have already done so. Although, the largest MFIs are mostly companies, some of the largest are still societies and trusts and intend to stay that way, especially as the bill will deny them the opportunity to mobilize thrift if they transform. Also, there is a possibility that the bill may be amended to include NBFCs and S25 companies, who do have such capacities. The attainment of profitability is a requirement that it often also suggested as a requirement for being allowed to mobilize voluntary savings.

24 While there is an agreement that federations should not usurp the function of the groups to make loans to their individual members, and should only make loans to their groups, some groups themselves want their federations to lend to individual members, usually by accessing loans from the banks, who feel more comfortable tracking loans in the name of individuals rather than groups (see Chapter 3).

25 This had been taken to mean that it will not apply to PACS, although a large part of PACS lending is for non-crop rural activities, or in other words constitutes microcredit in the usual sense of credit for non-crop activities. Both cooperative banks (district and state level) as well as PACS are part of the ongoing cooperative reform project – see endnote 27).

26 Speech by Thomas Carter of CLUSA at a conference of railway employees' thrift societies in Hyderabad on 6–7 February, 1986, who pointed out that it was from a trip to Bengal in the early 1900s that Edward Filene, the pioneer leader of thrift cooperatives in the US, drew his inspiration (circulated by CDF).

27 Carter in his speech in 1986 (see endnote 26) said, "I believe there are more than 23,000 thrift cooperatives in the country with close to 150 lakh members and savings of more than Rs. 1250 crores."

28 The package is being supported by the World Bank's $600 million "Strengthening Rural Cooperatives" project and an ADB loan. According to a World Bank press note dated on the project "Twelve Indian states have signed up to the reform program. Potentially viable CCBs" (defined to include PACS, DCCBs, and SCBs)" in those states will commit to a set of far-reaching legal, regulatory, governance and institutional reforms which will open the way to financial and operational restructuring. In the process, the CCBs will be recapitalized with grants to wipe out the accumulated losses, the value of

members' capital will be restored, and a minimum capital to risk weighted assets ratio (CRAR) of 7 percent will be achieved. The project will also provide technical assistance throughout the process to strengthen CCB governance, managerial, and operational performance, and support computerization for enhanced efficiency and transparency. CCB members, particularly small and marginal farmers, will receive training in areas such as financial literacy, and a strong project focus on monitoring and evaluation systems will include monitoring by CCB members themselves.

29 See note by Shashi Rajagopalan, "The Bill Relating to Micro-Finance Organizations," circulated by CDF. As she points out, the amount of thrift is agreed to by all members is usually the same for all members in absolute terms, or, in the case employees savings and credit cooperatives, a fixed percentage of their pay.

30 Or "self-reliant" or "self-help" or "self-supporting" or "autonomous" or "fraternal."

31 The MACS registrar has fewer powers than the registrar under the existing act in keeping with the lack of dependence of MACS on government. Indeed, MACS cannot accept government equity.

32 According to a personal communication from Shri Rama Reddy, President, CDF, "The Registrar under the MACS Act is entitled to receive annual financial statements from every MACS cooperative within 30 days from the holding of the annual general meeting; is empowered to get a special audit conducted at the cost of the MACS cooperative; is empowered to conduct an enquiry into specific affairs of a MACS cooperative; is empowered to convene a special general body meeting to explain to the members how their cooperative is being mismanaged; is empowered to request the Cooperative Tribunal to order the liquidation of a MACS cooperative if that MACS cooperative is not being run in accordance with the concept of cooperation and the provisions of the MACS Act."

33 Or "nominal members," "associate members," "B class members," etc.

34 According to Rama Reddy, "Neither the SHG Federation, nor the promoting GO, nor the promoting NGO, nor the registering DCO is interested in the functioning of the village organization as a MACS cooperative. They do not need any supervision and/or regulation, since they themselves are part and parcel of the governmental organizations or of the non-governmental organizations. On the one hand, as a policy, the State Government is interested in getting village organizations registered as MACS cooperatives and on the other hand, again as a matter of policy, the same government puts a ban on the registration of citizen-promoted genuine thrift cooperatives and dairy cooperatives under the MACS Act" (Personal communication).

35 Of the 129 MFIs covered by Sa-Dhan's Quick Report, 21 were MACS with 1.6 percent of the total number of borrowers, and 4 of them cooperatives with 3.9 percent. However, as noted above, there are thousands of thrift cooperatives in the country.

36 At least one state, AP, as noted above, is said to be opposed to it.

37 CGAP (2003) suggests a fourth alternative. It recommends that "financial cooperatives – at least large ones – should be prudentially supervised by a specialized financial authority, rather than by an agency that is responsible for all cooperatives."

38 There is no firm estimate even of the population of MFOs in the country.

39 According to one observer, "it is next to impossible to have a database at state level itself, leave alone the national level. The long and tortuous experience of the RBI, up to 1982, and of NABARD since 1982, in collecting, collating, and publishing basic data relating to three-tier rural cooperative thrift

and credit system (approximately 90,000 PACS, 375 DCCBs and 30 SCBs) should tell us that we are on very slippery ground as far as a database is concerned. From 1966 to 1982, the RBI supervised and regulated DCCBs and SCBs and, since 1982, they are being supervised by the NABARD and regulated by the RBI"... "The RBI and NABARD published data over a long period... Most of it is guesstimates manufactured manually till computers arrived. After the arrival of computers, the projections based on already manufactured data are presented as hard, primary data." (Rama Reddy, comments on this chapter). However, Misra (2007) observes that the MACS she studied do file audited annual returns to the registrar. She does not say whether they are scrutinized.

40 *According to a report in the Hindu dated 3 July, NABFINS would provide microcredit at "reasonable" rates with an authorized capital of Rs. 100 crores. It would have an issue capital of Rs. 20 crores and of which 51 percent would be subscribed to by NABARD and the rest by several banks and state governments. The MFI would start functioning in the two months by taking up a pilot project in Karnataka. In the second phase, it would be extended to Andhra Pradesh and Tamil Nadu and gradually other states. The Chairman of NABARD is reported to have pointed out that the major defects of MFIs are lack of transparency in account disclosures, high transaction costs, high rates of interest and coercive collection practices. "We want to show that an MFI can function without any defects and deliver microcredit at affordable interest rates and without coercive collection practices. The interest rates would be affordable, as the idea was to reduce transaction costs," he added.*

41 *See, for instance, Sinha (2007b). He suggests that the RBI's refusal to engage with microfinance is influenced by the recent failures of urban cooperative banks for which the RBI was blamed. He points out that its fear is unfounded for the reasons discussed earlier and also because it sends out the message that the "the lowly world of the poor does not need its attention."*

42 *"Banking" is defined in the Banking Regulation Act, 1949, as "the accepting, for the purpose of lending or investment, of deposits of money from the public, repayable on demand or otherwise, and withdrawable by cheque, draft, order, or otherwise."*

43 *The RBI has often been urged, further, to reduce the entry capital requirement from Rs. 2 crores at present to perhaps Rs. 50 lakhs to speed up the process of transformation of NGO–MFIs to incorporation as NBFCs. The initial version of the bill, as we have seen, envisaged entry capital for the new-window "MFIs" it envisaged, as Rs. 25 lakhs, but that was 2 years ago, and most MFIs should not find it difficult to raise Rs. 50 lakhs. However, the RBI takes the view that S 45-I A of the RBI Act, 1934, does not give it the latitude to distinguish between the various categories of NBFC in this respect. It points out that it sought such powers through a draft Financial Companies Regulation Bill submitted to the previous parliament, but the bill could not be enacted before the NDA government fell. The RBI could also lay down higher provisioning requirements for Microfinance-NBFCs.*

44 *The cap only applies to the commercial banks, and not to the RRBs or DCCBs, and only to priority sector loans, and not to personal loans. However, meeting priority sector targets is an important motivation for the commercial banks who accounted for 28 percent of all loans below Rs. 25,000, with the RRBs accounting for another 9 percent, in March 2006 (Speech by Deputy Governor, RBI at Sa-Dhan Annual Meeting, Chennai, 10 August 2007, Thorat 2007). Were the restriction removed, the number of commercial bank microloans is likely to increase dramatically (see Sinha 2007a, 2007b). The RBI has taken a step to remove the cap recently by allowing the banks to issue General Purpose Credit Cards (GCCs) with limits up to Rs. 25,000 and allowing 50 percent of the amounts utilized to be included in the priority sector. It is not known whether the scheme has taken off.*

45 *This recommendation in this section is based on the assumption that there will be no major amendments to the bill. It there are, the conclusion would have to be reviewed.*

46 The RBI did come out in May 2006 after the Krishna district episode with guidelines for NBFCs to abide by a "fair practices" code, but it does not have a field presence in the districts in the way the ombudsman could.

47 Also known as the SC Gupta committee report on the proposal for the states to register moneylenders as accredited loan providers out of funds borrowed form the banks.

48 Non-profit S25 company status requires no entry capital, and has provision for equity, but its prohibition of dividends makes it unattractive to investors and therefore to lenders also.

49 It is understood that in its interim suggestions the Committee for Financial Inclusion (headed by former RBI governor, C Rangarajan) has proposed amendments to S11(4) of the Income Tax Act so as to allow NGOs to invest in microfinance companies without prejudicing their tax status, S2(15) specifying microfinance as a charitable activity, and some others relating to tax concessions to NBFCs.

50 It was only at this stage that copies of the bill became freely available to the wider microfinance community, as the Standing Committee on Finance began inviting the views and suggestions of experts and persons and groups who wanted to be heard....

51 Chart is not included here.

References

APMAS, 2005, "A Report on Spandana's Microfinance Activity," Mimeo, APMAS, Hyderabad

APMAS, 2006, "Voice of the People on the Lending Practices of Microfinance Institutions in Krishna District of Andhra Pradesh," Mimeo, APMAS, Hyderabad

Bouman, FJA, 1989, "Small, Short, and Unsecured: Informal Rural Finance in India," Oxford University Press, New Delhi

CGAP, 2003, "Microfinance Consensus Guidelines: Guiding Principles on Regulation and Supervision of Microfinance," Washington, DC

CGAP, 2004, "Interest Rate Ceilings and Microfinance: The Story So Far," Occasional Paper, Washington DC

CGAP, 2005a, "Microfinance Consensus Guidelines: Developing Deposit Services for the Poor," Washington, DC

CGAP 2005b, "Protecting Microfinance Borrowers," Focus Note No. 27, Washington, DC

Das-Gupta, Arindam, CPS Nayar, and Associates, 1989, "Urban Informal Credit Markets in India," Study prepared for ADB by NIPFP, New Delhi

EDA Rural Systems, 2005, "The Maturing of Indian Microfinance: Findings of a microfinance assessment study (baseline) – implications for policy and practice," Study carried out for SIDBI, Gurgaon

EDA Rural Systems and APMAS, 2006, "Self-Help Groups in India: The Lights and Shades," for CRS, USAID, CARE and GTZ/NABARD, Microfinance India, New Delhi

Eschborn, 2004, "Emerging Scenarios for Microfinance Regulation in India: Some Observations from the Field," GTZ, Federal Ministry for International Cooperation, Germany

Ghate, Prabhu, 1992, "Informal Finance: Some Findings from Asia," OUP Hong Kong, for ADB, Manila

Ghate, Prabhu 2006, "Microfinance in India: A State of the Sector Report, 2006," Microfinance India, New Delhi, and "Indian Microfinance: The Challenges of Rapid Growth," Sage, New Delhi

Ghate, Prabhu, 2007a, "Consumer Protection in Indian Microfinance: Lessons from Andhra Pradesh and the Microfinance Bill," *Economic and Political Weekly*, March 31, Mumbai

Ghate, Prabhu, 2007b, "Financial inclusion via exclusion?" *Economic Times*, July 19, New Delhi

Misra, Rewa, 2007, "Case of SHGs and MACS — Does Federating Enable Remote Outreach?" paper for the Comparative Study of Member-Owned Institutions Offering Financial Services in Remote Rural Areas, Coady International Institute/Ford Foundation, Antigonish

PRS Legislative Research, 2007, "Legislative Brief: The Micro Financial Sector (Development and Regulation) Bill, 2007," Centre for Policy Research, New Delhi

Radcliffe, Daniel, and Rati Tripathi, 2006, "Sharpening the Debate: Accessing the Key Constraints in Indian Micro Credit Regulation," Centre for MicroFinance, Chennai

Rutherford, Stuart and Sukhwinder Singh Arora, 1997, "City Savers: How the poor, the DFID and its partners are promoting financial services in urban India," Discussion paper prepared for Urban Poverty Office, DFID, New Delhi

Rutherford, Stuart, 2005, "Why Do the Poor Need Savings Services? What They Get and What They Might Like," in Madeline Hirschland, editor, "Savings Services for the Poor," Kumarian Press, Bloomfield

Rutherford, Stuart, "Member Savings," MicroSave Briefing Notes on Grameen II # 2, MicroSave, Kenya, Uganda and India

Sa-Dhan, 2007, "Quick Report, 2007: A Snapshot of MFIs in India," New Delhi

Sinha, Sanjay, 2007a, "Microfinance Regulation for Financial Inclusion: The Street Child Needs Nurturing," Essays on Regulation and Supervision No. 22, CGAP and IRIS Center, Washington, DC, carried on www.cgap.org/regulation

Sinha, Sanjay, 2007b, "The financial exclusion bill," *Economic Times*, June 1, New Delhi

Sriram, MS, 2005, "Expanding Financial Services Access for the Poor: The Transformation of Spandana," WP No 2005-04-03, IIMA, Ahmedabad

Thorat, Usha, 2007, "Microfinance and financial inclusion," Speech at Sa-Dhan function to release "Quick Report, 2007," Chennai

Thorat, YSP and Wright, Graham, 2006 "Cooperatives — The Flawed Gem of Indian Rural Finance," MicroSave Briefing Note No. 56, MicroSave, Kenya, Uganda, and India

World Bank, 2007, "Microfinance in South Asia: Toward Financial Inclusion for the Poor," Washington DC

Wright, Graham, 2000, "Microfinance Systems: Designing Quality Financial Services for the Poor," University Press, Dhaka

Wright, Graham, and Leonard Mutesasira, "The Relative Risks to the Savings of Poor People," MicroSave Briefing Note No. 6, MicroSave, Kenya, Uganda, and India

Table A.1 Fact Sheet on Coverage and Growth of SHGs and MFIs, March 2006–07

Outreach

1	Cumulative number of persons in linked SHGs	41 million[1]
2	Total number of SHG members, currently linked	26.1 million[2]
3	Total number of MFI borrowers	11.5 million[3]
4	Total number of active MFI borrowers	8.3 million[4]
5	Total number of poor SHG members, currently linked	13.3 million[5]
6	Total number of poor, active, MFI borrowers	2.5 million[6]
7	Total number of poor current microfinance borrowers of SHGs and MFIs	15.8 million[7]
8	Growth of outreach of the SHG programme in 2006–07	31 percent[8]
9	Growth of outreach of MFIs, 2006–07	40–80 percent[9]

Loan outstanding

10	Loans outstanding under the SHG programme, March 2007	Rs. 10640 cr[10]
11	Loans outstanding under the MFI model	Rs. 3987 cr[11]
12	Growth of loans outstanding under the SHG programme in 2006–07	58 percent[12]
13	Growth of loans outstanding of MFIs in 2006–07	40–92 percent[13]
14	Average loans outstanding, SHG members	Rs. 4000[14]
15	Average loans outstanding, MFI borrower	Rs. 3400–5300[15]

Source:

1. Sa-Dhan, 2007, "Quick Report 2007: A Snapshot of Microfinance Institutions in India," New Delhi.

2. M-CRIL and MIX, 2007, "Indian Microfinance Review, 2007," M-CRIL, Gurgaon and MIX (Microfinance Information eXchange Inc.), Washington, DC.

Notes:

[1] 2.92 million SHGs ever linked (Table 2.1) times an average of 14 members each.

[2] Seventy-one percent of SHGs in row 1 estimated to be currently linked (Chapter 2), minus 10 percent estimated to have dropped out.

[3] Sa-Dhan's estimate of 10.49 million members served by 184 Sa-Dhan member MFIs as reported in Sa-Dhan's *Quick Report 2007* (Sa-Dhan 2007) adjusted upwards by 10 percent for members in MFIs that do not belong to Sa-Dhan.

[4] 11.5 million (row 3) times 0.72 estimated as the proportion of active borrowers to total members from M-CRIL/MIX's *Indian Microfinance Review* 2007 (M-CRIL and MIX, 2007).

[5] Row 2 times 0.51, the proportion of SHG members found to be poor by EDA and APMAS (2006).

[6] Thirty percent of active MFI borrowers in row 4. Thirty percent is the average proportion of borrowers below the international poverty line of $1 a day (PPP adjusted) for 12 MFIs recently assessed for their social performance by M-CRIL as reported in Chapter 6. Since the Indian poverty line is slightly lower, the proportion of borrowers below it will be slightly lower (Chapter 6).

[7] However, there are in addition microfinance borrowers of the banks, RRBs and PACs. The following table taken from Thorat (2007) shows the shares of all agencies making microfinance loans (defined for the purpose of the table as loans of below Rs. 25,000), and shows that microfinance borrowers of SHGs and MFIs constitute less than half the total, and that their share would be even lower if only currently linked SHGs were considered.

[8] This is the increase of 71 percent of the cumulative number of SHGs linked in March 2007 over 71 percent linked by March 2006 (Table 2.1).

[9] This is the range for three estimates, ranging from (i) the growth in membership of Sa-Dhan's 184 member MFIs to 10.5 million in March 2007 from 7.37 million (for 150 member MFIs) in March 2006, (ii) the growth in outreach of the 129 MFIs who responded to the survey reported in Sa-Dhan (2007) (60 percent in 2006–07), and (iii) the growth in outreach of M-CRIL and MIXs smaller sample of large MFIs, which was about 80 percent (Chapter 4).

[10] Estimated as 0.59 percent of cumulative bank loan disbursements (Table 2.1), using the ratio reported in Chapter 2.

[11] For Sa-Dhan's total membership in March 2007. Loans outstanding were Rs. 3065 crores for the 129 MFIs surveyed in the Quick Report (Table A.2).

[12] The increase in loans outstanding between March 2006 and March 2007, assuming 0.59 as the ratio of loans outstanding to cumulative disbursements, as reported in Chapter 2.

[13] Growth was estimated at (i) about 40 percent in the M-CRIL/MIX sample (Chapter 4), (ii) 60 percent for the 129 MFIs surveyed in the Quick Report, and (iii) 93 percent for Sa-Dhan's membership (which grew from Rs. 2070 crores in March 2006 to Rs. 3987 crores in March 2007 as reported in the Quick Report).

[14] Row 9 divided by 26.2 million (row 1) yields an estimate of about Rs. 4000.

[15] The lower bound of the range is estimated by M-CRIL, as reported in Chapter 4. The upper bound is derived from Sa-Dhan data in row 10 and footnote 3, after adjusting for inactive borrowers using the M-CRIL estimate in endnote 4, and works out to Rs. 5278.

Microfinance Accounts (Millions)

Agency	2005	% to total	2006	% to total
Commercial banks	28.3	29.3	29.4	27.7
RRBs	10.4	10.8	9.0	8.6
MFIs	6.7	6.9	7.3	6.9
SHG–Bank linkage	24.3	25.1	32.9	30.9
PACS	27.0	27.9	27.6	25.9
Total	96.7	100	106.2	100

Source: Thorat, Usha, 2007, "Microfinance and financial inclusion," Speech circulated at the launch of "Sa-Dhan's Quick Report," August 10, Chennai.

Table A.2 Information on 129 MFIs Covered in Sa-Dhan's Quick Report 2007

Sr No	Name of MFI	Location	Outreach	Gross loan portfolio (GLP) (Rs lakh)	Legal form	Delivery model	Borrowings (Rs lakh)	Net owned funds (Rs)	Interest rate (%)	Operating cost ratio (%)	Category (outreach)	Category (GLP)
1	Share Microfin Ltd.	Hyderabad, Andhra Pradesh	1,083,035	39,965	NBFC	GR, IL	36,985	3,735	22.0	10.8	Large	Large
2	Spandana Sphoorthy Innovative Financial Services Limited (SPANDANA)	Hyderabad, Andhra Pradesh	916,261	39,160	NBFC	GR	27,513	3,460	17.9	16.6	Large	Large
3	SKS Microfinance Pvt. Ltd.	Hyderabad, Andhra Pradesh	603,033	27,546	NBFC	GR	25,797	7,131	26.1	27.1	Large	Large
4	KAS Foundation	Bhubaneswar, Orissa	588,960	12,098	S25 Company	SHG, JLG	12,127	206	23.0	4.8	Large	Large
5	Shree Kshetra Dharmasthala Rural Development Projects (SKDRDP)	Dharmasthala, Karnataka	463,765	22,760	Trust	SHG	25,087	778	21.1	2.3	Large	Large
6	Bandhan Konnagar	Kolkata, West Bengal	433,324	12,613	Society	IL	10,023	1,085	26.2	18.9	Large	Large
7	Bharat Integrated Social Welfare Agency (BISWA)	Sambalpur, Orissa	364,325	9,422	Society	SHG	8,046	1,376	20.0	0.2	Large	Large
8	Shri Mahila Sewa Sahakari Bank Ltd. (SEWA Bank)	Ahmedabad, Gujrat	304,933	3,030	Cooperative	IL	175	652	17.0	12.0	Large	Large
9	BWDA Finance Ltd.	Villupuram, Tamil Nadu	236,388	7,209	NBFC	SHG, IL	6,966	513	15.5	0.1	Large	Large
10	Mahasemam	Madurai, Tamil Nadu	221,613	7,696	Trust	GR	12,630	8	10.0	23.3	Large	Large

(continued)

Sr No	Name of MFI	Location	Outreach	Gross loan portfolio (GLP) (Rs lakh)	Legal form	Delivery model	Borrowings (Rs lakh)	Net owned funds (Rs)	Interest rate (%)	Operating cost ratio (%)	Category (outreach)	Category (GLP)
11	Semam Microfinance Investment Literacy and Education Ltd.	Chennai, Tamil Nadu	221,613	5,877	NBFC	GR	2,987	620	19.0	5.6	Large	Large
12	CASHPOR Micro Credit	Varanasi, Uttar Pradesh	201,692	2,601	S25 Company	GR, JLG	10	567	26.0	27.3	Large	Large
13	BASIX	Hyderabad, Andhra Pradesh	198,282	13,970	NBFC	JLG	12,362	2,799	25.8	18.2	Large	Large
14	Activists for Social Alternatives (ASA)	Trichy, Tamil Nadu	196,224	8,025	Trust	GR	8,587	-	12.0	18.0	Large	Large
15	Evangelical Social Action Forum (ESAF)	Thrissur, Kerala	178,143	5,625	Society	GR	4,446	126	15.0	13.0	Large	Large
16	Sarvodaya Nano Finance Ltd. (SNFL)	Chennai, Tamil Nadu	126,211	6,425	NBFC	SHG	4,634	1,370	12.0	12.0	Large	Large
17	Kotalipara Development Society (KDS)	Kolkata, West Bengal	115,035	2,410	Society	IL	2,586	66	15.0	10.0	Large	Large
18	GR Koota	Bangalore, Karnataka	109,251	4,598	Trust	GR	4,715	490	23.2	15.0	Large	Large
19	Acts Mahila Mutually Aided Cooperative Thrift Society (AMMACTS)	Chitoor, Andhra Pradesh	82,904	4,572	MACS	GR	3,944	683	23.6	8.9	Large	Large
20	Sharadas Women's Association for Weaker Section (SWAWS)	Secunderabad, Andhra Pradesh	79,626	3,827	Society	GR, JLG, IL	4,017	104	15.5	10.1	Large	Large
21	Bharatha Swamukti Samsthe (BSS)	Bangalore, Karnataka	69,753	3,887	Trust	GR	3,200	346	28.5	23.8	Large	Large
22	Sreema Mahila Samity	Nadiya, West Bengal	62,024	1,635	Society	SHG	1,563	84	18.5	7.0	Large	Medium

23	Krishna Bhima Samruddhi Local Area Bank Ltd. (KBSLAB)	Mahaboobnagar, Andhra Pradesh	61,078	3,021	Local Area Bank	JLG, IL	4,228	589	19.0	18.0	Large	Large
24	Saadhana Microfin Society	Kurnool, Tamil Nadu	60,440	3,007	Society	IL	2,300	304	22.5	21.3	Large	Large
25	Indian Association for Savings and Credit (IASC)	Coimbatore, Tamil Nadu	55,539	1,740	S25 Company	SHG, IL	1,967	115	17.0	11.2	Large	Medium
26	Krushi	Karim Nagar, Andhra Pradesh	50,241	3,054	Society	SHG/ JLG	33	-	16.5	3.0	Large	Large
27	SE Investments Ltd. (SEIL)	Agra, Uttar Pradesh	45,924	12,722	NBFC	IL	13,540	2,769	27.0	7.0	Medium	Large
28	Rashtriya Seva Samiti (RASS)	Tirupati, Tamil Nadu	45,682	1,388	Society	SHG	1,123	247	15.0	4.0	Medium	Medium
29	Adhikar	Bhubaneswar, Orissa	43,335	1,209	Society	JLG, GR	1,425	43	25.8	5.3	Medium	Medium
30	Rashtriya Gramin Vikas Nidhi (RGVN)	Guahati, Assam	42,507	1,322	Society	SHG, JLG	1,420	33	15.0	9.4	Medium	Medium
31	Pragathi Seva Samiti (PSS)	Warangal, Andhra Pradesh	38,812	1,892	Society	SHG	1,615	346	14.0	2.9	Medium	Medium
32	Village Welfare Society (VWS)	Kolkata, West Bengal	35,394	1,525	Society	JLG, IL	1,425	271	22.2	18.6	Medium	Medium
33	Thirumalai Charity Trust (TCT)	Ranipet, Tamil Nadu	35,011	418	Society	SHG	1,533	21	24.0	13.0	Medium	Small
34	Karimangalam Ontriya Pengal Semipu Amaipu (SEARCH KOPSA)	Bangalore, Karnataka	32,247	1,003	S25 Company	SHG	1,211	343	14.0	10.9	Medium	Medium
35	Prochesta	Guwahati, Assam	31,927	44	Society	SHG	92	20	18.0	7.9	Medium	Small
36	Star Microfinance services Society	Kurnool, Andhra Pradesh	31,389	1,264	Society	GR	2,021	260	16.1	11.5	Medium	Medium

(continued)

Sr No	Name of MFI	Location	Outreach	Gross loan portfolio (GLP) (Rs lakh)	Legal form	Delivery model	Borrowings (Rs lakh)	Net owned funds (Rs)	Interest rate (%)	Operating cost ratio (%)	Category (outreach)	Category (GLP)
37	Mari-Sangatitha Mahila Mutually Aided Cooperative Societies Federation Ltd.	Warangal, Andhra Pradesh	30,084	226	MACs	SHG	302	74	18.0	23.0	Medium	Small
38	Nav Bharat Jagriti Kendra (NBJK)	Hajaribagh, Jharkhand	28,446	436	Society	SHG, JLG	177	371	24.0	11.0	Medium	Small
39	Village Micro Credit Services (VMCS)	Kolkata, West Bengal	27,579	1,136	S25 Company	JLG, IL	1,400	10	22.2	1.0	Medium	Medium
40	Liberal Association For Movement of People (LAMP)	Kolkata, West Bengal	27,332	210	Society	SHG, JLG	76	117	24.8	9.8	Medium	Small
41	Shalom Charitable Trust	Palakkad, Kerala	26,170	852	Trust	SHG	931	-	27.0	16.0	Medium	Medium
42	Nanayasurabhi Development Financial Services (NDFSO)	Trichy, Tamil Nadu	26,046	464	S25 Company	SHG	525	15	18.0	4.0	Medium	Small
43	Samuha	Bangalore, Karnataka	22,980	344	Society	SHG	421	7	10.5	6.4	Medium	Small
44	Welfare Services Ernakulam	Kochi, Kerala	22,645	33	Society	SHG	280	80	12.8	5.9	Medium	Small
45	Janodaya Public Trust (JPT)	Bangalore, Karnataka	22,500	817	Trust	SHG, IL	809	34	27.0	15.3	Medium	Medium
46	Ujjivan Financial Services Pvt. Ltd.	Bangalore, Karnataka	22,220	843	NBFC	GR	616	329	24.0	63.2	Medium	Medium
47	Social Education and Voluntary Action (SEVA)	Warangal, Andhra Pradesh	21,752	308	Trust	SHG	939	106	21.0	6.0	Medium	Small
48	Kalighat Society For Development Facilitation (KSDF)	Kolkata, West Bengal	20,976	375	Society	SHG, JLG	374	47	12.5	3.8	Medium	Small

No.	Name	Location			Legal form	Lending model						
49	Agricultural Science Foundation	Gadag, Karnataka	20,598	184	Society	SHG	186	20	22.8	4.7	Medium	Small
50	Disha Social Organization	Saharanpur, Uttar Pradesh	19,897	14	Society	SHG	50	2	24.0	7.5	Medium	Small
51	Village Financial Servies Pvt Ltd.	Kolkata, West Bengal	19,632	539	NBFC	JLG	431	112	23.0	15.5	Medium	Medium
52	Bandhan Financial Services Pvt. Ltd.	Kolkata, West Bengal	19,314	459	NBFC	IL	306	67	26.2	17.2	Medium	Small
53	Shramik Bharati	Kanpur, Uttar Pradesh	18,629	395	Society	SHG	-	388	11.4	6.0	Medium	Small
54	Cooperation Development Council (CDC)	Puri, Orissa	17,718	603	Trust	JLG, IL, GR	743	1	25.0	13.2	Medium	Medium
55	NIDAN	Patna, Bihar	17,562	189	Society	SHG	295	31	19.0	20.0	Medium	Small
56	Watershed Organization Trust (WOTR)	Ahmednagar, Maharashtra	17,086	363	Society	SHG	-	450	21.0	24.0	Medium	Medium
57	Swayamshree Micro Credit Services (SMCS)	Bhubaneswar, Orissa	15,868	645	S25 Company	SHG	570	29	16.0	5.2	Medium	Medium
58	Community Development Centre (CDC)	Theni, Tamil Nadu	15,680	675	Trust	SHG	673	-	18.0	15.0	Medium	Medium
59	Sanghamitra Rural Financial Services	Mysore, Karnataka	15,626	3,272	S25 Company	SHG	2,708	561	14.0	4.0	Medium	Large
60	Hope Foundation	Palakkad, Kerala	15,366	103	Trust	SHG	128	15	20.9	21.0	Medium	Small
61	South Indian Federation of Fishermen Societies	Trivendram, Kerala	14,566	672	Society	IL	225	245	12.0	12.6	Medium	Medium
62	Satin Credit Care Network Ltd.	Delhi	14,372	2,646	NBFC	IL	184	542	20.0	16.4	Medium	Large

(continued)

Sr No	Name of MFI	Location	Outreach	Gross loan portfolio (GLP) (Rs lakh)	Legal form	Delivery model	Borrowings (Rs lakh)	Net owned funds (Rs)	Interest rate (%)	Operating cost ratio (%)	Category (outreach)	Category (GLP)
63	Guide	Krishna, Andhra Pradesh	12,504	333	Society	SHG	222	12	18.5	19.0	Medium	Small
64	Sonata Finance Pvt. Ltd.	Puri, Orissa	11,393	498	NBFC	GR	602	150	36.0	42.7	Medium	Small
65	Sahabhagi Vikash Abhyan	Khurda, Orissa	11,176	127	Society	SHG	89	38	24.0	3.5	Medium	Small
66	The Payakaraopta Women's Mutually Aided Cooperative Thrift and Credit Society Ltd.	Vishakhapatnam, Andhra Pradesh	10,650	643	MACs	JLG,IL	850	25	18.5	5.2	Medium	Medium
67	Bhoruka Charitable Trust	Churu, Rajasthan	10,252	43	Trust	SHG	105	15	22.8	20.0	Medium	Small
68	Arohan	Kolkata, West Bengal	10,110	299	NBFC	JLG	211	125	30.0	64.0	Medium	Small
69	Vedika Credit Capital Limited	Ranchi, Jharkhand	9,421	997	NBFC	JLG,IL	713	885	24.0	16.0	Small	Medium
70	Initiatives For Development Foundation (IDF)	Bangalore, Karnataka	9,064	181	Trust	SHG	168	18	17.5	7.9	Small	Small
71	Hindustan Cooperative Credit Society Ltd.	Mumbai, Maharashtra	8,061	1,918	Cooperative	JLG,IL	1,135	317	18.0	8.0	Small	Medium
72	Ishara Foundation for Finance and Rural Development	New Delhi	7,251	58	S25 Company	SHG	58	15	27.0	21.9	Small	Small
73	Institute of Integrated Resource Management (IIRM)	Dekargaon, Assam	6,927	239	Society	JLG	333	-	15.0	18.5	Small	Small

74	Support	Hajaribag, Jharkhand	6,809	27	Society	SHG, JLG	57	-	22.8	8.0	Small	Small
75	Navachetana Foundation	Haveri, Karnataka	6,734	418	Society	GR	430	-	27.9	6.8	Small	Small
76	Raghunath Pathagar (RNP)	Ganjam, Orissa	6,540	458	Society	SHG, JLG	445	13	10.8	5.0	Small	Small
77	People's Action for Transformation	Trichy, Tamil Nadu	6,521	277	Trust	SHG	235	20	28.0	23.5	Small	Small
78	Bal-Mahila Vikas Samiti	Madhya Pradesh	6,075	21	Cooperative	SHG	20	1	34.2	38.1	Small	Small
79	Darabar Sahitya Sansad (DSS)	Khurda, Orissa	5,889	54	Society	SHG	98	2	19.0	10.8	Small	Small
80	Ullon Social Welfare Society	South 24 Pgs, West Bengal	4,967	108	Society	SHG,IL	-	199	24.0	7.8	Small	Small
81	Adarsa	Sambalpur, Orissa	4,917	37	Society	SHG	76	-	24.0	19.2	Small	Small
82	Sarala Women Welfare Society	Howrah, West Bengal	4,826	166	S25 Company	IL	150	19	33.0	8.7	Small	Small
83	Community Services Trust (CST)	Salem, Tamil Nadu	4,386	446	Trust	SHG	502	21	22.8	40.0	Small	Small
84	Pikepara Kamala Seva samity	24 Pgs, West Bengal	4,092	55	Society	SHG	13	-	24.0	8.0	Small	Small
85	Social Welfare Agency and Training Institute (SWATI)	Kandhmal, Orissa	3,885	16	Society	SHG, JLG, IL	3	-	18.0	5.0	Small	Small
86	Arman Lease and Finance Ltd.	Ahmedabad, Gujrat	3,770	1,786	NBFC	IL	867	597	19.5	11.8	Small	Medium
87	Guidance Society for Labour Orphans and Women (GLOW)	Vellore, Tamil Nadu	3,626	80	Society	JLG	100	19	22.8	16.5	Small	Small
88	Rajapur Seva Niketan (RSN)	Howrah, West Bengal	3,272	150	Society	SHG, JLG	184	28	15.2	4.6	Small	Small
89	Youth Volunteers Union	Wangamataba, Manipur	3,114	380	Society	SHG, JLG, IL	34	382	22.8	12.1	Small	Small

(continued)

Sr No	Name of MFI	Location	Outreach	Gross loan portfolio (GLP) (Rs lakh)	Legal form	Delivery model	Borrowings (Rs lakh)	Net owned funds (Rs)	Interest rate (%)	Operating cost ratio (%)	Category (outreach)	Category (GLP)
90	Sakhi Samudaya Kosh	Solapur, Maharashtra	3,072	140	S25 Company	SHG	125	63	20.0	42.2	Small	Small
91	Ajiwika Society	Deoghar, Jharkhand	2,515	228	S25 Company	SHG, JLG	148	9	18.0	6.0	Small	Small
92	Mother Theresa Mahila MACCS Ltd.	Krishna, Andhra Pradesh	2,501	78	MACs	SHG	19	60	7.1	12.0	Small	Small
93	Society for Model, Gram Bikas Kendra	Kolkata, West Bengal	2,453	73	Society	GR	27	3	35.8	2.9	Small	Small
94	Priyasakhi Mahila Sangh, Indore	Indore, Madhya Pradesh	2,350	53	Society	SHG	34	11	21.8	24.4	Small	Small
95	People's Action for National Integration (PANI)	Faizabad, Uttar Pradesh	2,324	148	Society	SHG	45	103	22.8	10.0	Small	Small
96	Jeevika Livelihoods Support Organization Max Wealth Trust	Jabalpur, Madhya Pradesh	2,100	57	Society	JLG, GR	56	11	38.0	45.0	Small	Small
97	Mahila Kalyan Samiti Dhori, Bokaro	Bokaro, Jharkhand	1,865	25	Society	JLG	36	15	34.2	18.0	Small	Small
98	Manab Sewa Sangh (MSS)	Guwahati, Assam	1,750	4	Society	SHG, JLG	60	2	18.0	12.0	Small	Small
99	Hope Integrated Rural Development Society	Kurnool, Andhra Pradesh	1,710	6	Society	GR	96	2	31.0	35.5	Small	Small
100	Max Wealth Trust	Hyderabad, Andhra Pradesh	1,425	61	Trust	SHG	68	-	23.5	115.5	Small	Small
101	Social Action for Rural Community (SARC)	Sambalpur, Orissa	1,208	6	Society	SHG	1	1	25.0	42.7	Small	Small
102	Swadhar Finances	Mumbai, Maharashtra	1,125	43	S25 Company	JLG	25	20	35.8	203.0	Small	Small

No.	Name	Location										
103	Ma tarani Prathamika Mahila Sanchaya Samabaya Ltd.	Nayagarh, Orissa	982	17	MACs	SHG, IL	12	18	19.5	16.0	Small	Small
104	CHINYARD	Dharwad, Karnataka	918	50	Trust	SHG/ JLG	50	12	12.5	7.7	Small	Small
105	Society for Empowerment and Women Advancement (SERV–SEVA)	Hajaribag, Jharkhand	886	23	Society	SHG	18	12	22.8	1.8	Small	Small
106	GramIn Vikas Mandal	Beed, Maharashtara	882	37	Society	SHG	37	-	34.2	3.1	Small	Small
107	Indian Institute for Rural Development (IIRD)	Jaipur, Rajasthan	773	58	Society	JLG	50	50	25.7	7.0	Small	Small
108	Nari Jagruti Prathamika Mahila Sanchaya Samabaya Ltd.	Cuttack, Orissa	750	24	MACs	IL	9	24	21.3	13.5	Small	Small
109	Sramajibi Bikas Prathamika Mahila Sanchaya Samabaya Ltd.	Khurda, Orissa	740	15	MACs	IL	12	20	18.7	12.7	Small	Small
110	Mahila Vikas Prathamika Sanchaya Samabaya Ltd.	Khurda, Orissa	682	17	Cooperative	SHG, JLG	9	11	24.0	8.0	Small	Small
111	Mahalaxmi Prathamika Mahila Sanchaya Samabaya Ltd.	Nayagarh, Orissa	598	18	MACs	SHG, IL	8	20	16.1	11.6	Small	Small
112	Mimo Finance	Dehradun, Uttaranchal	570	30	NBFC	JLG, SHG, GR	20	30	32.3	100.0	Small	Small
113	Nava Jagriti	Saran, Bihar	512	32	Society	SHG	32	-	18.0	16.0	Small	Small
114	Upkar	Nimapara, Orissa	482	3	Society	SHG, IL	7	3	34.2	2.0	Small	Small

(continued)

Sr No	Name of MFI	Location	Outreach	Gross loan portfolio (GLP) (Rs lakh)	Legal form	Delivery model	Borrowings (Rs lakh)	Net owned funds (Rs)	Interest rate (%)	Operating cost ratio (%)	Category (outreach)	Category (GLP)
115	Padmabati Prathamika Mahila Sanchaya Samabaya Ltd.	Nayagarh, Orissa	470	9	MACs	IL	5	7	18.9	16.8	Small	Small
116	Ma Sakti Prathamika Mahila Sanchaya Samabaya Ltd.	Cuttack, Orissa	435	3	MACs	SHG, IL	2	6	19.8	16.4	Small	Small
117	Ma Adisakti Prathamika Mahila Sanchaya Samabaya Ltd.	Cuttack, Orissa	310	2	MACs	IL	1	1	22.1	18.9	Small	Small
118	Nari Bikas Prathamika Mahila Sanchaya Samabaya Ltd.	Bhubaneswar, Orissa	308	11	MACs	IL	6	14	21.4	15.4	Small	Small
119	Devisakti Prathamika Mahila Sanchaya Samabaya Ltd.	Cuttack, Orissa	219	1	MACs	IL	1	1	16.7	23.1	Small	Small
120	Gram Swaraj Seva Trust	Wardha, Maharashtra	208	12	Society	SHG, JLG	NA	26	24.0	23.0	Small	Small
121	Ma Matrusakti Prathamika Mahila Sanchaya Samabaya Ltd.	Cuttack, Orissa	188	1	MACs	SHG, IL	1	1	19.3	20.3	Small	Small
122	Khandual Prathamika Mahila Sanchaya Samabaya Ltd.	Cuttack, Orissa	181	2	MACs	IL	1	2	12.8	12.7	Small	Small
123	Khetrapal Prathamika Mahila Sanchaya Samabaya Ltd.	Khurda, Orissa	148	2	MACs	IL	2	2	13.7	10.6	Small	Small
124	Potolei Prathamika Mahila Sanchaya Samabaya Ltd.	Cuttack, Orissa	143	1	MACs	IL	1	3	20.6	18.8	Small	Small

125	Saktimayeeni Prathamika Mahila Sanchaya Samabaya Ltd.	Khurda, Orissa	141	2	MACs	IL	2	2	10.2	8.7	Small	Small	Small
126	Ma Jogamaya Prathamika Mahila Sanchaya Samabaya Ltd.	Cuttack, Orissa	104	1	MACs	SHG, IL	1	1	14.5	15.3	Small	Small	Small
127	Jhanshirani Prathamika Mahila Sanchaya Samabaya Ltd.	Khurda, Orissa	102	1	MACs	IL	1	1	8.0	10.1	Small	Small	Small
128	Swayamsakti Prathamika Mahila Sanchaya Samabaya Ltd.	Cuttack, Orissa	69	0	MACs	IL	0	0	9.3	21.3	Small	Small	Small
129	Nirantara Community Services	Bidar, Karnataka	30	2	Society	GR	10	-	29.0	27.5	Small	Small	Small
	Total		8,231,026	306,475			274,412	38,675					

Notes:

1. *Self-reported data as of 31 March 2007, taken from Sa-Dhan's Quick Report 2007: A Snapshot of Microfinance Institutions in India.*

2. *Gross Loan Portfolio = sum total of all the loans outstanding of the MFI. This includes portfolio on the balance sheet as well as off the balance sheet.*

3. *GR = Grameen, IL = Individual Loan, JLG = Joint Liability Groups (JLG). The JLG model refers to group lending models, which do not strictly follow the five member, up to eight group, center concept.*

4. *The interest rate is the annual effective rate of interest charged by the MFI to its borrowers.*

5. *Operating cost ratio is calculated by dividing the total operating costs (salaries, travel, depreciation, and other administrative costs) by average loans outstanding.*

Table A.3 Lending By Selected Apex Financing Institutions and Banks to MFIs

Sr No	Apex financing institution/Bank	Partners		Outstanding (Rs crores)	
		31 March 06	31 March 07	31 March 06	31 March 07
1	SIDBI	NA	100	329	548
2	FWWB	NA	102	67	104
3	Maanaveeya Holdings	NA	24	NA	50
4	ICICI Bank	100	NA	2350	1392
5	HDFC Bank	NA	66	250	300
6	Axis Bank	40	65	103	269
7	ABN-AMRO Bank	19	27	87	161
8	Yes Bank	NA	7	NA	62
9	Standard Chartered Bank	12	12	50	38
10	Other private sector banks	NA	NA	NA	400
11	Public sector banks	NA	NA	NA	195
12	Others[*]	NA	NA	NA	25

[*]Grameen Trust, Grameen Foundation, Oikocredit, etc.

Notes:

1. The amounts for ICICI Bank include lending under the SHG model and individual jewel loans, and thus, are not comparable with those for the other banks.

2. Items Nos. 1–8 are based on information provided by the apex financing institutions/banks.

3. Items Nos. 9–11 are based on information compiled from the annual reports/annual financial statements of 48 MFIs.

Table A.4 Salient Features of Selected India-Oriented Equity Investors

	Bellwether	Lok Capital	Aavishkaar Goodwell India Microfinance Development Company	Michael and Susan Dell Foundation	Unitus Equity Fund
Indian/Offshore	Indian	Offshore	Offshore	Offshore	Offshore
Size at first closing	$22 million	Size at first closing $12 million (expecting 2nd close of greater than $15 million)	USD 8.4 Mn	A foundation with an endowment of more than US $1 billion, which also makes equity investments	US$23.5m
Life of Fund	15 Years	10 years	10 years, extendable by 2 years	NA	10 yrs
Main Investors	Individual & Institutional (Hivos Triodos, Gray Ghost and FMO)	IFC, KfW, CDC, FMO (In process of closing investment from ACCION)	Institutional (Goodwell MDC, IFC, FMO, DB)	NA	Mix of social and commercial investors
Investees so far (in India)	12 of which Equity (8), Convertible Debt (2) and debt (2).	2 of which both are equity	One MFI – Equity investment	2 equity investments, 2 grants of donated equity to non profit MFIs, 1 incubation grant	2 equity
Investees so far (in India)	12 of which Equity (8), Convertible Debt (2) and debt (2).	2 of which both are equity	One MFI – Equity investment	2 equity investments, 2 grants of donated equity to non profit MFIs, 1 incubation grant	2 equity
Pipeline	2 Existing MFIs and 2 start-ups	MFIs, spread across 10 states, half of which are start-up or early-stage MFIs. Expecting to close 2 further investments by end of 2007.	3 existing entities, 2 start ups franchisee companies	3–4 additional MFIs over the next year	Expect 2–3 additional equity investments in India by end of year
Coverage Goals	By year 5, aims to successfully transform 7 MFIs, of which at least 3 will be start ups. Expects 40 percent of investments to be outside southern states, and a rural urban balance.	Targeting 12-15 investments in total, which will be diversified through geographies, growth stages and product/market specializations.	The fund would invest in established MFIs, transforming MFIs, to foster and encourage the spread of MF across the country, in small start up entities as well in partnership with Intellecash franchisee program	3–4 new MFIs every year	8-10 leading MFIs worldwide with the first fund

(continued)

	Bellwether	Lok Capital	Aavishkaar Goodwell India Microfinance Development Company	Michael and Susan Dell Foundation	Unitus Equity Fund
Arrangements for TA	Will access grants for partners from other sources	TA Lok Foundation will have the ability to finance $2–3 million worth of TA services to investee MFIs. Partnerships have been established with both Indian as well as international TA providers.	Will channel TA to enable fulfilling its mandate of spreading MF across the country and encouraging start up entities	As a Foundation, can offer grant finances	Affiliate of Unitus through whom a breadth of capacity building, capital advisory, functional solutions and network linkages are offered. Unitus currently has 16 MFI Partners worldwide (10 in India).
Emphases and Special features	Apart from social returns, investees must offer clear prospects of attractive returns on equity.	Lok Capital is an India-focused MF fund. Apart from social returns, investees must offer clear prospects of attractive returns on equity. Lok Capital seeks longer term investment timelines of 5–7 years, and looks to provide significant value-add services to its investees.	To maximize value through superior risk – adjusted social and financial returns, by focusing on scalability, efficiency and leverage and by applying a private equity approach within a mission driven setting. The geographic focus is India.	Focuses exclusively on early-stage urban microfinance institutions which are (potentially) scalable and sustainable model. Emphasis on financial and social performance parameters. Also supports non-profit MFIs	Demonstrate that industries which serve the poor in a commercially sustainable manner, such as microfinance, are viable investment vehicles.

Investees

Bellwether	Satin Credit Care (Debt), Ujjivan Financial Services Pvt Ltd. (Equity), Sharda's Women's association for Weaker Sections (SWAWS) – Equity, MAS Financial Services (Debt), Sonata Finance Pvt. Ltd. (Equity), Arohan Financial Services (Equity), Indur MACS Federation (Debt), BISWA Microfinance Services (Equity and Debt), Janalakshmi Financial Services (Equity and Debt), Swayamshree Micro Credit Services (Debt plus option), MIMO Finance (Equity and debt).
Lok Capital	Spandana Sphoorty Financial Services Ltd., Janalakshmi Financial Services (Equity)
Aavishkaar Goodwell India Microfinance Development Company	Share Microfin Limited
MSDF	Janalakshmi Financial Services (Equity), Swadhaar Finances (Grant), Ujjivan Financial Services Pvt. Ltd. (Equity), Nirmaan Bharati Arthik and Samajik Sansthan (Grant)
Unitus Equity Fund	Ujjivan Financial Services Pvt. Ltd. (Equity), SKS Microfinance Ltd. (Equity).

Source: Self-reported.

Table A.5 Insurance coverage by selected MFIs

Sr No	MFI	Customers covered under life insurance	Customers covered under health insurance	Customers covered under accident insurance only	Number of livestock insured	Number of micro enterprises insured	No of weather insurance customers
1	Bharat Integrated Social Welfare Agency (BISWA)	58,743	153223	47386	237	3,862	-
2	KAS Foundation	2,794		190357	1,934	5,505	-
3	Kotalipara Development Society (KDS)	25,000	5,000	-	-	25,000	-
4	CASHPOR Micro Credit	27,879	-	-	-	-	-
5	Satin Credit Care Network Ltd	-	-	-	-	-	-
6	SE Investments Ltd. (SEIL)	-	-	-	-	-	-
7	Activists for Social Alternatives (ASA)	49,623	-	-	-		
8	BASIX	372,344	356,545	-	10,098	1,263	10,711
9	Evangelical Social Action Forum (ESAF)	287	13,510	68,521	-	-	-
10	Krishna Bhima Samruddhi Local Area Bank Ltd. (KBSLAB)	17,892	17,892	-	953	-	1,005
11	Mahasemam Trust	221,613	30,498	-	-	-	-
12	Saadhana Microfin Society	101,901	-	-	-	-	-
13	Sarvodaya Nano Finance Ltd. (SNFL)	-	-	-	-	-	-
14	Sharadas Women's Association for Weaker Section (SWAWS)	48,154	48,154	-	-	-	-
15	Shree Kshetra Dharmasthala Rural Development Projects (SKDRDP)	-	721,203	-	-	-	-
16	SKS Microfinance Pvt. Ltd.	603,933	990	-	-	-	-
17	Spandana Sphoorthy Innovative Financial Services Limited (SPANDANA)	10,20,000	-	-	-	-	-
	Total	**1,530,163**	**1,537,372**	**115,907**	**13,222**	**35,630**	**11,716**

Source: Information provided by MFIs on the basis of a questionnaire.

Table A.6 List of selected transformations

SHARE, Andhra Pradesh transformed from a society to an NBFC – Share Microfin Limited
Swayam Krishi Sangam **(SKS), Andhra Pradesh** transformed from a society to an NBFC – SKS Microfinance Pvt. Ltd.
Spandana, Andhra Pradesh transformed from a society to an NBFC – Spandana Sphoorty Innovative Financial Services Limited
Bullockcart Worker's Development Association **(BWDA), Tamil Nadu** transformed from a society to an NBFC – BWDA Finance limited
CASHPOR, Uttar Pradesh transformed from a society to a S25 company – Cashpor Micro Credit (CMC)
The Microfinance programme of Swayam Sikshan Prayog **(SSP), Maharastra** transformed from a Society to a S25 Company Sakhi Samudaya Kosh (SSK)
The Microfinance Programme of **NEEDS, Jharkhand** has transformed in to a S25 Company – AJIWIKA
Evangelical Social Action Forum **(ESAF), Kerala** is in the process of transforming from a society to an NBFC – ESAF Microfinance Limited
Konnagar Bandhan, West Bengal is in the process of transforming from a society to the NBFC – Bandhan Financial Services Limited
Village Welfare Society **(VWS), West Bengal** is in the process of transforming from a society to an NBFC – Village Financial Services Limited
Shardas Women's Association for Weaker Sections **(SWAWS), Andhra Pradesh** is in the process of transforming in to an NBFC
Mahasemam Trust, Tamil Nadu is in the process of transforming its microfinance programme to an NBFC, Semam Microfinance Investment Literacy and Empowerment (SMILE)
Microfinance programme of **SHEPHERD, Tamil Nadu** has transformed in to a S25 Company – Nanyasurabhi Development Financial Services
Microfinance programme of **CYSD, Orissa** has transformed in to a S25 Company – Swayanshree Microcredit Services
The microfinance programme of **Gram Utthan, Orissa** microfinance programme is in the process of transformation into a S25 Company – Kalyani Microfinance Foundation
The microfinance programme of **BISWA, Orissa** is in the process of transforming in to an NBFC – Credible Securities and Finance Private Ltd.
The microfinance programme of **ADHIKAR, Orissa** has been transformed into a S25 Company – Sanchayika.
Council of Professional Social Workers **(CPSW), Orissa** is in the process of transforming its microfinance programme in to a S25 Company – Amba Jibika
Organization for Development Coordination **(ODC), Orissa** is also in the process of transforming into a S25 Company – Jana Jibika Foundation

Note:

This information has been compiled on the basis of interaction with various stakeholders. It is not a comprehensive list, but may be of interest. For the purpose of this table, only transformation from a society/trust to a S25 Company or an NBFC has been considered.